BOESMAN AND LENA

and other plays

ALSO BY

ATHOL FUGARD

Statements
(including *Sizwe Bansi is Dead* and *The Island* by
Athol Fugard, John Kani, and Winston Ntshona, and
Statements after an Arrest under the Immorality Act)

Dimetos and Two Early Plays
(including *No-good Friday* and *Nongogo*)

BOESMAN AND LENA

and other plays

THE BLOOD KNOT
PEOPLE ARE LIVING THERE
HELLO AND GOODBYE
BOESMAN AND LENA

ATHOL FUGARD

OXFORD UNIVERSITY PRESS
Cape Town

33577.

Oxford University Press
OXFORD NEW YORK TORONTO
DELHI BOMBAY CALCUTTA MADRAS KARACHI
PETALING JAYA SINGAPORE HONG KONG TOKYO
NAIROBI DAR ES SALAAM CAPE TOWN
MELBOURNE AUCKLAND

AND ASSOCIATES IN
BERLIN IBADAN

OXFORD is a trade mark of Oxford University Press

Introduction © Athol Fugard 1974, 1978
The Blood Knot © Athol Fugard 1963, 1964
People are Living There © Athol Fugard 1970
Hello and Goodbye © Athol Fugard 1973
Boesman and Lena © Athol Fugard 1973
First South African Impression 1980
Second Impression 1981
Third Impression 1982
Fourth Impression 1984
Fifth Impression 1985
Sixth Impression 1985
Seventh Impression 1986
Eighth Impression 1987
Ninth Impression 1988

These plays are fully protected by copyright and application
for public performance should be made to William Morris
Agency (UK) Ltd., 147/149 Wardour Street, London WIV
3TB, or to William Morris Agency, Inc., 1350 Avenue of the
Americas, New York, N.Y. 100019, U.S.A.

ISBN 0 19 570197 6

Printed and bound by Citadel Press, Lansdowne, Cape
Published by Oxford University Press, Harrington House,
Barrack Street, Cape Town 8001, South Africa

B438/L

CONTENTS

INTRODUCTION

I was born in Middelburg, a small village in the semi-desert Karroo region of South Africa, on 11 June 1932. My mother is an Afrikaner, my father an English-speaking South African, possibly of Irish descent. I have an elder brother and a younger sister. At the time of my birth my parents owned a small general dealer's store in the village, but we sold this when I was about three years old and moved to Port Elizabeth, which has been my home ever since. Port Elizabeth is an almost featureless industrial port on the Indian Ocean. It is assaulted throughout the year by strong south-westerly and easterly winds. Close on half a million people live here—black, white, Indian, Chinese, and Coloured (mixed-race). It is also very representative of South Africa in the range of its social strata, from total affluence on the white side to the extremest poverty on the non-white. I cannot conceive of myself as separate from it. It is the setting for all three plays in this book.

Korsten, where *The Blood Knot* is set, is a non-white slum adjoining one of our factory areas. The Valley Road of *Hello and Goodbye* is a poor-white area close to the centre of the city. The mudflats, where Boesman and Lena confront each other, is at a point seven miles outside the city where the Swartkops River flows into the sea. The other places referred to in the last play—Kleinskool, Veeplaas, Missionvale, etc.—are shanty-towns on the outskirts of the city.

My life away from Port Elizabeth has included three years of studying philosophy and social anthropology at the University of Cape Town, a six-month hitch-hiking trip up Africa, two years as a seaman in the Far East, and a few trips overseas when I worked in theatre and television in England, America, and Europe.

I first became actively involved in theatre after my return from the Far East when I met my wife—Sheila Meiring—who was working as an actress in Cape Town. We formed an experimental drama group for which we wrote most of the material. In 1958, the second year of our marriage, we moved to Johannesburg, where I found a job as clerk in a Native Commissioner's Court.

Every black man and woman in South Africa has to carry a pass-book, with endorsements which decide where he may live, work, seek work, travel, etc., etc. Any violation of these endorsements is a statutory offence and is dealt with in a Native Commissioner's Court. The usual sentence is from two weeks imprisonment. My time in the Fordsburg Court in Johannesburg was traumatic for me as a white South African. We were kept very busy, averaging about one case every three minutes. During my six months in that Court Room I saw more suffering than I could cope with. I began to understand how my country functioned.

At the same time I made my first black friends and began to visit them in the ghetto townships. Out of this life I wrote my first full-length play, *No-Good Friday*, which described the lives of black people in those townships, threatened as always by white laws and black gangsters. Through personal contacts my wife and I managed to assemble the necessary cast of ten (only a few of whom had any previous stage experience) and we began to rehearse wherever and whenever possible. *No-Good Friday* received considerable attention when first presented.

By the end of the run of *No-Good Friday* I had left the Native Commissioner's Court and was working as a paid Stage Manager for the white National Theatre Organisation. I began immediately to write another play for a black cast. *Nongogo* (a woman for 25 cents) had a more intimate subject—a woman who had been a mine worker's whore. This had a cast of five and like *No-Good Friday* was rehearsed and performed wherever possible.

In 1960 my wife and I went to Europe, where we worked in theatre, returning home after a year when she fell pregnant. During this period overseas I began to keep a notebook. It became a daily ritual to record anything that happened to me which seemed of significance—sensual fragments, incidents, quotations, speculations. Writing now, I find in them the content of all I can possibly say about my work. The first entry in the first notebook deals with Korsten and my idea for a play about two brothers living in one of the shacks in the slum. Writing *The Blood Knot* was a compulsive and direct experience and this note is the only reference I can find to it:

1960 (London)

Korsten: The Berry's Corner bus, then up the road past the big motor-assembly and rubber factories. Turn right down a dirt road—badly potholed, full of stones, donkeys wandering loose, Chinese and Indian grocery shops—down this road until you come to the lake. Dumping ground for waste products from the factories. Terrible smell. On the far side, like a scab, Korsten location. A collection of shanties, pondoks, lean-to's. No streets, names, or numbers. A world where anything goes.

When the wind blows in from the east the inhabitants of Korsten live with the terrible smell of the lake.

In one of these shacks the two brothers—Morrie and Zach. Morrie is a light-skinned Coloured who has found out that to ignore the temptations to use his lightness is the easiest way to live. Rather than live with the fear and uncertainty that would have come from 'trying for white', he has settled for being Coloured. He has some education—can read and write. In contrast, his brother Zach—dark-skinned Coloured, virtually African in appearance. Zach has no education, has made no attempt to acquire any, will never have any. Zach can never be anything other than what he is—a black man. There are no choices for him.

The appearance of Ethel in their lives. Morrie wants to have nothing to do with her. He is frightened of her. Zach wants her but can't have her. It is masochism and revenge that make Zach insist that his brother meet her. Zach could in the beginning, and eventually does, envy Morrie the lightness of his skin.

Their relationship as brothers. . . . Zach is confused. Suspicion and envy. The question haunting him . . . Why? It was the same mother! Why?

The blood tie linking them has chained them. They are dead or dying because of it.

The situation of the two brothers (imprisonment in a blood tie) cannot continue after the appearance of Ethel. Too much has surfaced—Zach's envy and hate, Morrie's crippling sense of guilt and responsibility.

A last confrontation.

Close to this note are two others which I now recognize as the seeds of *Hello and Goodbye*. We had returned to South Africa at this point and were staying with my parents in Port Elizabeth. My father was seriously ill, and died a few months later, shortly after the birth of our daughter Lisa.

11/5/61

Dad's pain. Fluttering, throbbing, soft as a dove. Pussy-paws kneading away at the tender part. Occasionally a claw slipped out, caught a nerve, and plucked from his consciousness a sharp, raw note. Caressing his pain. Crying out, alone in the dark, in the silent, sleeping house. In the other bed his wife, sleeping. In the other room, also sleeping, the young woman with child, the young man.

The face of a man, a fine face, the face of a noble man, but when he opened his mouth in the dark the whimper and whine of a child. Utterly without protest or anger. A final, total resignation. Asking only to be able to sound his suffering.

The habit of suffering. The inward wait and watch for pain. The Lesson of a life. He knows it, the anatomy of pain, the way other old people know their pets. The secret places where it plays—the chest, toe-nails, stump,. cramp in the good leg. This and the habit of dependence, the habit of humiliation, of loneliness. A man withdrawn, marooned finally on the last unassailable island of the individual consciousness . . . pain.

The pill. In the dark, between his trembling finger-tips, so small, so round. Visions of mighty pain-killing properties, of relief, of sleep, like the others in their beds. He never took them with water. Went straight onto his tongue and lay there until they crumbled apart and soaked away with his spit.

15/5/61

Tonight, after two weeks of pain, of sleepless nights, of crying and whining in the dark, of vain imploring . . . Jeeesus! Christ Almighty help me! . . . Dad broke down and cried like a child. Tears and flat spit bubbles between his lips. We searched around for pills, for Nerve-Pain Specific, for anything we could lay our hands on that might help, and dosed him with the lot. He pulled himself together and just before I left called to me: 'Come here, my boy.' He started to say something then floundered and drowned in another flood of tears. He eventually got it out. 'Don't let them do anything to my leg. Don't let them take it off.'

So that's it. Behind the bland, withdrawn expression, that is the terror of the midnight hours—that the second leg, his final vestige of independence, of manhood, would go.

The Blood Knot was the opening production of the Rehearsal Room—a private club-style theatre sponsored by AMDA, the African Music and Drama Association. The Rehearsal Room was on the third floor of Dorkay House, an abandoned factory, which stands between Johannesburg's busiest thoroughfare and an African men's hostel. Performances had to cope with traffic noises on one side, and the drums and chanting of mine dances on the other. From the Rehearsal Room the play was taken over by a commercial management and toured the country for six months. In 1962 it was still possible for a black man and a white man to appear on the same stage before a mixed audience, provided the management of the theatre involved was prepared to let this happen. But since major plays, one by Pinter and one by Bolt, were being performed for whites only, I wrote an open letter to British playwrights asking them to make it a condition in granting the rights to their plays that all audiences be non-segregated. The letter, and the debate that followed, precipitated the now established boycott of South African theatre by most English-speaking overseas playwrights.

After the tour of *The Blood Knot* I returned to Port Elizabeth to write a play called *People Are Living There*. In many respects this appears to be an aberrant work. It has neither a Port Elizabeth setting nor, seemingly, a socio-political context of any significance. It deviates from my other work in still a third respect: it was written more directly from life than any of the other plays. During the period when I was employed as a clerk in the Johannesburg Native Commissioner's Court my wife and I stayed in the Braamfontein rooming-house that provides the setting for *People Are Living There*. All of the characters involved and many of the dramatic incidents are almost literal transcriptions of our experiences in that rambling, near derelict, double-storeyed house at the bottom of Hospital Hill. Speaking for myself personally, however, the play is in no sense an 'aberrant' work. For six years my attempts to understand the possibility of affirmation in an essentially morbid society were dominated by and finally invested in three women: Mildred Constance Jenkins was the first, Hester Smit the second, and Lena the culmination. As with *The Blood Knot*, I can find only one reference to it in my notebooks.

14/5/62
The novel has aborted. Read what I had written to Sheila last night. Her silence and my own feelings as I progressed from one muddled paragraph to another were enough. I don't consider the work wasted. The characters are with me now. They'll come out one day. In any

case this business of writing 'prose' because a publisher wants 'prose', is wrong. I'm a playwright.

So tomorrow I start again. How many false starts before one finds a beginning that leads through to an end! But I am hopeful. One image has resurrected an old complex of ideas: Milly's panic when she realizes late at night that she's spent the whole day in her dressing gown.

Her cri-de-coeur: 'Is this all we get?' Hurt or outrage? Obviously both. Certainly not despair.

It was during this period at home that I was approached by a group of men and women from New Brighton (Port Elizabeth's African township; population approx. 200,000) and asked to help start a drama group along the lines of the one I had left working in the Rehearsal Room. This was the beginning of Serpent Players. Our first production, in May 1963, was a free adaptation to a township setting of Machiavelli's *The Mandrake*. Seven years later there was a revival of that production here in Port Elizabeth which we staged together with *Friday's Bread on Monday*—an improvised essay into hunger and desperation in the townships. In the years between, among our productions were Büchner's *Woyzeck*, Brecht's *Caucasian Chalk Circle*, and Sophocles' *Antigone*, all of which had an urgent relevance to the lives of the people of the township.

We function as an amateur group—that is to say, nobody gets paid and we do most of our rehearsing at night. At the moment Serpent Players consists of myself and another white as non-acting members, and ten members from the township. Of the latter one is a school-teacher, one a social worker, four are factory workers, two messengers, and two domestic servants. Most of our performances take place in the townships, though we do manage to give a few white friends a chance to see our work by way of private performances. We have been refused permission to perform publicly for whites. In the eight years of our existence Serpent Players have had to cope with the imprisonment of some members on political charges and with police harassment and isolation—Africans are given virtually no chance to see any of the white theatre that is staged in Port Elizabeth. As regards performances and rehearsals, we work under the most primitive physical circumstances imaginable. Apart from the talent of one individual in white theatre, the work of this group is the only significant provocation and stimulus to myself as writer and director that I have encountered in South Africa. In the context of theatre in this country I think it is the only group of actors with a unique and important identity, a truly creative potential which if one day fully realized might be our most meaningful contribution to theatre.

I began working seriously on *Hello and Goodbye* towards the end of 1963. My notebooks have a more extensive record of both the genesis of this play and my problems in writing it.

19/5/63

From time to time I keep remembering, and still see occasionally on the streets, one face from my youth. That of a man who, for as long as I can remember, could be seen at night standing motionless against the wall on the corner of Jetty and Main Streets. Large unsmiling eyes, heavy lids. Bitter mouth. Must have seen him a hundred times, yet I have no recollection of any expression other than this one of morbid withdrawal. Saw him about a week ago—entrance to the public lavatory behind the Town Hall. Has taken to standing there these days. I watched him for a few minutes. He stood motionless, staring at nothing. Face is now bloated, eyes glazed, shabbily dressed. Next to him stood a young Coloured boy, watching the white man with amused contempt. My man said something to the boy (without looking at him), then lurched away down the street. He was dead drunk.

Remember my father. He had the same way of telling people, even strangers, the next move in their enormously trivial game of life, and then doing it. 'Well, better be on my way.' 'Think I'll make it an early night.'

When I think of the places where this man could live, I get excited. The Valley for example.

Johnnie (Boetie to his family).

Johnnie Smit.

Johnnie Le Gransie.

19/6/63

Still thinking about Johnnie. A Port Elizabeth story. I see and feel him in terms of Jetty Street, the Valley, South End and his tireless vigil on the Union Castle Corner at night, and beside Queen Victoria's statue during the day. Not to forget of course that that is where the bus drivers gather with their tin boxes of tickets and time-sheets.

16/9/63

Last night before sleep found myself thinking about Johnnie—the local street-corner derelict I made a few notes about some months back. I remembered a thought I had about a sister and suddenly I saw very clearly the germinal situation of a play. Thinking about it this morning I am again excited.

Johnnie living with his father in a two-room shack in Valley Road. The father is blind and a cripple . . . victim of a blasting accident when he worked for the South African Railways. Johnnie looks after him—feeding, washing, dressing, carrying. They exist on the old man's pension—old age or disability. One night, after ten or fifteen years absence, his sister arrives back unexpectedly at the little house. All she possesses in the world she has with her in an old and battered suitcase. Her purpose is revealed. She believes the old man was paid 'hundreds of pounds compensation' by the S.A.R. for the accident. It is in a box under his bed. She wants the money. Is ready to steal. Eventually even prepared to kill the old man to get it. None of these possibilities happens. She leaves Johnnie and the old man together.

First problem. Do we see the old man? Or only Johnnie and his sister? (Her name?) Even if not seen, the old man's presence must be felt . . . a bigotry and meanness of spirit as twisted and misshapen as his physical reality.

The sister a common prostitute. Even before leaving home for Johannesburg she had men. Sailors (war years). In fact the reason for her leaving home—her father found out. Her past fifteen years in Johannesburg—an experience that has taken her to the limits of physical violence and crudity. Carnal reality.

'I'm not a woman any more. What's a woman? Not me. They fuck me but I'm not a woman.' All that is left for her is the 'happiness' in the box 'under daddy's bed'. What does she mean by happiness?

What defeats her?

Johnnie does not recognize his sister when she walks in with her old suitcase. She has to tell him, 'I'm . . . .'

The sister: All hope (blind) and meaning in 'the box under daddy's bed'. An obsession that allows of neither right nor wrong, yes or no. She must get it. This is what life has come down to. Apart from that there are only memories, and most of them provoke her to either anger, hate, or disgust. One other reality—her bruises, her physical self. Flesh that has said fuck-you to the spirit.

The old man: His cries, pain, plight—a drug which keeps Johnnie numb.

25/9/63

Almost certain now that the next play is going to be about Johnnie and Hester Smit. Central images becoming increasingly obsessional. How many themes does a writer really have? How *few* can he have? This play—the idea—is in one sense a fusion of elements in *The Blood Knot* and *People Are Living There*. If I can realize my intentions though, it should be closer to the former in style and structure— tense and tight. Main problem remains whether to have only two characters, or whether the father should also be seen.

29/9/63

Certain now that there will only be two characters—Johnnie and Hester. At one level this worries me a little because it means the inevitable comparison with *The Blood Knot*. Once I get past this fear though and concern myself only with what is real, it seems so pointless to even consider 'adding' another character. In Hester and Johnnie I find a *complete* expression of the complex of ideas and images that have generated this play.

Two acts, one interval.

The First Act—Hester's arrival, her reason for returning, the first suitcase.

The Second Act—suitcase after suitcase, box after box, their contents spilling out onto the floor. A growing chaos in which Hester flounders, almost drowns, as she finds her past, her promise, her life, and finally sees clearly their ruin in the present. And leaves.

19/12/63

Thinking and making notes almost continuously now about the Valley play. Difficulty in the mechanics of the climax, when Hester 'loses hope' and 'learns she must die'. Suspicious of what I feel is a stock pattern or formula in my resolution of the climactic moment, i.e. *growing desperation*, leading to *emotional crisis*, leading to *the leap*.

Thinking about it for a moment I realize that I am wrong to see this as a formula common to all my other plays. *The Blood Knot* doesn't have it. Far from leaping, Morrie and Zach wake up heavy and hopeless, almost prostrate on the earth.

Yes, that is it! What I am searching for in the new play is the moment when Hester 'wakes up'. Three experiences: Loss of hope, knowledge of death, and finally the only certainty, the flesh . . . 'truths the hand can touch'.

What could be more obvious than that I should be drawn to, overwhelmed by Camus. Wasn't I trying to do that to Morrie and Zach at the end of *The Blood Knot*—two men who were going to try to live without hope, without appeal. In effect Morrie is trying to say, in that final beat of the play: Now we Know.

At this point my work on *Hello and Goodbye* was interrupted by a trip to Zambia (then Northern Rhodesia) to direct a production of Brecht's *Caucasian Chalk Circle*. This production never reached a stage. I was forced to leave the country after being threatened with deportation for stating publicly that I had encountered less understanding and communication between the races in that country than in South Africa. I returned to my work on *Hello and Goodbye* in the second half of 1964.

4/9/64
Hester gives me a chance for the ruthless honesty I so admire in Faulkner. Also Camus' 'Courageous Pessimism'. Isn't Hester the closest I've yet come to the bone? Even in Milly *(People Are Living There)* there is still too much 'meat'—something that must rot or be cut away before the hard, white truth is exposed.

11/1/65
Title: *Hello and Goodbye.*
   'To my father, who lived and died in the next room.'
   Resumed work after the New Year. 1st Act in rough draft. Second Act in outline and a mass of notes.
   Strong sense of Hester's moral anarchy. Have abandoned the idea of Hester forgetting about the money while she searches through the boxes for something *specific* and *special* from her childhood, and which when found will trigger off a cathartic reliving of a moment in her youth. Instead, she still forgets the compensation from time to time, but is searching for something she herself cannot identify.
   What does Hester want? To begin with, the compensation. But only *to begin with*, because she walks into that room unconscious of her life; 'in it' as she says at the end. But one level of her experience with the boxes and all that comes out of them is a growing alienation, a removal from her characteristic intense 'being myself'. At this level she is searching for something that will counter the absurdity spilling out of the boxes.

13/1/65
Succeeded yesterday in an Act Two speech in defining Hester's resentment of the world, the 'revolt of the back streets'. How much of this will remain in the final draft, in fact how important it is to the main statement, I do not yet know. But it is certainly a part of Hester's reality, and if not dwelt upon must at least be felt. An expression of her moral anarchy.

14/1/65

Important step forward yesterday. Plotted the sequence that takes the play through to the last box and Hester's climax on discovering that the next room is empty, that her father is dead. Two major gains in my rough outline of the play. First, and specifically, I see the way to a full and complete expression of the absurdity that overwhelms Hester ('There is no God!'). Secondly, and more generally, I see a pattern, not just a plot, a chance to weave together all that Johnnie and Hester mean separately—the 'simultaneous' moment with all its complexity in design and depth that I achieved unconsciously in *The Blood Knot* and was not able to repeat in *People Are Living There*.

18/2/65

A question I cannot fully answer. (Yet? Ever?) What is it that draws Johnnie to the crutches? Any number of 'little' answers. Tantalized by the thought that there is one 'final' answer that still eludes my thinking? Do I need to know it? Because I *feel* the absolute reality of his fascination with his father's crutches, I see him so clearly drawing closer and closer to the moment when he goes onto them permanently.

28/2/65

To master the idiom—thought and speech—of a character. The problem is never 'what' Hester and Johnnie think, but 'how' they think it. A constant challenge in all the plays.

The first presentation of *Hello and Goodbye* in Johannesburg in October 1965 brought me into a fresh confrontation with the problem of segregated audiences. In the three years that had passed since the run of *The Blood Knot*, the Government had enacted legislation which made it impossible to have either mixed casts or audiences at a *public* performance. In this context it was a question of either accepting this compromise or doing nothing at all. I decided on the former. Since *Hello and Goodbye* all my plays have gone before segregated audiences, on the condition that whenever staged both white and non-white communities be given a chance to see them.

It is very difficult for me to indicate the full extent of the inner debate involved in agreeing to this compromise. Since 1965 I have doubted the wisdom and decency of this decision as many times as I have reaffirmed it. Fairly recently I was forced yet again to evaluate my standpoint on this issue and I decided I would still rather attempt to relate to fellow South

Africans under these conditions than not at all. Some of my thinking and feeling about all this is reflected in the following extracts from my notebook and a letter to Mary Benson, a friend in London.

3/5/68

Work of the past ten days disturbed by a sudden resurgence of the playwrights' boycott issue. Sparked by an interview Laurens van der Post gave on his arrival back in London, in which he quoted me correctly as saying that I thought the situation in South Africa would now be better served by abandoning the boycott. First, two incredibly agitated and irritable letters from Mary: Was van der Post right? Surely not! Timing of statement appalling! . . . death of Luther King, Olympic Games issue, racial troubles in Britain, etc., etc. Would I please write straight away to the London *Times*, giving a full statement.

Spent the whole weekend trying to examine my conscience and feelings for a personal reply to her when the papers came on the phone for a statement. I gave Maisch (Levin, of the South African *Sunday Times*) the following:

'When I first advocated the boycott by playwrights five years ago, my decision to do so related directly to the circumstances then prevailing in South Africa. I felt the gesture might provoke some reaction from the theatrical managements in this country who had accepted the principle of segregated audiences long before they were in fact forced to do so by law. Now the laws are on the statute books and the timid and indifferent among us have a perfect excuse. But the five years that have passed have seen far profounder changes in our society than the loss of just this one opportunity. Virtually all significant opposition to the Government has been silenced . . . either in our jails, by being despatched into exile, by banning orders, censorship, or just plain intimidation. The ultimate irony is that the same period has seen the emergence of the myth of an 'outward-going' South Africa, of a policy (separate development) which given a fair chance would show itself to be ultimately decent.

'One of the consequences of this is a complacency among the majority of whites in South Africa that threatens our future more certainly than any of the dire communist plots the Government keeps warning us about. It is frightening to see to what extent white South Africans have been bluffed or intimidated into accommodating the appalling consequences of the policies of this Government.

'My point is obvious. Anything that will get people to think and feel for themselves, that will stop them delegating these functions to the politicians, is important to our survival. Theatre has a role to play in this. There is nothing John Balthazar Vorster and his Cabinet would like more than to keep us isolated from the ideas and values current in the Free Western World. These ideas and values find an expression in the plays of contemporary writers. I think we South Africans should see these plays.'

My reply to Mary was on a private and personal level—an attempt to explain to her (and understand for myself) my survival impulses ... maybe reflexes is a better word. It boiled down finally to one point, one dilemma: That I appear to, and might well be, accommodating a big evil in order to sustain a little good. As I said to her:

'The issue is people—it's the fact that men can be good, that the good must be sustained and that it's almost impossible to imagine a situation on this earth where it is harder to survive with any decency than here and now in S.A. I can't think of any moral dilemma more crucifying than this one—to destroy the evil at the cost of what little good there is, or to seem to accommodate the evil by sustaining the good. *I am not sure. I do not know.* I don't think I ever will. But to sit in moral paralysis while the days of my one life, my one chance to discover the brotherhood of other men, pass is obviously so futile and pointless it is not worth talking about. So without the support of reason, or a clear conviction as to consequences— relying only on an instinct (blind as it is) at the core ... I have chosen to act.'

It is not that the executioners are ineffective. I suppose the contrary is the terrible truth. But I don't want to be one of them.

My passport was withdrawn by the Government in June 1967, a few days after the screening in Britain of the B.B.C. Television production of *The Blood Knot*. Whether there is any connection here I do not know. The Government consistently refused to give any reasons for its action against me. My own feeling is that the act was meant to intimidate and so force me into leaving the country permanently on a one-way ticket, the so-called 'Exit Permit'. The Government has made frequent use of the withdrawal of passports, particularly in cases where it cannot 'get at' the person involved by actual imprisonment or does not want to use a banning order, as means of purging the society of what it regards as undesirable elements. Between 1967 and 1970 I tried on three separate occasions, when the opportunity for work abroad presented itself, to have my passport returned. My application was refused each time. Then in 1971, following on a petition to the Government which friends here had organized on my behalf, I tried again so as to be able to take up an offer to direct *Boesman and Lena* for the Theatre Upstairs in London. This time my application was partially successful. My passport was returned to me for a limited period of one year with my travelling restricted to the United Kingdom. Although I felt very strongly the loss of the opportunity to travel outside South Africa—particularly as this cut me off from direct contact with new developments in theatre in England, America, and the Continent—the thought of leaving my country permanently was, and remains, intolerable.

I first began working on *Boesman and Lena* in October 1967. I find these two entries in my notebook.

2/10/67

Boesman—self-hatred and shame, focused on Lena, who is, after all, his life . . . tangible and immediate enough to be beaten, derided, and, worst of all, needed. His jealousy and bewilderment in her relationship with the old man. Her discovery of value, of herself as having value. Boesman's loneliness at that moment.

Boesman and Lena facing each other across the scraps and remnants of their life.

'I'll carry my share.'

'This is all we are . . . all we've got.'

Love. Desertion.

25/10/67

An essay on the translation of poetry—form and content of one language as opposed to another (English and Afrikaans here in S.A.)—prompts the thought that an important element in my own writing is this question of 'translating' from Afrikaans to English. Particularly conscious of it this time with *Boesman and Lena*. To begin with, so much of it was in Afrikaans—some phrases are still and seem to defy translation into an English equivalent that will have the same texture or feel, e.g., *nog 'n vrot ou huisie vir die vrot mens*.

Lowell's *Imitations*.

I shelved *Boesman and Lena* to work on an original television script for the B.B.C., *Mille Miglia*, based on the background to Stirling Moss's victory in this famous motor race. I came back to *Boesman and Lena* ten months later and then stayed with it until its completion.

2/6/68
Boesman and Lena: Just by accident, in paging back through this notebook, found the first entry and images I noted down just under a year ago. These, plus a sudden realization of personal parallels, of the possibility of making a personal statement, make the thought of these two reject characters very provocative.

A little surprised to find how fully realized the Boesman and Lena story already is, how much of it is implicit in those early images. Why had I shelved it? Boesman shouldering all they have, and then Lena taking her share and joining him! Will see what happens.

4/7/68
First act down in the roughest of rough drafts, skeleton for the second. More difficulty than I expected in finding the substance to this man-woman relationship. Struggling for objectivity and distance. For example: Boesman's hatred and abuse of Lena. Easy enough to formulate this as an 'idea' but a struggle to reveal the full carnal reality of it in incident and dialogue.

Unrelieved squalor of their situation demands that I write this one very carefully. Flowers on the dung-heap. Where has all my 'joy' gone? Morrie and Zach had it. Hester and Johnnie had it. Realized that the genesis of this play lies possibly in an image from over ten years ago—Coloured man and woman, burdened with all their belongings, whom I passed somewhere on the road near Laingsburg. It was sunset and they were miles from the nearest town. Then of course also the old woman near Cradock on the drive back from Norman's trial. 'Put your life on your head and walk.'

Again: Brecht's 'ease' (Messingkauf Dialogues). Lightness and laughter.

6/7/68
A Lena on the banks of the Swartkops River yesterday while fishing with Don.

Saw her as we were leaving our spot on the Canal wall. Either drunk or hung-over—number of bait-diggers and Coloured fishermen had spent the night there. Bitterly cold. Bottles of cheap wine to help them live through it.

Scarf on her head, faded maroon blouse, and an old blue skirt. Barefoot. Unseeing eyes, focused if anything on the ground just ahead. We were merely 'whitemen'—nothing could have been more remote from her life, from her experience of herself, at that moment. Walked like a somnambulist. Face shrivelled and distorted by dissipation, resentment, regrets. Strangely no surprise at seeing her.

To Don: '. . . just a sense of the possibility of the sacrilegious and the sacred, of the demand that the truth be told, that I must not bear false witness.'

Physical texture of the place—mud.

13/7/68

Memory of another Coloured woman who gives weight to my image of Lena. Lived somewhere in the bush along the Glendore Road. Worked for us for a short period about two years ago. Sense of terrible physical and spiritual destitution, of servility. Did the housework without a sound, without the slightest flicker of 'self'. For some reason left us after about two months, then came back some time later to see if we had any work. Stiflingly hot day—Berg wind blowing. In the course of the few words I had with her she seemed in an even more desperate condition—not so much physically as in a sense of her disorientation, almost derangement, as if only a fraction of herself was committed to and involved in the world around her.

After our telling the woman we had no work she left to try a few other houses. Last sight of her about two hours later. Heat even more fierce. Obviously unsuccessful in her search for work, she was trudging up the hill on her way back to the Glendore bush.

That hill, that sun, that walk! Possibly even a walk that my Lena has not yet made, but *will* one day in the course of the little time that lies ahead of her as she takes up her load and follows the frightened Boesman across the mudflats. A walk beyond the moment of rebellion—that possibility past, even forgotten—a walk beyond the battles, the refusals, the last few tears. A walk into the final ignominy of silence, burdened at that moment as never before by those unanswerable little words . . . Why? How? Who? What?

16/7/68

Floundering in first act, specifically Lena's first long soliloquy when she tries to unravel and order her memories of the past, tries to work out how she got to where she is. Very clear on the function and 'feel' of this moment, but can't get it down on paper. Same in a sense true for the whole first movement of the play . . . from their arrival to the appearance of Outa. Sure I experienced the same problem with *Hello and Goodbye*—made a note about skating on a hard surface reality, waiting for it to break somewhere, somehow, so that I could fall in and be forced to survive in 'depth'.

I'm sure the Zen precept is right—the harder you try the more it will elude you. (Beating a drum while hunting the fugitive.) Spontaneity. Must rediscover this in my writing. Without it there can be no 'happy accidents'. Will leave the first act for the moment and sketch in, wherever I feel I want to, the second act. So often the paradox in writing—discover your beginning when you reach the end.

19/7/68

To be careful that I do not pitch Boesman at a level of monotonous hatred and abuse. Not just the technical problem of variety of tone and tempo—the more basic issue that it is not as simple as Lena being the victim and Boesman the oppressor. Both are ultimately victims of a common, a shared predicament, and of each other. Which of course makes it some sort of love story. They are each other's fate.

So for Boesman as total a statement as for Lena. What is mutilated and why? The key I am sure is to reveal and dramatize his self-hatred as focused on Lena. What he really hates is himself.

Thus:

Lena . . . sense of injustice, implying therefore a value of self.

Boesman . . . no value, or rather a denial of value as the price of his uneasy and violent acceptance of the world he finds himself in. His fear and loneliness when Lena chooses the old man at the end of Act One . . . *because Boesman's greatest fear is discovering he has value.*

Must do something about a decent title.

23/7/68

The complex of central images survives the frequent assault of my doubts about validity, significance, etc. On top of this they have now also become obsessional—increasingly impatient with any time spent away from them. Now also working in the afternoons. Any number of blanks remain though. Lena and the old man . . . I do not yet have any image of her 'choice'. Why does she choose to sit out there in the cold with him? Any number of ideas as answers, but still no image.

Pound . . . Image is that which releases an emotional and psychological complex in an instant of time.

21/8/68

Good work on Boesman and Lena (must find title).

Strong and clear sense of the dynamics to the first act. Most important consequence is that Lena now has a drive, is 'moving' and not just sitting there in the mud floundering in her predicament. Reading Laing's *Politics of Experience* and *Bird of Paradise* has added new dimensions to my thinking about Boesman and Lena. Ontological insecurity: Lena in her demand that her life be witnessed. Not just a sense of injustice and abuse.

Growing sense also of the pattern of the whole of being able to find the right (and only) moment for images and actions.

23/8/68

In Pretoria tried without much success to find or remember for Mary an example of what I call the 'accident' in my writing. An example of it five minutes ago. Sorting out my ideas and images for the ending of Act One—Lena at the fire with Outa, sharing her mug of tea and piece of bread, kept hearing her say, 'This mug . . .' 'This bread' . . . 'My life . . .'. Suddenly, and apparently irrelevantly, remembered Lisa the other day reading a little book on the Catholic Mass. There it was. Lena's Mass—the moment and its ingredients became sacramental, the whole a celebration of her life.

9/9/68

Two or three more days and I should have a skeleton outline for the second act. Two fulcrums in the dynamic of Lena's predicament.

1) Calling Outa into her life—her sense of her life, her feeling for it, involvement in it, demand that it be witnessed.

2) Outa's death—her alienation. 'I'm alone.' 'So that is all. Hold on tight, and then let go.' She lets go. But you can't be dead before you die, so . . . 'Give me mine.' She takes herself back for another walk, possibly her last.

Do I know what this means! ! !

The naïveté of these notes. Like maps of the world before they discovered the earth was round.

Title: *Boesman and Lena.*

Significantly, in my days at this table I don't look at the map [Port Elizabeth and environs] on my wall any more, but at blank paper. When I started work on the play it was that little stippled area [the mudflats] beside the washed blue of the river that riveted my attention. Fruitless hours staring at it. The answers to all my questions lay in the still greater mystery of blank foolscap paper. Before the magic of the 'word' the clotted, choking reality of blank paper. Every, but every possibility. I choose one.

11/9/68

The thought today that *Boesman and Lena* is the third part of a trilogy, that together with *The Blood Knot* and *Hello and Goodbye* it should be called *The Family*.

First brother and brother, then child and parent, and now in *Boesman and Lena*, parent and parent, man and woman.

Economy. To write the line which, coupled with the actor's gesture, will say the 'whole' and not one jot more . . . or better still which *needs* the actor's gesture to complete it.

26/12/68

Ernst Fischer and his description of the Marxist artist as being 'commissioned by his society'. My whole dilemma, specifically now with *Boesman and Lena*, focused in this. Do I want a commission? Have I got one? Must I function without one? Is my context as artist irremediably Bourgeois? How do I align myself with a future, a possibility, in which I believe but of which I have no clear image? A failure of imagination.

The social content of *Boesman and Lena*. Nagging doubts that I am opting out on this score, that I am not saying enough. At one level their predicament is an indictment of this society which makes people 'rubbish'. Is this explicit enough?

The thought that this play is really a one-acter, that there should be no interval.

When *Boesman and Lena* was first presented in South Africa in 1969 I had serious misgivings about running into trouble with our Censorship Board. Censorship of theatre, books, publications, and films produced *in* South Africa had been enacted since the time of *The Blood Knot*. To judge by the results, I doubt very much whether the Censorship Board would have allowed *The Blood Knot* to be staged without insisting on drastic cuts. In the case of *Boesman and Lena*, however, there was no trouble. With this play I was again able to present it to all sections of the community: performances to 'whites only' audiences, and in the African, Indian, and Coloured townships. I think this means nothing more than that I was lucky. The threat of censorship is one of the most inhibiting factors in the South African artistic scene. There are several ideas I have for plays which I just know would not be allowed to reach the stage or, if they did, would be shut down very soon after opening.

That is that. I've said all I want to, and maybe all I can, about myself as a South African and a writer. Like everyone else in this country, black and white, my horizons have shrunk, and will continue to do so. Today's future barely includes tomorrow. At times I see the situation deteriorating still further, to the point where even the thought of a tomorrow will be a luxury. I'm trying to live and work in preparation for that eventuality.

ATHOL FUGARD
Port Elizabeth

THE
BLOOD KNOT

A PLAY
IN SEVEN SCENES

CHARACTERS

There are two characters, ZACHARIAH *and* MORRIS. *Zachariah is dark-skinned and Morris is light-skinned.*

All the action takes place in a one-room shack in the Non-White location of Korsten, near Port Elizabeth, South Africa. The walls are a patchwork of scraps of corrugated iron, packing-case wood, flattened cardboard boxes, and old hessian bags. There is one door, one window (no curtains), two beds, a table, and two chairs. Also in evidence is a cupboard of sorts with an oil-stove, a kettle, and a few pots. The shack is tidy and swept, but this only enhances the poverty of its furnishings. Over one of the beds is a shelf on which are a few books and an alarm-clock.

THE BLOOD KNOT was first produced at the Rehearsal Room (African Music and Drama Association), Johannesburg, on 23 October 1961 with the following cast:

MORRIS	Athol Fugard
ZACHARIAH	Zakes Mokae

SCENE ONE

Late afternoon.

   Lying on his bed, the one with the shelf, and staring up at the ceiling, is Morris. *After a few seconds he stands up on the bed, looks at the alarm-clock, and then lies down again in the same position. Time passes. The alarm rings and Morris jumps purposefully to his feet. He knows exactly what he is going to do. First, he winds and resets the clock, then lights the oil stove and puts on a kettle of water. Next, he places an enamel washbasin on the floor in front of the other bed and lays out a towel. He feels the kettle on the stove and then goes to the door and looks out. Nothing. He wanders aimlessly around the room, for a few more seconds pausing at the window for a long look at whatever lies beyond. Eventually he is back at the door again and, after a short wait, he sees someone coming. A second burst of activity. He places a packet of foot-salts beside the basin, turns off the stove, pours hot water into the basin, and finally replaces the kettle.*

   Zachariah *comes in through the door.*

   Their meeting is without words. Morris nods and Zachariah grunts on his way to the bed where he sits down, drags off his shoes, and rolls up his trousers. While he does this Morris sprinkles foot-salts into the basin and then sits back on his haunches and waits. Zachariah dips his feet into the basin, sighs with satisfaction, but stops abruptly when he sees Morris smile. He frowns, pretends to think, and makes a great business of testing the water with his foot.

ZACHARIAH. Not as hot as last night, hey?

MORRIS. Last night you said it was too hot.

ZACHARIAH [*thinks about this*]. That's what I mean.

MORRIS. So what is it? Too hot or too old?

ZACHARIAH. When?

MORRIS. Now.

ZACHARIAH. Luke-ish. [*Bends forward and smells.*] New stuff?

MORRIS. Yes.

ZACHARIAH. Oh! Let's see.

   [*Morris hands him the packet. Zachariah first smells it, then takes out a pinch between thumb and forefinger.*]

   It's also white.

3

MORRIS. Yes, but it is different stuff.

ZACHARIAH. The other lot was also white but it didn't help, hey?

MORRIS. This is definitely different stuff, Zach. [*Pointing.*] See. There's the name. Radium Salts. [*Zachariah is not convinced. Morris fetches a second packet.*] Here's the other. Schultz's Foot Salts.

ZACHARIAH [*taking the second packet and looking inside*]. They look the same, don't they? [*Smells.*] But they smell different. You know something? I think the old lot smells nicest. What do you say we go back to the old lot?

MORRIS. And you just said it didn't help!

ZACHARIAH. But it smells better.

MORRIS. It's not the smell, Zach. You don't go by the smell, man.

ZACHARIAH. No?

MORRIS. It's the healing properties.

ZACHARIAH. Maybe.

MORRIS [*taking back the new packet*]. Listen to this. . . . [*Reads.*] 'For all agonies of the joints: lumbago, rheumatism, tennis elbows, housemaid's knees; also ideal for bunions, corns, callouses' . . . that's what you got . . . 'and for soothing irritated skins.'

[*Zachariah lets him finish, examining the old packet while Morris reads.*]

ZACHARIAH. How much that new stuff cost?

MORRIS. Why?

ZACHARIAH. Tell me, man!

MORRIS [*aware of what is coming*]. Listen, Zach. It's the healing properties. Price has got nothing. . . .

ZACHARIAH [*insistent*]. How—much—does—that—cost?

MORRIS. Two and six.

ZACHARIAH [*with a small laugh*]. You know something?

MORRIS. Yes, yes, I know what you're going to say.

ZACHARIAH. This old stuff, which isn't so good, is three bob. A sixpence more! [*He starts to laugh.*]

MORRIS. So? Listen, Zach. No. Wait, man! Price, Zach . . . ZACH! Do you want to listen or don't you? [*Zachariah is laughing loud in triumph.*] PRICE HAS GOT NOTHING TO DO WITH IT!!

ZACHARIAH. Then why is this more money?

MORRIS. Profit. He's making more profit on the old stuff. Satisfied?

ZACHARIAH. So?

MORRIS. So.

ZACHARIAH. Oh. [*Slowly.*] So he's making more profit on the old stuff. [*The thought comes.*] But that's what you been buying, man! *Ja* . . . and with my money, remember! So it happens to be my profit he's making. Isn't that so? I work for the money. Not him. He's been making my profit.

[*Zachariah is getting excited and now stands in the basin of water.*]

Ja. I see it now. I do the bloody work . . . all day long . . . in the sun. Not him. It's my stinking feet that got the hardnesses. But he goes and makes my profit.

[*Steps out of the basin.*]

I want to work this out, please. How long you been buying that old stuff? Four weeks? That makes four packets, hey? So you say sixpence profit . . . which comes to . . . two bob . . . isn't that so? Whose? Mine. Who's got it? Him . . . him . . . some dirty, rotting, stinking, creeping, little. . . .

MORRIS. But we are buying the cheap salts now, Zach! [*Pause.*] He's not going to get the profits any more. And what is more still, the new salts is better.

[*The thread of Zachariah's reasoning has been broken. He stares blankly at Morris.*]

ZACHARIAH. I still say the old smells sweeter.

MORRIS. I tell you what. I'll give you a double dose. One of the old and of the new . . . together! That way you get the healing properties and the smell. By God, that sounds like a cure! Hey? How's that, Zach? Okay?

ZACHARIAH. Okay.

[*He goes to the bed, sits down, and once again soaks his feet.*]
You got any more warm?

[*Morris pours the last of the hot water into the basin. Zachariah now settles down to enjoy the luxury of his footbath. Morris helps him off with his tie and afterwards puts away his shoes.*]

MORRIS. How did it go today?

ZACHARIAH. He's got me standing again.

MORRIS. At the gate?

ZACHARIAH. *Ja.*

MORRIS. But didn't you tell him, Zach? I told you to tell him that your feet are calloused and that you wanted to go back to pots.

ZACHARIAH. I did.

MORRIS. And then?

ZACHARIAH. He said, 'Go to the gate or go to hell.'

MORRIS. That's an insult.

ZACHARIAH. What's the other one?

MORRIS. Injury!

ZACHARIAH. No. The long one, man.

MORRIS. Inhumanity!

ZACHARIAH. *Ja.* That's what I think it is. My inhumanity *from him.* 'Go to the gate or go to hell.' What do they think I am?

MORRIS. What about me?

ZACHARIAH [*anger*]. Okay. What do you think I am?

MORRIS. No, Zach! Good heavens! You got it all wrong. What do *they* think *I* am, when they think what *you* are?

ZACHARIAH. Oh.

MORRIS. Yes. I'm on your side, they're on theirs. There's always two sides to a sad story and I mean . . . I couldn't be living here and not be on yours, could I? [*Morris is helping Zachariah off with his coat. When Zachariah is not looking he smells it.*]

Zach, I think we must borrow Minnie's bath again.

ZACHARIAH. Okay.

MORRIS. What about me? Do I smell?

ZACHARIAH. No. [*Pause.*] Have I started again?

[*Morris doesn't answer. Zachariah laughs.*]

MORRIS. Yes, you do.

ZACHARIAH [*with sly amusement*]. How?

MORRIS. Sweat. . . .

ZACHARIAH. Go on.

MORRIS. You're still using paper the way I showed you, hey?

ZACHARIAH. *Ja*. What's that thing you say, Morrie? The one about smelling?

MORRIS [*quoting*]. 'The rude odours of manhood.'

ZACHARIAH. 'The rude odours of manhood.' And the other one? The long one?

MORRIS. 'No smell'? [*Zachariah nods.*]
'No smell doth stink as sweet as labour.
'Tis joyous times when man and man
Do work and sweat in common toil,
When all the world's my neighbour.'

ZACHARIAH. 'When all the world's my neighbour.' [*Zachariah starts drying his feet with the towel. Morris empties the basin and puts it away.*] Minnie.

MORRIS. What about Minnie?

ZACHARIAH. Our neighbour. Strange thing about Minnie. He doesn't come any more.

MORRIS. I don't miss him.

ZACHARIAH. You don't remember. I'm talking about before you.

MORRIS. Of course I remember. Didn't he come that once when I was here? And sit all night and say nothing?

ZACHARIAH. Before that, Morrie. I'm meaning before your time, man. He came every night. *Ja*! [*Little laugh.*] Me and him use to go out . . . together you know . . . quite a bit. [*Pause.*] Hey!

MORRIS. What's the matter?

ZACHARIAH. How did I forget a thing like that!

MORRIS. What are you talking about?

ZACHARIAH. Me and Minnie going out! Almost every night . . . and I've forgotten. [*Pause.*] How long you been here?

MORRIS. Let's see. About a year.

7

ZACHARIAH. Only one miserable year and I forgotten just like that! Just like it might not hardly have never happened!

MORRIS. Yes, Zach. The year has flown by.

ZACHARIAH. You never want to go out, Morrie.

MORRIS. So I don't want to go out.

ZACHARIAH. That's all.

MORRIS. No. Wait. Why? Ask me why and I'll tell you. Come on.

ZACHARIAH. Why?

MORRIS. Because we got plans, remember? We're saving for a future, which is something Minnie didn't have.

ZACHARIAH. *Ja.* He doesn't come no more.

MORRIS. You said that already, you know. I heard you the first time.

ZACHARIAH. I was just thinking. I remembered him today. I was at the gate. It was lunchtime. I was eating my bread.

MORRIS. Did you like the peanut butter?

ZACHARIAH. I was eating my bread. All of a suddenly like, I know I'm alone, eating my bread at the gate, and it's lunchtime.

MORRIS. You can have it again tomorrow.

ZACHARIAH. And then it comes, the thought: What the hell has happened to old Minnie?

MORRIS. Zach, I was asking you. . . .

ZACHARIAH. Wait, man! I'm remembering it now. He used to come, I thought to myself, with his guitar to this room, to me, to his friend, old Zachariah, waiting for him here. Friday nights it was, when a *ou*'s got pay in his pocket and there's no work tomorrow and Minnie is coming. There was friend for a man! He could laugh, could Minnie, and drink! He knew the spots, I'm telling you, the places to be and the good times and . . . and what else? *Ja!* [*Reverently.*] Minnie had music! Listen, he could do a *vastrap*, that man, non-stop, on all strings, at once. He knew the lot. Polka, *tickey-draai, opskud en uitkap, ek sê* . . . that was jollification for you, with Minnie. So, when I'm waiting here, and I hear that guitar in the street, at my door, I'm happy!

8

It's you, I shout. He stops. I know it's you, I say. He pretends he isn't there, you see. Minnie, I call. Minnie! So what does he do then? He gives me a quick *chik-a-doem* in G. He knows I like G. It's Friday night, Minnie, I say. *Chik-a-doem-doem*. Are you ready? *Doem-doem*, he says. And then I'm laughing. You bugger! You motherless bastard. So I open the door, and what do I see? Minnie! And what's that he got in his hand? Golden Moments at two bob a bottle. Out there, Morrie. Standing just right on that spot out there in the street with his bottle and his music and laughing with me. Zach, he says, *Ou pellie*, tonight is the night. . . . [*The alarm goes off.*] . . . is the night . . . tonight. . . .

[*Zachariah loses the thread of his story. By the time the alarm stops, he has forgotten what he was saying. The moment the alarm goes off Morris springs to his feet and busies himself at the table with their supper. Zachariah eventually goes back to the bed.*]

What's for supper tonight?

MORRIS. Fish, as usual. [*Watching Zachariah surreptitiously from the table.*] I been thinking, Zach. It's time we started making some definite plans. I mean . . . we've agreed on the main idea. The thing now is to find the right place. [*Pause.*] Zach? [*Pause.*] We have agreed, haven't we?

ZACHARIAH. About what?

MORRIS. Hell, man. The future. It is going to be a small two-man farm, just big enough for you and me; or what is it going to be?

ZACHARIAH. *Ja*.

MORRIS. Right. We agree. Now, I'm saying we got to find the right place. [*Pause.*] Zach! What's the matter with you?

ZACHARIAH. I was trying to remember what I was saying about Minnie. There was something else.

MORRIS. Now listen, Zach! I'm sorry, but I'll have to talk to you now. What's the matter with you? Hey? You said yourself he doesn't come no more. So what are you doing thinking about it? Here am I putting our future to you and you don't even listen. The farm, Zach! Remember, man? The things we're going to do. Picture it! Picking our own fruit. Chasing those damned baboons helter-skelter in the *koppies*. Chopping the firewood trees . . . and a cow . . . and a horse . . . and little chickens. Isn't it exciting? Well, I haven't been sitting still, Zachie. I been saying to myself: What's the problem? The right place, I replied. And that's a problem all right. It's a big world this. A big, bloody world. Korsten, my friend, is just the beginning. [*Morris fetches an old map from the shelf over his bed.*] Now, I want you to take a look at this. You want to know what it is? A map. Of what? . . . you might ask. Of Africa, I reply. Now, this is the point, Zach. There . . . and there . . . and there . . . and down here. . . . Do you see it? Blank. Large, blank spaces. Not a town, not a road, not even those thin little red lines. And, notice, they're green. That means grass. So what, you say. So this. I reckon we should be able to get a few acres in one of these blank spaces for next to nothing. I look at it this way.

[*Zachariah, bored, leaves the bed and goes to the window and looks out.*]

You listening, Zach?

ZACHARIAH. *Ja.*

MORRIS. This is not just talk, you know. It's serious. I'm not smiling. One fine day, you wait and see. We'll pack our things in something and get to hell and gone out of here.

Yes! Now that I come to think of it. You say I don't want to get out? My reply is that I do, but I want to get right out. You think I like it here more than you? You should have been here this afternoon. The wind was blowing again. Coming this way it was, right across the lake. You should have smelt it. I'm telling you that water has gone bad. Really rotten! And what about the factories there on the other side? Hey? And the lavatories all around us? They've left no room for a man to breathe.

Go out, you say. But go out where? On to the streets? Are they any better? Where do they lead? Nowhere. That's my lesson. City streets lead nowhere . . . just corners and lamp-posts. And roads are no different, let me tell you . . . only longer, and no corners and no lamp-posts which, in a way, is even worse. I mean . . . I've seen them, haven't I? Leading away into the world—the big empty world.

But when we go, Zach, together, and we got a place to go, our farm in the future . . . that will be different.

[*Zachariah has been at the window all the time, staring out. He now sees something which makes him laugh. Just a chuckle to begin with, but with a suggestion of lechery.*]

What's so funny?

ZACHARIAH. Come here.

MORRIS. What's there?

ZACHARIAH. Two donkeys, man. You know.

[*Morris makes no move to the window. Zachariah stays there, laughing from time to time.*]

MORRIS. Yes. It's not just talk. When you bring your pay home tomorrow and we put away the usual, guess what we will have? Go on. Guess. Forty-five pounds. If it wasn't for me you wouldn't have nothing. Ever think about that. You talk about going out, but forty-five pounds. . . .

ZACHARIAH [*breaking off in the middle of a laugh*]. Hey! I remember now! By hell! About Minnie. [*His voice expresses vast disbelief.*] How did I forget? Where has it gone? It was . . . ja . . . ja. . . . It was woman! That's what we had when we went out at night. Woman!!

[*Morris doesn't move. He stares at Zachariah blankly. When the latter pauses for a second Morris speaks again in an almost normal voice.*]

MORRIS. Supper is ready.

[*Zachariah loses the train of his thought, as with the alarm-clock, earlier. Morris sits down.*]

So . . . where were we? Yes. Our plans. When, Zach? That's another thing we got to think about. Should we take our chance with a hundred pounds, one hundred and fifty? I mean . . . we can even wait till there is three hundred, isn't that so? [*Zachariah is still standing.*] Bring that chair over there, man, and sit down and eat.

[*Morris has already started on his supper. As if hypnotized by the sound of the other man's voice, Zachariah fetches the chair and sits.*]

So what are we going to do, you ask? This. Find out what the deposit, cash, on a small two-man farm, in one of those blank spaces, is. There are people who handle this sort of thing. So we'll find one. Have no worry about that. We'll hunt him down.

Take some bread, man. [*Offering a slice.*]

For all we know, only a couple of months more over here, and then. . . .

ZACHARIAH. No! [*Hurls, into a corner, the slice of bread he took from Morris.*]

MORRIS. What's this?

[*With even greater violence Zachariah sweeps away the plate of food in front of him.*]

What's that?

ZACHARIAH. You're not going to make me forget. I won't. I'm not going to. We had woman, I tell you. [*Pounding the table with his fists.*] Woman. Woman! Woman!

MORRIS. Do you still want the farm?

ZACHARIAH. Stop it! I won't listen!

[*Jumps up from the table. Rushes across to the other side where his jacket is hanging. Begins to put it on.*]

ZACHARIAH. What do you think I am, hey? Guess! Two legs and trousers. I'm a man. And in this world there is also woman, and the one has got to get the other. Even donkeys know that. What I want to know now, right this very now, is why me, Zach, a man, for a whole miserable little year has had none. I was doing all right before that, wasn't I? Minnie used to come. He had a bottle, or I had a bottle, but we both had a good time, for a long time. And then you came . . . and. . . . [*Pause.*]

MORRIS. Say it.

ZACHARIAH. . . . then you came. That's all.

[*Zachariah's violence is ebbing away. Perplexity takes its place.*]

You knocked on the door. It was Friday night. I remember. I got a fright. A knocking on my door on Friday night? On *my* door? Who? Not Minnie. Minnie's coming all right, but not like that. A knocking on my door on a Friday night? So I had a look, and it was you standing there, and you said something, hey?

What did I say? 'Come in.' Didn't I? 'Come in,' I said. And when we had eaten I said again, 'Come out with me and a friend of mine, called Minnie.' Then you said, 'Zach, let us spend tonight talking.' *Ja*, that's it. That's all. A whole year of spending tonights talking, talking. I'm sick of talking. I'm sick of this room.

MORRIS. I know, Zach. [*He speaks quietly, soothingly.*] That's why we got plans for the future.

ZACHARIAH. But I was in here ten years without plans and never needed them!

MORRIS. Time, Zach. It passes, and a man gets sick of things. It's happened to you.

ZACHARIAH. I was in here ten years and didn't worry about my feet, or a future, or having supper on time!

MORRIS. The body, Zach. It gets old. A man feels things more.

ZACHARIAH. But I had fun and Minnie's music!

MORRIS. That's life for you. The passing of time and worthless friends.

ZACHARIAH. I want woman.

MORRIS. I see. I see that, Zach. Believe me, I do. But let me think about it. Okay? Now finish your supper and I'll think about it.

[*Morris puts his own plate of food in front of Zachariah and then moves around the room picking up the food that Zachariah swept to the floor.*]

You get fed up with talking, I know, but it helps, doesn't it? You find the answers to things, like we are going to find the answer to your problem. I mean. . . . Look what it's done for us already. Our plans! Our future! You should be grateful, man. And remember what I said. You're not the only one who's sick of this room. It also gets me down. I say: A whole year . . . and sigh . . . but to myself. That's why you never hear. A whole year, I say, and sigh, and always the smell of the rotting waters. In between my cleaning and making the room ready when you're at work, I look at the lake. Even when I can't smell it I just come here to the window and look. [*Morris is now at the window and looking at the lake.*] It's a remarkable sheet of water. Have you noticed it never changes colour? On blue days or grey days it stays the same dirty brown. And so calm, hey, Zach! Like a face without feeling. But the mystery of my life, man, is the birds. Why, they come and settle here and fly around so white and beautiful on the water and never get dirty from it too!

[*Turning to Zachariah.*] How you doing, chap?

[*Leaving the window.*] Have you noticed, Zach, the days are getting shorter again, the nights longer? Autumn is in our smelly air. It's the time I came back, hey! About a year ago! We should have remembered what day it was, though. Would have made a good birthday, don't you think? A candle on a cake for the day that Morrie came back to Zach. Yes. That's bitter. Not to have remembered what day it was. I mean . . . so much started for both of us, and it wasn't easy, hey? I reckon it's one of the hard things in life to begin again when you're already in the middle.

[*Zachariah leaves the table and goes to his bed.*]

You finished?

ZACHARIAH. *Ja*.

MORRIS. Jam or peanut butter tomorrow?

ZACHARIAH. Jam.

MORRIS. Don't you like the peanut butter?

ZACHARIAH. It's all right.

MORRIS. Shall we make it peanut butter then?

ZACHARIAH. *Ja*, okay.

MORRIS. I knew you'd like it.

[*Pause. Morris makes the sandwiches.*]

Has it helped, Zach?

ZACHARIAH. What?

MORRIS. The talking.

ZACHARIAH. Helped what?

MORRIS. About . . . woman.

ZACHARIAH. No. It's still there. You said you was going to think about it and me.

MORRIS. I'm still busy, Zach. It takes time. Shall I talk some more?

14

ZACHARIAH. Let me!

[*He speaks eagerly. The first sign of life since the outburst.*]

Let me talk about . . . woman?

MORRIS. You think it wise?

ZACHARIAH. You said it helps. I want to help.

MORRIS. Go on.

ZACHARIAH. You know what I was remembering, Morrie? As I sat here?

MORRIS. No.

ZACHARIAH. Guess.

MORRIS. I can't.

ZACHARIAH [*soft, nostalgic smile*]. The first one. My very first one. You was already gone. It was in those years.

MORRIS [*looking at Zachariah with interest*]. Tell me about her.

ZACHARIAH [*visibly moved*]. Hell man! You say a thing like that! You know, about being young and not caring a damn.

MORRIS. 'So sweet did pass that summer time,
Of youth and fruit upon the tree,
When pretty girls and laughing boys
Did hop and skip and all were free.'

ZACHARIAH. 'Did skop and skip the pretty girls.' [*Sigh.*] Her name was Connie.

MORRIS. That's a lovely name, Zach.

ZACHARIAH. Connie Ferreira.

MORRIS. You were happy, hey?

ZACHARIAH. *Ja.*

MORRIS. Don't be shy. Tell me more.

ZACHARIAH. We were young.

MORRIS. Shame! That's a moving thought. Must have been a sad sight. You and Connie.

ZACHARIAH. Her mother did washing. Connie used to buy blue soap from the Chinaman on the corner.

MORRIS. Your sweetheart, hey!

ZACHARIAH. I waited for her.

MORRIS. Was it true love?

ZACHARIAH. She called me a black *hotnot*, the bitch, so I waited for her. She had tits like fruits. So I waited for her in the bushes.

MORRIS [*absolute loss of interest*]. Yes, Zach.

ZACHARIAH. She was coming along alone. Hell! Don't I remember Connie now! Coming along alone, she was, and I was waiting in the bushes. [*Laugh.*] She got a fright, she did. She tried to fight, to bite. . . .

MORRIS. All right, Zach!

ZACHARIAH. She might have screamed, but when I had her. . . .

MORRIS. That's enough!!

[*Pause.*]

ZACHARIAH. That was Connie.

[*He broods.*]

MORRIS. And I was away.

ZACHARIAH. *Ja.* It was the years when you was away.

MORRIS. Feeling better?

ZACHARIAH. A little.

MORRIS. Talking helps, doesn't it? I said so. You find the answers to things.

ZACHARIAH [*undressing for bed*]. Talking to one would help me even more.

MORRIS. Yes. . . . [*Pause.*] You mean to a woman?

ZACHARIAH. I'm telling you, Morrie, I mean it, man. With all my heart.

MORRIS [*the idea is coming*]. There's a thought there, Zach.

ZACHARIAH. There is?

MORRIS. In fact I think we got it.

ZACHARIAH. What?

MORRIS. The answer to your problem, man.

ZACHARIAH. Woman?

MORRIS. That's it! You said talking to one would help you, didn't you? So what about writing? Just as good, isn't it, if she writes back?

ZACHARIAH. Who . . . who you talking about?

MORRIS. A pen-pal, Zach! A corresponding pen-pal of the opposite sex! Don't you know them? [*Zachariah's face is blank.*] It's people, Zach, who write letters to each other. My God! Why didn't I think of it before! It's a woman, you see! She wants a man friend, but she's in another town, so she writes to him . . . to you!

ZACHARIAH. I don't know her.

MORRIS. You will. You're her pen-pal!

ZACHARIAH. I don't write letters.

MORRIS. I will.

ZACHARIAH. Then it's your pen-pal.

MORRIS. No, Zach. You tell me what to say. I write just what you say. You see, she writes to you. She doesn't even know about me. Can't you see it, man? A letter to Mr. Zachariah Pietersen . . . you . . . from her.

ZACHARIAH. I don't read letters.

MORRIS. I'll read them to you.

ZACHARIAH. From a woman.

MORRIS. From a woman. You can take your pick.

ZACHARIAH [*now really interested*]. Hey!

MORRIS. There's so many.

ZACHARIAH. Is that so!

MORRIS. Big ones, small ones.

ZACHARIAH. What do you know about that!

MORRIS. Young ones, old ones.

ZACHARIAH. No. Not the old ones, Morrie. [*Excited.*] The young ones, on the small side.

MORRIS [*happy*]. Just take your pick.

ZACHARIAH. Okay. I will.

MORRIS. Now listen, Zach. When you get your pay tomorrow, take a *tickey*, go into a shop, and ask for a newspaper with pen-pals.

ZACHARIAH [*repeating*]. . . . with pen-pals.

MORRIS. That's it. We'll study them and you can make your pick.

ZACHARIAH. And I can say what I like?

17

MORRIS [*hesitant*]. Y-e-s . . . but she's a lady remember, so you must be decent.

ZACHARIAH. And she will write back?

MORRIS. That's what they're there for. . . . That's pen-pals.

ZACHARIAH. Hell, Morrie!

MORRIS. Tomorrow you'll see.

ZACHARIAH. And she's going to write to me. Hey, what do you know! Pen-pals!

MORRIS. That's it!

[*Zachariah flops back on his bed laughing. Morris drifts to the window.*]

MORRIS. Wind's coming up. You sleepy?

ZACHARIAH. It's been a long day.

MORRIS. Okay, we'll cut it short.

[*Morris fetches a Bible from the shelf over his bed. He hands it to Zachariah who, with his eyes tightly closed, opens it and brings his finger down on the page.*]

Four?

[*Zachariah nods. Morris reads.*]

'And if thou bring an oblation of a meat offering baken in the oven, it shall be unleavened cakes of fine flour with oil or unleavened wafers anointed with oil: And if thy oblation be a meat offering baken in a pan it shall be of fine flour, unleavened, mingled with oil: Thou shalt part it in pieces and pour oil thereon. It is a meat offering.'

ZACHARIAH. Sounds nice.

MORRIS. Yes. But we haven't got a pan.

[*He replaces the Bible, finds needle and cotton, and then takes Zachariah's coat to the table.*]

I'm helping you, aren't I, Zach?

ZACHARIAH. *Ja*, Morrie.

MORRIS. I want to believe that. You see. . . . [*Pause.*] . . . there was all those years, when I was away.

ZACHARIAH. Why did you come back?

MORRIS. I was passing this way.

ZACHARIAH. Why did you stay?

MORRIS. We are brothers, remember.

[*A few seconds pass in silence. Morris threads his needle and then starts working on a tear in Zachariah's coat.*]

That's a word, hey! Brothers! There's a broody sound for you if ever there was. I mean. . . . Take the others. Father. What is there for us in . . . Father? We never knew him. Even Mother. Maybe a sadness in that one, though, I think, at times. Like the wind. But not much else. She died and we were young. What else is there? Sister. Sissy, they say, for short. Like something snaky in the grass, hey? But we never had one, so we can't be sure. You got to use a word a long time to know its real meaning. That's the trouble with 'Mother'. We never said it enough.

[*He tries it.*] Mother. Mother! Yes. Just a touch of sadness in it, and maybe a grey dress on Sundays, and soapsuds on brown hands. That's the lot. Father, Mother, and the sisters we haven't got. The rest is just the people of the world. Strangers, and a few friends. And none of them are blood.

But brothers! Try it. Brotherhood. Brother-in-arms, each other's arms. Brotherly love. Ah, it breeds, man! It's warm and feathery, like eggs in a nest. [*Pause.*] I'll tell you a secret now, Zach. Of all the things there are in this world, I like most to hear you call me that. Zach?

[*He looks at Zachariah's bed.*]

Zachie? Zachariah!

[*He is asleep. Morris takes the lamp, goes to the bed, and looks down at the sleeping man. He returns to the table, picks up the Bible, and after an inward struggle speaks in a solemn, 'Sunday' voice.*]

'And he said: What hast thou done? The voice of thy brother's blood crieth unto me!'

[*Morris drops his head in an admission of guilt.*]

Oh Lord! Oh Lord! So he became a hobo and wandered away, a marked man, on a long road, until a year later, in another dream, He spake again: Maybe he needs you, He said. You better go home, man!

[*Pause.*]

So he turned around on the road, and came back. About this time, a year ago. Could have been today. I remember

19

turning off the road and coming this way across the veld. The sun was on my back. Yes! I left the road because it went a longer way around . . . and I was in a hurry . . . and it was autumn. I had noticed the signs on the way. Motor-cars were fewer and fast. All of them were crowded and never stopped. Their dust was yellow. Telephone poles had lost all their birds . . . and I was alone . . . and getting worried.

I needed comfort. It's only a season, I said bravely. Only the beginning of the end of another year. It happens all the time! Be patient! . . . which was hard hurrying home after all those years. . . . Don't dream at night! You must get by without the old dreams. Maybe a few new ones will come with time . . . and in time, please! . . . because I'm getting desperate, hey! . . . I remember praying.

Then I was off the road and coming here across the veld, and I thought: It looks the same. It was. Because when I reached the first *pondokkies* and the thin dogs, the wind turned and brought the stink from the lake and tears, and a clear memory of two little *outjies* in khaki *broeks*.

No one recognized me, after all those years. I must have changed. I could see they weren't sure, and wanting to say 'Sir' at the end of a sentence and ask me for work and wanting to carry my bundle for a *tickey*. At first I was glad . . . but then came a certain sadness in being a stranger in my old home township. I asked the time. It's not late, they said. Not really dark, don't worry. It always gets this way when the wind blows up the factory smoke. The birds are always fooled and settle down too soon to sleep . . . they assured me.

I also asked the way. Six down, they said, pointing to the water's edge. So then there was only time left for a few short thoughts between counting the doors. Will he be home? Will I be welcome? Be remembered? Be forgiven . . . or forgotten, after all those years? Be brave, Morris! Because I had arrived at that door here about a year ago. I remember I reached it . . . and held my breath . . . and knocked . . . and waited . . . outside in the cold . . . hearing a move inside here . . . and then there was my heart as well, the smell of the water behind my back, his steps beyond the door, the slow terrible turning of the knob, the squeak of a rusty hinge, my sweat, until at last, at long last after a lonely road he stood before me . . . frowning.

[*Pause.*]

You were wearing this coat. It's been a big help to me, this warm old coat . . . then . . . and in the days that followed. But specially then. It was all I saw at first! I didn't dare look up, because your eyes were there, and down below on the ground were your sad, square feet, and coming out to me, your hands . . . your empty hands. So I looked at your coat! At the buttons. At the tears, and your pockets hanging out . . . while we talked.

And that night, in the dark, when you slept, I put it on . . . because, I've got to get to know him again, I said, this brother of mine, all over again.

[*Morris puts on Zachariah's coat. . . . It is several sizes too large.*]

It was a big help. You get right inside the man when you can wrap up in the smell of him, and imagine the sins of idle hands in empty pockets and see the sadness of snot smears on the sleeve, while having no lining and one button had a lot to say about what it's like to be him . . . when it rains . . . and cold winds. It helped a lot. It prepared me for your flesh, Zach. Because your flesh, you see, has an effect on me. The sight of it, the feel of it . . . it . . . it feels, you see. Pain, and all those dumb dreams throbbing under the raw skin, I feel, you see. . . . I saw you again after all those years . . . and it hurt.

SCENE TWO

The next evening.

Zachariah sits disconsolately on the bed, his feet in the basin. Morris is studying a newspaper.

MORRIS. Well, Zach, you ready? There's three women here. The young ladies Ethel Lange, Nellie de Wet, and Betty Jones.

ZACHARIAH. So what do we do?

MORRIS. I'll get the ball rolling with this thought: They are all pretty good names.

ZACHARIAH. That's for true.

MORRIS. Ethel, Nellie, and Betty. Good, simple, decent, clean, common names. About equal, I'd say.

ZACHARIAH [*hopefully*]. There's no Connie, is there, Morrie?

MORRIS. No. Now, before you decide, I suppose I'd better tell you about them.

ZACHARIAH. What do you know about them?

MORRIS. It's written down here, man. That's why you bought the paper. Listen.... [*Reads.*] 'Ethel Lange, 10 de Villiers Street, Oudtshoorn. I am eighteen years old and well-developed and would like to correspond with a gent of sober habits and a good outlook on life. My interests are nature, rock-and-roll, swimming, and a happy future. My motto is, "Rolling stones gather no moss." Please note: I promise to reply faithfully.' How's that?!

ZACHARIAH. Well-developed.

MORRIS. She gives a *ou* a clear picture, hey! Here's the next one. [*Reads.*] 'Nellie de Wet' . . . she's in Bloemfontein . . . 'Twenty-two and no strings attached. Would like letters from men of the same age or older. My interests are beauty contests and going out. A snap with the first letter, please.' [*Pause.*] That's all there is to her. I think I preferred Ethel. I mean . . . there was more to her, it sounds to me and . . . well . . . Nellie's greedy, isn't she?

ZACHARIAH. *Ja.* And what do I know how old I am?

MORRIS. Exactly, Zach! I mean . . . it was years ago, hey!

Maybe forty or more, taking a quick look at you. Where does she think she comes from . . . 'my age or older'?

ZACHARIAH. Bloemfontein.

MORRIS. Yes. Last one. [*Reads.*] 'Betty Jones. Roodepoort. Young and pleasing personality. I'd like to write to gentlemen friends of maturity. No duck-tails need reply. My hobby at the moment is historical films, but I'm prepared to go back to last year's, which was autograph-hunting. I would appreciate a photograph.' She's got a education. Anyway . . . it's up to you. Take your pick.

ZACHARIAH [*after thinking about it*]. Hey, Morrie! Let's take all three.

MORRIS. No, Zach.

ZACHARIAH. *Ag*, come on.

MORRIS. You don't understand.

ZACHARIAH. Just for sports, man!

MORRIS. I don't think they'd allow that.

ZACHARIAH [*losing interest*]. Oh.

MORRIS [*emphatic*]. No, they wouldn't. [*Pause.*] Listen, Zach, you must take this serious.

ZACHARIAH. Okay.

MORRIS [*losing patience*]. Well, it's no good saying 'Okay' like that!

ZACHARIAH. Okay!

MORRIS. Must I talk to you again? Hey! What's the use, Zach? You ask me to help you, and when I do, you're not interested any more. What's the matter?

ZACHARIAH. I can't get hot about a name on a piece of paper. It's not real to me.

MORRIS [*outraged*]. Not real! [*Reads.*] 'I am eighteen years old and well-developed.' . . . eighteen years old and well-developed! If I called that Connie it would be real enough, wouldn't it?

ZACHARIAH [*his face lighting up*]. *Ja*!

MORRIS. So the only difference is a name. This is Ethel and not Connie . . . which makes no difference to being eighteen years old and well-developed! Think, man!

ZACHARIAH [*without hesitation*]. Look, Morrie, I'll take her.

MORRIS. That's better. So it's going to be Miss Ethel Lange at 10, de Villiers Street, Oudtshoorn, who is eighteen years old and well-developed and would like to correspond with a gent of sober habits and a good outlook on life. [*Putting down the paper.*] Yes, she's the one for you all right. Your outlook is quite good, Zach. You have a friendly smile—especially when you're sober, which is what she wants. And I know what we do. How about asking Ethel to take a snapshot of herself? The others done it. Nellie and Betty. We'll get one from Ethel so that you can know what *her* outlook is. Then . . . just think of it . . . you can see her, hear from her, write to her, correspond with her, post your letter off to her. . . . Hell, man! What more do you want?! [*Zachariah smiles.*] No! Don't tell me. That's something else. This is pen-pals, and you got yourself Ethel in Oudtshoorn. Now, come and eat and we'll talk about our first letter to her. [*At the table.*] I got polony and chips tonight. Variety spiced with life, as they say. [*Zachariah sits down at the table and starts eating.*] You want to hear about Oudtshoorn, Zach? I been there.

ZACHARIAH. Okay.

MORRIS. Sort of give you the picture, so that you can see it.

ZACHARIAH. What's the difference? [*Morris looks at him sharply.*] One town, another town. This place, her place. She lives in a room in a street, like us.

MORRIS. So you're not interested in Oudtshoorn. Is that it?

ZACHARIAH. What's it got to do with it? We're going to send a letter to this. . . .

MORRIS. Her name is Ethel Lange.

ZACHARIAH. That's right. [*Continues eating. Morris waits.*]

MORRIS. Well? Finish what you were going to say.

ZACHARIAH. When?

MORRIS. You said, 'We're going to send a letter to this. . . .'

ZACHARIAH. Her name is Ethel Lange.

MORRIS. That's right. [*Pause.*] Okay. Fine. And I was going to tell you about Oudtshoorn where she lives because I been there, wasn't I? Yes. Well . . . it's about four days from here with good lifts. I been along that road twice and both times it was four days. But I've met those who done it in two . . . even one! Anyway, about Oudtshoorn. I think they call it the dusty uplands of the Karroo, that part where it is behind the mountains. Dry country, man. White, white thorns and the bushes grey and broken off. They roll about the veld when the wind blows. And, of course, there's the dust as well. Dusty as hell it is, when that wind blows. To get there, Zach, you turn your back on the sea and go north through the mountains. The sky gets big and the earth ends up flat and round like a penny. I want to say this: I'm surprised there's a pen-pal in Oudtshoorn. It doesn't strike in my memory as a pally sort of place at all. I remember mostly yellow walls and red roofs. That's what you see when you reach there where the road bends beside a river running dry. It was summer, you see, and I was going in on a lorry. We passed people walking to town. They just stopped, and stood there in the dust, and watched us go by. They were our sort. You get them everywhere. Country folk, simple folk. They always stop and watch you go by. Now for Oudtshoorn itself. I'll give it to you clear. Not too big, as I remember; not too small, either, because it was a long walk through to the other end where the road carried on. Houses, like I said. Red roofs, yellow walls . . . that yellow, sunny wall, you know, with fig trees on the other side, and, of course, the people. Both times I went straight through. I didn't make no friends there. [*Pause.*] Anything else you want to know, Zach?

ZACHARIAH. Nothing.

MORRIS. Aren't you interested in the climate?

ZACHARIAH. *Ja.*

MORRIS. That's a question all right. Well, I thought I was going to die of thirst until that lorry stopped.

ZACHARIAH. Thirsty.

MORRIS. And what about the major industries?

ZACHARIAH. Them too.

MORRIS. Well, as I was saying, I didn't stop long, but I reckon you could get work there like any place else. [*Zachariah leaves the table.*] You finished?

ZACHARIAH. *Ja.*

MORRIS. Left your chips, Zach. What's wrong?

ZACHARIAH. Not nice chips.

MORRIS. Same as always. Ferreira's.

ZACHARIAH. I—said—they—aren't—nice—chips!

MORRIS. And the bread, too?

ZACHARIAH. *Ja.* And the bread too.

MORRIS. Okay. [*Starts clearing the table.*] But we always have polony and chips on a Friday. [*Zachariah says nothing.*] I mean . . . that was an agreement, like fish on Thursday.

ZACHARIAH [*in a rage*]. Well, I'm telling you now! They— aren't—nice—chips! [*Morris looks blankly at him. This enrages Zachariah even more.*] Look at them, will you! Look! This one! Now I just want to know one thing! Does that look like it came from a potato? Hey? And this one? Now tell me. Would you even give this to a horse?

MORRIS. Why a horse?

ZACHARIAH. Why not? Some stinking horse.

MORRIS. They don't eat. . . .

ZACHARIAH. You just keep quiet, Morris, and let me finish this time, and don't think I'm going to get lost in my words again. That bloody clock of yours doesn't go off till bedtime, so I got plenty of time to talk. So just you shut up, please! Now this chip . . . and the other one I showed you . . . and the whole, rotten, stinking lot. [*Zachariah is throwing them all round the room.*] If my profit is tied up in this as well, I'll go out and murder the bastard. Well? Is it?

MORRIS. I don't think so.

ZACHARIAH. So you don't think so. How much you pay for them?

MORRIS. Sixpence. Like always.

ZACHARIAH. Like always. Well, all I can say is that he's lucky, because if I ever meet that Ferreira, I'm going to ask him what he thinks I am. A *hotnot*! A *swartgat kaffer*!

MORRIS. Stop it!

[*Morris jumps forward with his arm raised as if to hit Zachariah. This silences Zachariah, who looks at his brother, first with surprise,*

26

then amusement, which finally starts him laughing. His laughter becomes uproarious and he has to sit down on the bed. Morris turns away.]

ZACHARIAH. Your face! Your poor bloody face! Hey, Morrie? Why's it you get like that?

MORRIS. I don't know what you're talking about.

ZACHARIAH. Come on, man. I was just making a joke.

MORRIS. A joke!

ZACHARIAH. This *hotnot* joke. But it always gets you, hey? Now come on. There's a question. To hell with Oudtshoorn, and tell me why it always gets you like that?

MORRIS. I don't like to hear it.

ZACHARIAH [*a pause, then realizing his question hasn't been answered*]. But why?

MORRIS. Because you're my brother! [*Zachariah shakes his head and turns away.*] What's wrong?

ZACHARIAH. There is something in the way you say that word, that. . . .

MORRIS. What?

ZACHARIAH. Something. . . .

MORRIS. Go on.

ZACHARIAH. . . . in that word. . . .

MORRIS. Brother?

ZACHARIAH. . . . and the way you say it like . . . say it.

MORRIS. Brother.

ZACHARIAH. Like a soft sound.

MORRIS [*trying it out*]. Brother!

ZACHARIAH. And a dark sound, too. It's. . . .

MORRIS. Brothers!

ZACHARIAH. When I heard it for the first time, I said it means something. He means something, I thought, does Morrie when he says it so often. . . . So soft and . . . I don't know! What?

MORRIS. Why not, Zach? It's us. Our meaning. Me and you . . . in here.

ZACHARIAH. Warm. A warm word.

MORRIS. Ah! Now you're on to it. A woolly one. Like old

27

brown jackets a size too big. But what does that matter, as long as it keeps out the cold, and the world?

ZACHARIAH [*breaking away to the window*]. Hell, it's hot tonight. You want to know something? I'd like to jump into that lake and swim away.

MORRIS. Mustn't do that. You've seen the notices.

ZACHARIAH. I don't read notices.

MORRIS. They're warnings. It's unfit for human consumption being full of goggas that begin with a B. I can never remember.

ZACHARIAH. Then it's no bloody use, is it?

MORRIS. Just a dead bit of water. They should drain it away, now that winter's coming and the birds are gone. Pull out the plug and fill up with fresh.

ZACHARIAH. You say a thing about it. The one that gives me the creeps.

MORRIS.   'No fish nor fowl,
         Did break the still hate of its face.'

ZACHARIAH. Hell!

MORRIS [*breaking the mood*]. Well, what about Ethel? What about writing to her all alone in her eighteen well-developed years up Oudtshoorn way, where I've been. What do you say, Zach? Do you still want her?

ZACHARIAH [*fervently*]. Do I still want her!

MORRIS. Or Nellie?

ZACHARIAH. Nellie.

MORRIS. Or Betty? Do you still want Ethel?

ZACHARIAH. Or Betty, or Nellie. [*Pause.*] Bellie. [*Pause.*] Nelly's belly.

MORRIS [*encouragingly*]. That's good, Zach! A little game like that with a word or two.

ZACHARIAH [*sitting on his bed*]. You know, Morrie, it's a long time since I called a woman's name.

MORRIS. Now you got three to pick from.

ZACHARIAH. In a woman's name, man, there is. . . . [*Pause, and a gesture.*] When you call it out loud on a Friday night, you know, outside her door, it's like. . . . [*Pause, and a gesture.*]

When you whisper it, man, in the grass, in the wet grass, when you start to fiddle and she makes her little cries, it's . . . it's. . . . [*Pause, and a gesture.*] Hey! It's a long time since I called a woman's name. You know, Morrie, you know the one I called with the gladdest heart?

MORRIS. Connie.

ZACHARIAH. No man. Then I was in hiding. It was by surprise, that time, and only once. I never saw her again. No . . . no, man. The one that gave me the happiest heart was Hetty.

MORRIS. That's a new one.

ZACHARIAH. New one! [*Zachariah laughs broadly.*] New one! You don't know what you mean. She was second-hand. The whole world had fingered her. Connie was new, but Hetty was second-hand . . . something old and a long time ago. It was my youth. You took your chance, you see. You went to her window and called her name and she came when the sound was right. I'm telling you, Morrie, some of them used to come back six times and try, with a *dop* in between to give them hope. No one knew what the right sound was, you see. Some days she liked it soft, another day loud, or maybe with a little laugh. I was a shy boy with pimples. Old Sarah sent me to borrow a candle, because Joseph was dying and she needed the light. So I stood in the street, very shy, and called: Hetty . . . Hetty! I only wanted a candle for old Sarah to see Joseph dying, but Hetty came to the window because she liked the sound. She took me and taught me. And you know something? It always worked if I did it that way. And not just Hetty. Sannie too, and Maria . . . they always came if I spoke—like asking for candles. I'm telling you, man, Morrie, not even Minnie. . . . [*Pause.*] *Ai . . . ai . . . ai!* What the hell has happened to old Minnie?

MORRIS. You said that yesterday.

ZACHARIAH. I'm thinking it again now.

MORRIS. A man can't spend his life with only one thought, Zach.

ZACHARIAH. But why doesn't he come no more?

MORRIS. Maybe he's sick.

ZACHARIAH. Never. Not a day in his long life did he caught a cold.

MORRIS. Then maybe he got old, if it was such a long life as you say. Yes. There's a thought for you.

ZACHARIAH [*horrified*]. Minnie—old?

MORRIS. It happens . . . to men . . . before their time . . . after women and too much life. Can't you see him?

ZACHARIAH. Minnie?

MORRIS. Yes. Take a good look with your mind's eye. No more dancing. No more drinking there! Gone are the *vastraps* and *tickey-draais*.

ZACHARIAH. Why?

MORRIS. His legs are stiff with old age.

ZACHARIAH. Grey hair, too?

MORRIS. If he's got any left. It falls out, you know.

ZACHARIAH. Bald head?

MORRIS. . . . cold bones . . . and nowhere to rest them.

ZACHARIAH. No home?

MORRIS. He's all alone, man, and on the streets, drifting sadly from lamp-post to lamp-post.

ZACHARIAH. With his old guitar, hey, Morrie!

MORRIS. No! He sold that for food. [*Zachariah has nothing left to say.*] Yes. You ever thought about that? Having to sell things for food. Having to leave this room because you couldn't pay the rent, so you sold it for food. Where would you go, hey? With that last little loaf wrapped up in newspaper. What would you do when it was finished? You've lost your job, remember . . . and like Minnie, you're alone. Unhappy thoughts, aren't they? And they would be, if I wasn't here. As it is, I am. But only because we're brothers. So you see, you mustn't let that word frighten you. It means there won't be no cold old age for us. We're saving for the future, for the best years of a man's life, when we'll have a place to go and things to do. And, in the meantime, there is Ethel. Which is a good idea, you'll see. She'll fill those empty hours without wasting you away. Which brings us round to your letter. Ready to write it? [*Pause.*] Come on, Zach. Cheer up, man.

Don't be so lustless. [*Nudging him slyly.*] Eighteen years and well-developed. You still want her? [*Zachariah looks up.*] That's better. [*Morris moves to the table where he sorts out a piece of writing-paper, a pencil, and an envelope.*] I've got everything ready. One day I must show you how. Maybe have a go at a letter yourself. Address in the top right-hand corner. Mr Zachariah Pietersen, Korsten P.O., Port Elizabeth. Okay, now take aim and fire away. [*He waits for Zachariah.*] Well?

ZACHARIAH. What?

MORRIS. Speak to Ethel.

ZACHARIAH [*shy*]. Go jump in the lake, man.

MORRIS. No, listen, Zach. I'm sitting here ready to write. You must speak up.

ZACHARIAH. What?

MORRIS. To begin with, address her.

ZACHARIAH. What!

MORRIS. Address her.

ZACHARIAH. Oudtshoorn.

MORRIS. You're not understanding. Now imagine, if there was a woman, and you want to say something to her, what would you say? Go on.

ZACHARIAH. Cookie . . . or . . . Bokkie. . . .

MORRIS [*quickly*]. You're getting hot, but that, Zach, is what we call a personal address, but you only use it later. This time you say: Dear Ethel.

ZACHARIAH. Just like that?

MORRIS. You got her on friendly terms. Now comes the introduction. [*Writes.*] 'With reply to your advert for a pen-pal, I hereby write.' [*Holds up the writing-paper.*] Taking shape, hey! Now tell her who you are and where you are.

ZACHARIAH. How?

MORRIS. I am . . . and so on.

ZACHARIAH. I am Zach and I. . . .

MORRIS. . . . ariah Pietersen . . . go on.

ZACHARIAH. And I am at Korsten.

MORRIS. 'As you will see from the above.'

ZACHARIAH. What's that?

MORRIS. Something you must add in letters. [*Newspaper.*] She says here: My interests are nature, rock-and-roll, swimming, and a happy future. Well, what do you say to that?

ZACHARIAH. Shit! [*Pause. Frozen stare from Morris.*] Sorry, Morrie, Nature and a happy future. *Ja.* Good luck! How's that? Good luck, Ethel.

MORRIS. Not bad. A little short, though. How about: I notice your plans, and wish you good luck with them.

ZACHARIAH. Sure, sure. Put that there. [*Morris writes, then returns to the newspaper.*]

MORRIS. 'My motto is: Rolling stones gather no moss.' [*Pause.*] That's tricky.

ZACHARIAH. I can see that.

MORRIS. What does she mean?

ZACHARIAH. I wonder.

MORRIS. Wait! I have it. How do you feel about: 'Too many cooks spoil the broth'? That's my favourite.

ZACHARIAH. Why not? Why not, I ask?

MORRIS. Then it's agreed. [*Writes.*] 'Experience has taught me to make my motto: Too many cooks spoil the broth.' Now let's get a bit general, Zach.

ZACHARIAH [*yawning*]. Just as you say.

MORRIS [*after a pause*]. Well, it's your letter.

ZACHARIAH. Just a little bit general. Not too much, hey!

MORRIS [*not fooled by the feigned interest*]. No. [*Pause.*] I can make a suggestion.

ZACHARIAH. That's fine. Put that down there, too.

MORRIS. No, Zach. Here it is. How about: I have a brother who has seen Oudtshoorn twice?

ZACHARIAH. You.

MORRIS. Of course. [*Pause.*] Well?

ZACHARIAH. Maybe.

MORRIS. You mean . . . you don't like it?

ZACHARIAH. I'll tell you what. Put in there: I'd like to see

Oudtshoorn. I've heard about it from someone. [*Morris writes.*]

MORRIS. What else?

ZACHARIAH. I'd like to see you too. Send me a photo.

MORRIS. . . . 'please' . . . I'm near the bottom now.

ZACHARIAH. That's all.

MORRIS. 'Please write soon. Yours. . . .'

ZACHARIAH. Hers?

MORRIS. . . . faithfully. Zachariah Pietersen. [*Zachariah prepares for bed. Morris addresses and seals the envelope.*] I'll get this off tomorrow. Remember, this is your letter, and what comes back is going to be your reply.

ZACHARIAH. And yours?

MORRIS. Mine?

ZACHARIAH. There's still Nellie. Or Betty. Plenty of big words there, as I remember.

MORRIS. One's enough. [*Zachariah lies down on his bed and watches Morris who has taken down the Bible.*] My turn tonight. [*Opens the Bible and chooses a passage.*] Matthew. I like Matthew. [*Reads.*] 'And Asa begat Josaphat, and Josaphat begat Joram, and Joram begat Ozias, and Ozias begat Joatham, and Joatham begat Achaz, and Achaz begat Ezekias, and Ezekias begat Manasses, and Manasses begat Amon, and Amon begat Josias!' [*Pause.*] That must have been a family. [*Puts away the Bible and prepares his own bed.*] Why you looking at me like that, Zach?

ZACHARIAH. I'm thinking.

MORRIS. Aha! Out with it.

ZACHARIAH. You ever had a woman, Morris? [*Morris looks at Zachariah blankly, then pretends he hasn't heard.*] Have you?

MORRIS. What do you mean?

ZACHARIAH. You know what I mean.

MORRIS. Why?

ZACHARIAH. Have—you—ever—had—a—woman?

MORRIS. When?

ZACHARIAH. Why have I never thought of that before? You

been here a long time now, and never once did you go out, or speak to me about woman. Not like Minnie did. Anything the matter with you?

MORRIS. Not like Minnie! What's that mean? Not like Minnie! Maybe it's not nice to be like Minnie. Hey? Or maybe I just don't want to be like Minnie! Ever thought about that? That there might be another way, a different way? Listen. You think I don't know there's woman in this world, or that I haven't got two legs and trousers too? That I haven't longed for beauty? Well, I do. But that's not what you're talking about, is it? That's not what Minnie means, hey! That's two bloody donkeys on a road full of stones and Connie crying in the bushes. Well, you're right about that. I am not interested. I touched the other thing once, with my life and these hands, and there was no blood, or screaming, or pain. I just touched it and felt warmth and softness and wanted it like I've never wanted anything in my whole life. Ask me what's the matter with me for not taking it when I touched it. That's the question. Do you want to know what was the matter with me? Do you? Zach? [*Pause, then softly.*] Zach?

[*Zachariah is asleep. Morris takes the blanket off his own bed and covers the sleeping man. He puts out the light and goes to bed.*]

SCENE THREE

A few days later.

Morris is at the table counting their savings—banknotes and silver. The alarm-clock rings. He sweeps the money into a tin which he then carefully hides among the pots on the kitchen dresser. Next he resets the clock and prepares the footbath as in the first scene. Zachariah appears, silent and sullen, goes straight to the bed, where he sits.

MORRIS. You look tired tonight, old man. [*Zachariah looks at him askance.*] Today too long? I watched you dragging your feet home along the edge of the lake. I'd say, I said, that that was a weary body. Am I right, old fellow?

ZACHARIAH. What's this 'old fellow' thing you got hold of tonight?

MORRIS. Just a figure of speaking, Zach. The shape of round shoulders, a bent back, a tired face. The Englishman would say 'old boy' . . . but we don't like that 'boy' business, hey?

ZACHARIAH. *Ja.* They call a man a boy. You got a word for that, Morrie?

MORRIS. Long or short?

ZACHARIAH. Squashed, like it didn't fit the mouth.

MORRIS. I know the one you mean.

ZACHARIAH. Then say it.

MORRIS. Prejudice.

ZACHARIAH. Pre-ja-dis.

MORRIS. Injustice!

ZACHARIAH. That's all out of shape as well.

MORRIS. Inhumanity!

ZACHARIAH. No. That's when he makes me stand at the gate.

MORRIS. Am I right in thinking you were there again today?

ZACHARIAH. All day long.

MORRIS. You tried to go back to pots?

ZACHARIAH. I tried to go back to pots. My feet, I said, are killing me.

MORRIS. And then?

ZACHARIAH. Go to the gate or go to hell . . . boy!

35

MORRIS. He said boy as well?

ZACHARIAH. He did.

MORRIS. In one sentence?

ZACHARIAH. Prejudice and inhumanity in one sentence!
[*He starts to work off one shoe with the other foot and then dips the bare foot into the basin of water. He will not get as far as taking off the other shoe.*]

ZACHARIAH. When your feet are bad, you feel it.

MORRIS. Try resting your legs.

ZACHARIAH. It's not so much in the legs.

MORRIS. Find a chair, then. Support your back.

ZACHARIAH. Chair! [*Scorn and contempt.*] A chair over there! What you talking about? A chair at the gate! Wake up, man! Anyway, it's not so much in my back also. It's here. [*A hand over his heart.*]

MORRIS. Ah, yes. *That* weariness.

ZACHARIAH. What is it?

MORRIS. The muscles of your heart.

ZACHARIAH. *Ja. Ja*! That sounds like it all right. The muscles of my heart are weary. That's it, man! Inside me, just here, I'm so tired, so damn tired to the bottom of my body of . . . what?

MORRIS. Beating. That's what a heart does to a man.

ZACHARIAH [*gratitude*]. By God, Morrie, you're on to it tonight. I'm tired of beating, beating, every day another beating. [*Pause.*] What's all this beating for anyway?

MORRIS. Blood.

ZACHARIAH. It gets worse and worse, hey! [*Pause.*] I looked at the stuff once, on my hands. It was red, so red as. . . .

MORRIS. Pain.

ZACHARIAH. *Ja.* [*Little laugh.*] But it wasn't mine. So it's my heart, is it? Getting tired. Tell me about it, Morrie. [*Morrie says nothing, but holds up his hand and rhythmically clenches and unclenches his fist.*] What's that?

MORRIS. Your heart.

ZACHARIAH. *Eina*! [*Morris continues.*] Give it a rest.

MORRIS. Doesn't rest.

ZACHARIAH. Not at all?

MORRIS. All the time.

ZACHARIAH. All the day?

MORRIS. And the night.

ZACHARIAH. Day and night?

MORRIS. In your bed.

ZACHARIAH. At the gate?

MORRIS. Until. . . . [*He breaks the rhythm. Keeps his fist clenched.*] Do you know what that is?

ZACHARIAH. No.

MORRIS. A failure. Dead.

ZACHARIAH [*upset.*] No, man!

MORRIS. Put your hand on your chest. You can feel it.

ZACHARIAH. Oh no, oh no!

MORRIS. Like I just showed you.

ZACHARIAH. I don't want to see it.

MORRIS. Don't be scared, man. [*Zachariah shakes his head.*] Then let me. [*Puts his hand over Zachariah's heart. Zachariah tenses.*]

ZACHARIAH. Still beating?

MORRIS. Yes.

[*Pause.*]

ZACHARIAH. Still there?

MORRIS. Yes. It's going: Dub-dub dub-dub dub-dub. . . . [*The strain is too much for Zachariah. He pushes Morris away.*]

ZACHARIAH. That's enough.

MORRIS. Come on. . . .

ZACHARIAH. I'm all right now. It's feeling fine. Tiredness gone.

MORRIS. Okay [*Starts helping Zachariah take off his coat.*] Funny, you know. I never thought about that before. That old heart of yours, beating away all the time, all the years when I was away. It's a sad thought. [*At this point Morris finds an envelope in the inside pocket of Zachariah's coat. He examines it*

37

secretly. Zachariah broods on, one foot in the basin.] Did you stop by the Post Office on your way back?

ZACHARIAH. *Ja.*

MORRIS. Nothing again? [*Pause.*] Looks like she's not replying.

ZACHARIAH. Who?

MORRIS. Ethel.

ZACHARIAH. *Ja.* There was a letter.

MORRIS. I know there was. [*Holding up the envelope.*] I just found it.

ZACHARIAH. Good.

MORRIS. Good? What do you mean good?

ZACHARIAH. You know . . . good, like Okay.

MORRIS [*excited and annoyed*]. What's the matter with you?

ZACHARIAH [*hand to his heart*]. What's the matter with me?

MORRIS. Don't you realize? This is your pen-pal. This is your reply from Ethel!

ZACHARIAH. In Oudtshoorn.

MORRIS. But Zach! You must get excited, man! Don't you want to know what she said?

ZACHARIAH. Sure.

MORRIS. Shall we open it then?

ZACHARIAH. Why not?

[*Morris tears open the letter.*]

MORRIS. By God, she did it! She sent you a picture of herself.

ZACHARIAH [*first flicker of interest*]. She did?

MORRIS. So this is Ethel!

ZACHARIAH. Morrie . . . ?

MORRIS. Eighteen years . . . and fully . . . developed.

ZACHARIAH. Let me see, man! [*He grabs the photograph. The certainty and excitement fade from Morris's face. He is obviously perplexed at something.*] Hey! Not bad. Now that's what I call a goosie. Good for old Oudtshoorn, I say. You don't get them like this over here. That I can tell you. Not with a watch! Old Hetty couldn't even tell the time. But she's got one. You see that, Morrie. Good for old Ethel, all right. Pretty smart, too. No *doek*. Nice hair. Just look at those locks. And how's that for a wall she's standing against? Ever seen a wall like that, as big as that, in Korsten? I mean it's made of bricks, isn't it?

MORRIS [*snatching the photograph out of Zachariah's hands and taking it to the window where he has a good look*]. Give it to me!

ZACHARIAH. Hey! What's the matter with you? It's my pen-pal, isn't it? It is!

MORRIS. Keep quiet, Zach!

ZACHARIAH. What's this 'keep quiet'? It's my room, isn't it? It is!

MORRIS. Where's the letter?

ZACHARIAH. You had it.

MORRIS. Where did I put it?

[*He throws the photograph down on the bed and finds the letter, which he reads feverishly. Zachariah picks up the photograph and continues his study.*]

ZACHARIAH. You're acting like you never seen a woman in your life. Why don't you get you a pen-pal? Maybe one's not enough.

MORRIS [*having finished the letter, his agitation is now even more pronounced*]. That newspaper, Zach. Where is the newspaper?

ZACHARIAH. I don't know.

MORRIS [*anguish*]. Think, man!

ZACHARIAH. You had it. [*Morris is scratching around frantically.*] What's the matter with you tonight? Maybe you threw it away.

MORRIS. No. I was keeping it in case. . . . [*Finds it.*] Thank God! Oh please, God, now make it that I am wrong!

ZACHARIAH. What the hell are you talking about?

[*Morris takes a look at the newspaper, pages through it, and then drops it. He stands quite still, unnaturally calm after the frenzy of the previous few seconds.*]

MORRIS. You know what you done, don't you?

ZACHARIAH. Me?

MORRIS. Who was it then? Me?

ZACHARIAH. But what?

MORRIS. Who wanted woman?

ZACHARIAH. Me.

MORRIS. Right. Who bought the paper?

ZACHARIAH. Me.

MORRIS. Right. Who's been carrying on about Minnie, and Connie, and good times? No me.

ZACHARIAH. Morrie! What are you talking about?

MORRIS. That photograph.

ZACHARIAH. I've seen it.

MORRIS. Well, have another look.

ZACHARIAH [*he does*]. It's Ethel.

MORRIS. *Miss* Ethel Lange to you!

ZACHARIAH. Okay, I looked. Now what?

MORRIS. Can't you see, man? Ethel Lange is a white woman! [*Pause. They look at each other in silence.*]

ZACHARIAH [*slowly*]. You mean that this Ethel . . . here. . . .

MORRIS. Is a white woman!

ZACHARIAH. How do you know?

MORRIS. Use your eyes. Anyway, that paper you bought, it's white. There's no news about our sort.

ZACHARIAH [*studying the photo*]. You're right, Morrie. [*Delighted.*] You're damn well right. And she's written to me, to a *hotnot*, a *swartgat*. This white woman thinks I'm a white man. That I like! [*Zachariah bursts into laughter. Morris jumps forward and snatches the photograph out of his hand.*] Hey! What you going to do?

MORRIS. What do you think?

ZACHARIAH [*hopefully*]. Read it?

MORRIS. I'm going to burn it.

ZACHARIAH. No!

MORRIS. Yes.

ZACHARIAH. I say no! [*Zachariah jumps up and comes to grips with Morris who, after a short struggle, is thrown violently to the floor. Zachariah picks up the letter and the photograph. He stands looking down at Morris for a few seconds, amazed at what he has done.*] No, Morrie. You're not going to burn it.

MORRIS. You hit me!

ZACHARIAH. I didn't mean it.

MORRIS. But you did, didn't you? Here on my chest.

ZACHARIAH. You was going to burn it.

MORRIS [*vehemently*]. Yes, burn it! Destroy it!

ZACHARIAH. But it's my pen-pal, Morris. Now, isn't it? Doesn't it say here: Mr. Zachariah Pietersen? Well, that's me . . . isn't it? It is. My letter. You just don't go and burn another man's letter, Morrie.

MORRIS. But it's an error, Zach! Can't you see? The whole thing is a error.

ZACHARIAH. You must read it to me first. I don't know.

[*The alarm rings.*]

MORRIS. Supper time.

ZACHARIAH. Later.

MORRIS. Listen. . . .

ZACHARIAH. Letter first.

MORRIS. Then can I burn it?

ZACHARIAH. Read the letter first, man. Let's hear it. [*Handing Morris the letter.*] No funny business, hey!

MORRIS [*reading*]. 'Dear Zach, many thanks for your letter. You asked me for a snap, so I'm sending you it. Do you like it? That's my brother's foot sticking in the picture behind the bench on the side. . . .'

ZACHARIAH. She's right! Here it is.

MORRIS. 'Cornelius is a . . . policeman.'

[*Pause.*]

ZACHARIAH [*serene*]. Go on.

MORRIS. 'He's got a motor-bike, and I been with him to the dam, on the back. My best friend is Lucy van Tonder. Both of us hates Oudtshoorn, man. How is P.E.? There's only two bios here, so we don't know what to do on the other nights. That's why I want pen-pals. How about a . . . picture . . . ?'

[*Pause.*]

ZACHARIAH [*still serenely confident*]. Go on.

MORRIS. 'How about a picture of you? You got a car? All for now. *Totsiens*, Ethel. P.S. Please write soon.' [*Morris folds the letter.*] Satisfied?

ZACHARIAH [*gratefully*]. Thank you, Morrie.

[*Holds out his hand for the letter.*]

MORRIS. Can I burn it now?

ZACHARIAH. Burn it! It's a all right letter, man. A little bit of this and a little bit of that.

MORRIS. Like her brother being a policeman.

ZACHARIAH [*ignoring the last remark*]. Supper ready yet? Let's talk after supper, man. I'm hungry. What you got, Morrie?

MORRIS. Boiled egg and chips.

ZACHARIAH. Sounds good. Hey! We never had that before.

MORRIS [*sulking*]. It was meant to be a surprise.

ZACHARIAH. But that's wonderful. [*Zachariah is full of vigour and life.*] No. I mean it, Morrie. Cross my heart and hope to die. Boiled egg! I never even knew you could do it.

[*Zachariah takes his place at the table, and stands up the photograph in front of him. When Morris brings the food to the table, he sees it and hesitates.*]

ZACHARIAH. Just looking, Morrie. She sent it for me to look at her, didn't she? [*Eats. Morris sits down.*] What's it got here on the back?

MORRIS [*examines the back of the photograph*]. 'To Zach, with love, from Ethel.'

[*Another burst of laughter from Zachariah. Morris leaves the table abruptly.*]

ZACHARIAH [*calmly continuing with his meal*]. What's the matter?

MORRIS. I'm not hungry.

ZACHARIAH. You mean, you don't like to hear me laugh?

MORRIS. It's not that. . . .

ZACHARIAH. It is. But it's funny, man. She and me. Of course, it wouldn't be so funny if it was you who was pally with her.

MORRIS. What does that suppose it means?

ZACHARIAH. Don't you know?

MORRIS. No. So will you kindly please tell me?

ZACHARIAH. You never seen yourself, Morrie?

MORRIS [*trembling with emotion*]. Be careful, Zach! I'm warning you now. Just you be careful of where your words are taking you!

ZACHARIAH. Okay. Okay. [*Eats in silence.*] You was telling me the other day about Oudtshoorn. How far you say it was?

MORRIS [*viciously*]. Hundreds of miles.

ZACHARIAH. So far, hey?

MORRIS. Ah! I get your game. Don't fool yourself. It's *not* far enough for safety's sake. Cornelius has got a motor-bike, remember.

ZACHARIAH. *Ja.* But we don't write to him, man.

MORRIS. Listen, Zach, if you think for one moment that I'm going to write. . . .

ZACHARIAH. Think? Who says? I been eating my supper. It was good, Morrie. The eggs and chips. Tasty.

MORRIS. Don't try to change the subject-matter!

ZACHARIAH. Me? I like that. You mean, what's the matter with you? You was the one that spoke about pen-pals first. Not me.

MORRIS. So here it comes at last. I've been waiting for it. I'm to blame, am I? All right. I'll take the blame. I always did, didn't I? But this is where it ends. I'm telling you now, burn that letter, because when they come around here and ask me, I'll say I got nothing more to do with it.

ZACHARIAH [*bluff indignation*]. Burn this letter! What's wrong with this letter?

MORRIS. Ethel Lange is a white woman!

ZACHARIAH. Wait . . . wait . . . wait . . . not so fast. I'm a sort of slow man. We were talking about this letter, not her. Now tell me, what's wrong with what you did read? Does she call me names? No. Does she laugh at me? No. Does she swear at me? No. Just a simple letter with a little bit of this and a little bit of that. Now comes the clue. What sort of chap is it that throws away a few kind words? Hey, Morrie? Aren't they, as you say, precious things these days? And this pretty picture of a lovely girl? I burn it! What sort of doing is that? Bad. Think of Ethel, man. Think! Sitting up there in Oudtshoorn with Lucy, waiting . . . waiting . . . for what? For nothing. For why? Because bad Zach Pietersen burnt it. No, Morrie. Good is good, fair is fair, and I may be a shade of black, but I go gently as a man.

MORRIS. Are you finished? [*Pause.*] I just want to remind you, Zach, that when I was writing to her you weren't even interested in a single thing I said. *Ja* . . . *Ja* . . . Okay . . . Okay. . . . That's all that came from you. But now, suddenly, now you are! Why? Why, I ask myself . . . and a suspicious little voice answers: Is it maybe because she's white? [*Pause.*] Well?

ZACHARIAH. Okay. Do you want to hear me say it? [*Morris says nothing.*] It's because she's white! I like this little white girl! I like the thought of this little white girl. I'm thinking it, now. Look at me. *Ja*. Can't you see? I'm serious, but I'm also smiling. I'm telling you I like the thought of this little white Ethel better than our future, or the plans, or getting away, or foot-salts, or any other damned thing in here. It's a warm thought for a man in winter. It's the best thought I ever had and I'm keeping it. So maybe it's a error as you say. Well, that's just too bad. We done it, and now I got it and I'm keeping it, and don't you try no tricks like trying to get it away from me. Who knows? You might get to liking it too. [*Morris says nothing. Zachariah comes closer.*] *Ja.* There's a thought there. What about *you*, Morrie? You never had it before? . . . that thought? A man like you, specially you, always thinking so many things? A man like you who's been places! You're always telling me about the places you been. Wasn't there ever no white woman thereabouts? I mean. . . . You must have smelt them someplace. That sweet, white smell, you know. They leave it behind. [*Nudging Morris.*] Of course you did. Hey? I bet you had that thought all the time. I bet you been having it in here. Hey? You should have shared it, Morrie. I'm a man with a taste for thoughts these days. It hurts to think you didn't share a good one like that with your brother. Giving me all that shit about future and plans, and then keeping the real goosie for yourself. You weren't scared, were you? That I would tell? Come on. Confess. You were scared, hey! A little bit poopy. I've noticed that. But you needn't worry now. I'm a man for keeping a secret, and anyway, we'll play this very careful . . . very, very careful. Ethel won't never know about us, and I know how to handle that brother. Mustn't let a policeman bugger you about, man. So go get your pencil and piece of paper. [*Morris defeated. He sits at the table. Zachariah paces.*] We'll go gently with this one. There'll be others . . . later. So we'll take her on friendly terms again. [*Pause.*] 'Dear Ethel, . . . [*Morris writes.*] I think you might like to know I got your letter, and the picture. I'd say Oudtshoorn seems all right. You were quite all right too. I would like to send you a picture of me, but it's this way. It's winter down here now. The light is bad, the lake is black, the birds have gone. Wait for spring, when things improve. Okay? Good. I heard you ask about my car. Yes. I have it. We pumped the tyres today. Tomorrow I think I'll put in some petrol. I'd like to take you for a drive, Ethel, and Lucy too. In fact, I'd like to drive both of you. They say over here, I'm fast. I'll tell you this. If I could drive you, I would do it so fast, Ethel, and Lucy too, both of you, so fast I would, it would hurt. . . .'

MORRIS. Okay, Zach!!

ZACHARIAH [*pulling himself together*]. 'Ja! But don't worry. I got brakes. [*Pause.*] I notice your brother got boots. All policemen got boots, I notice. Good luck to him, anyway, and Lucy too. Write soon. Zachariah Pietersen.' [*Pause.*] Okay, Morrie. Do your business on the envelope, but I'll post it. There, you see! Nothing to it, was there? A little bit of this and a little bit of that and nothing about some things. When Ethel gets it, she'll say: He's okay. This Zachariah Pietersen is okay, Lucy! Say something, Morrie.

MORRIS. I'm okay.

ZACHARIAH. That's better. Don't you think it was a good letter? For a man who hasn't done one before?

MORRIS. I have a feeling about it Zach, about this whole business.

ZACHARIAH. A feeling about Ethel? [*Laughs.*] I told you!

MORRIS. Zach! Listen to me without getting angry. [*Pause.*] Let me burn it.

ZACHARIAH. My letter?

MORRIS. Yes.

ZACHARIAH. The one we just done?

MORRIS. Yes.

ZACHARIAH. Ethel's letter, now my letter! [*He gets up and takes the letter in question away from Morris.*] You're in a burning mood, all right.

MORRIS. Please, Zach. You're going to get hurt.

ZACHARIAH [*aggression*]. Such as by who?

MORRIS. Ethel. [*Zachariah laughs.*] Then yourself! Yes. Do you think a man can't hurt himself? Let me tell you, he can. More than anybody else can hurt him, he can hurt himself. I know. What's to stop him dreaming forbidden dreams at night and waking up too late? Hey? Or playing dangerous games with himself and forgetting where to stop? I know them, I tell you, these dreams and games a man has with himself. That. There in your hand. To Miss Ethel Lange, Oudtshoorn. You think that's a letter? I'm telling you it's a dream, and the most dangerous one. Maybe, just maybe, when the lights are out, when you lie alone in the darkest hour of the night, then, just maybe, a man can dream that one for a little while. But remember, that even then, wherever you lie, breathing fast and dreaming, God's Watching With His Secret Eye to see how far you go! You think he hasn't seen us tonight? Now, you got it on paper as well! That's what they call evidence, you know. [*Pause.*] God, Zach, I have a feeling about this business, man!

ZACHARIAH. Cheer up, Morrie.

MORRIS. You won't let me burn it?

ZACHARIAH. Like you said, it's just a game.

MORRIS. But you're playing with fire, Zach!

ZACHARIAH. Maybe. But then I never had much to play with.

MORRIS. Didn't you?

ZACHARIAH. Don't you remember? You got the toys.

MORRIS. Did I?

ZACHARIAH. *Ja.* Like that top, Morrie. Don't you? I have always specially remembered that top. That brown stinkwood top. She gave me her old cotton-reels to play with, but it wasn't the same. I wanted a top.

MORRIS. Who? Who gave me the top?

ZACHARIAH. Mother.

MORRIS. Mother!

ZACHARIAH. *Ja.* She said she only had one. There was always only one.

MORRIS. Zach, you're telling me a thing now!

ZACHARIAH. Did you forget her?

MORRIS. No, Zach. I meant the top. I can't, for the life of me, remember that top.

ZACHARIAH. And the marbles?

MORRIS. Was there marbles, too?

ZACHARIA. *Ja.* One time. A bag of them with a big green *ghoen.* Such a *ghoen,* man! Another time there was the little soldiers.

MORRIS [*shaking his head*]. No. . . .

ZACHARIAH. And what about the tackies?

MORRIS. Tackies . . . ? Yes, yes I do! I remember her calling and putting them on and taking me to church. How it comes back, hey! And what about her, Zach? There's a memory for you. I tried it out the other day. Mother, I said, Mother! A sadness, I thought.

ZACHARIAH. *Ja.*

MORRIS. Just a touch of sadness.

ZACHARIAH. A soft touch with sadness.

MORRIS. And soapsuds on brown hands.

ZACHARIAH. And her feet.

[*Pause. Morris looks at Zachariah.*]

MORRIS. What do you mean?

ZACHARIAH. There was her feet.

MORRIS. Who had feet?

ZACHARIAH. Mother, man.

MORRIS. I don't remember her feet, Zach.

ZACHARIAH [*serenely confident*]. *Ja,* man. The toes was crooked,

47

the nails skew, and there was pain. They didn't fit the shoes.

MORRIS [*growing agitation*]. Zach, are you sure that wasn't somebody else?

ZACHARIAH. It was mother's feet. She let me feel the hardnesses and then pruned them down with a razor-blade.

MORRIS. No, Zach. You got me worried now! A grey dress?

ZACHARIAH. Maybe.

MORRIS [*persistent*]. Going to church. She wore it going to. . . .

ZACHARIAH. The butcher shop! That's it! That's where she went.

MORRIS. What for?

ZACHARIAH. Offal.

MORRIS. Offal! Stop, Zach. Stop! We must sort this out, man. I mean . . . it sounds like some other mother.

ZACHARIAH [*gently*]. How can that be?

MORRIS. Listen, Zach. Do you remember the songs she sang?

ZACHARIAH. Do I! [*He laughs and then sings.*]
>My skin is black,
>The soap is blue,
>But the washing comes out white.
>
>I took a man
>On a Friday night;
>Now I'm washing a baby too.
>
>Just a little bit black,
>And a little bit white,
>He's a Capie through and through.

[*Morris is staring at him in horror.*] What's the matter?

MORRIS. That wasn't what she sang to me.

ZACHARIAH. No?

MORRIS. Lullaby-baby it was . . . '. . . you'll get to the top.'

ZACHARIAH. I don't remember that at all.

MORRIS [*anguish*]. This is some sort of terrible error. What . . . wait! I've got it . . . I think. Oh, God, let it be that I've got it. [*To Zachariah.*] How about the games we played? Think, Zach. Think carefully! There was one special one. Just me and you. I'll give you a clue. Toot-toot. Toot-toot.

ZACHARIAH [*thinking*]. Wasn't there an old car?

MORRIS. Where would it be?

ZACHARIAH. Rusting by the side of the road.

MORRIS. Could it be the ruins of an old Chevy, Zach?

ZACHARIAH. It could.

MORRIS. And can we say without tyres and wires and things?

ZACHARIAH. We may.

MORRIS. . . . and all the glass blown away by the wind?

ZACHARIAH. Dusty.

MORRIS. Deserted.

ZACHARIAH. Sting bees on the bonnet.

MORRIS. Webs in the windscreen.

ZACHARIAH. Nothing in the boot.

MORRIS. And us?

ZACHARIAH. In it.

MORRIS. We are? How?

ZACHARIAH. Side by side.

MORRIS. Like this? [*He sits beside Zachariah.*]

ZACHARIAH. That's right.

MORRIS. Doing what?

ZACHARIAH. Staring.

MORRIS. Not both of us!

ZACHARIAH. Me at the wheel, you at the window.

MORRIS. Okay. Now what?

ZACHARIAH. Now, I got this gear here and I'm going to go.

MORRIS. Where?

ZACHARIAH. To hell and gone far away, and we aren't coming back.

MORRIS. Wait! What will I do while you drive?

ZACHARIAH. You must tell me what we pass. Are you ready? Here we go! [*Zachariah goes through the motions of driving a car. Morris looks eagerly out of the window.*]

MORRIS. We're slipping through the streets, passing homes and people on the pavements who are quite friendly and wave as we drive by. It's a fine, sunny sort of a day. What are we doing?

ZACHARIAH. Twenty-four.

MORRIS. Do you see that bus ahead of us? [*They lean over to one side as Zachariah swings the wheel. Morris looks back.*] Chock-a-block with early morning workers. Shame. And what about those children over there, going to school? Shame again. On such a nice day. What are we doing?

ZACHARIAH. Thirty-four.

MORRIS. That means we're coming to open country. The white houses have given way to patches of green, and animals and not so many people any more. But they still wave . . . with their spades.

ZACHARIAH. Fifty.

MORRIS. You're going quite fast. You've killed a cat, flattened a frog, frightened a dog . . . who jumped!

ZACHARIAH. Sixty.

MORRIS. Passing trees, and haystacks, and sunshine, and the smoke from little houses drifting up . . . shooting by!

ZACHARIAH. Eighty!

MORRIS. Birds flying abreast, and bulls, billy-goats, black sheep. . . .

ZACHARIAH. One hundred!

MORRIS. . . . cross a river, up a hill, to the top, coming down, down, down . . . stop! stop!

ZACHARIAH [*slamming on the brakes*]. Eeeeeooooooooaaah! [*Pause.*] Why?

MORRIS. Look! There's a butterfly.

ZACHARIAH. On your side?

MORRIS. Yours as well. Just look.

ZACHARIAH. All round us, hey!

MORRIS. This is rare, Zach! We've driven into a flock of butterflies. [*Zachariah smiles and then laughs.*] You remember, hey! We've found it, Zach. We've found it! This is our youth!

ZACHARIAH. And driving to hell and gone was our game.

MORRIS. Our best one.

ZACHARIAH. What about chasing donkeys in the veld? Remember that?

MORRIS. And the trees! Me and you in the trees. Tarzan and his ape.

ZACHARIAH. Teasing the girls.

MORRIS. Stealing the fruit.

ZACHARIAH. Catching the birds.

MORRIS. My God! The things a man can forget!

ZACHARIAH. *Ja.* Those were the days!

MORRIS. God knows!

ZACHARIAH. Goodness, hey!

MORRIS. They were that.

ZACHARIAH. And gladness, too.

MORRIS. Making hay, man, come and play, man, while the sun is sinking . . . which it did.

ZACHARIAH. What's that . . . that . . . that nice thing you say, Morrie?

MORRIS. 'So sweet did pass that summer time,
        Of youth and fruit upon the trees,
        When pretty girls and laughing boys
        Did hop and skip and all were free.'

ZACHARIAH. Did skop and skip the pretty girls. They did, too.

MORRIS. Hopscotch.

ZACHARIAH. That was it.

MORRIS. We played our games, Zach.

ZACHARIAH. We could. There was no work.

MORRIS. Or worries.

ZACHARIAH. No hurry.

MORRIS. That's true. We took our time and our chances. There were a few falls of course. I mean . . . can a man climb without a fall?

ZACHARIAH. You got to come tumbling down sometime, the laughing boys and pretty girls.

MORRIS. But you picked yourself up. . . .

ZACHARIAH. And the scabs off your knees. . . .

MORRIS. And carried on. A few inner hurts, too, from time to time.

ZACHARIAH. What was those?

MORRIS. Don't you remember?
    Kaffertjie, Kaffertjie, waar is jou pas?

ZACHARIAH [*taking up the jingle*]. But my old man was a white man.

MORRIS. *Maar, jou ma was 'n Bantoe,*
    So dis nou jou ras.

ZACHARIAH [*shaking his head*]. *Ja.* That hurt.

MORRIS. But on the whole it was fun.

ZACHARIAH. While it lasted, which wasn't for long.

MORRIS. It had to happen, Zach. We grew upright, mother lay down and died, so I went away. I took the long road away.

ZACHARIAH. And me? What did I do?

MORRIS. Connie.

ZACHARIAH. That's right.

MORRIS. And Minnie.

ZACHARIAH. That was all right.

MORRIS. So then I came back.

ZACHARIAH. And now?

MORRIS. See for yourself. Here we are, later. And now there's Ethel as well, and that makes me frightened.

ZACHARIAH. Sounds like another game, hey?

MORRIS. Yes. But not ours . . . this time. [*They sit together, overshadowed by the presence in their words.*] I often wonder.

ZACHARIAH. Same here.

MORRIS. I mean . . . where do they go? The good times in a man's life?

ZACHARIAH. And the bad ones?

MORRIS. Yes. That's a thought. Where do they come from?

ZACHARIAH. Oudtshoorn.

SCENE FOUR

An evening later.

Zachariah is seated at the table, eating. He is obviously in good spirits, radiating an inward satisfaction and secrecy. Morris is moving about nervously behind his back.

MORRIS. So it has come to this. Who would have thought it, hey! That one day, one of us would come in here with a secret and keep it to himself! If someone had tried to tell me that, I would have thrown up my hands in horror. To Morrie and Zach! . . . I would have cried. No! Emphatically not. [*Pause.*] Which just goes to show you. Because I was wrong, wasn't I? There is a secret in this room, at this moment. This is how friendships get wrecked, you know, Zach, in secrecy. It's the hidden things that hurt and do the harm. [*Pause. Morris watches Zachariah's back.*] So. Do you want to tell me?

ZACHARIAH. What are you talking about, Morrie?

MORRIS. You got a letter today, didn't you?

ZACHARIAH. Who?

MORRIS. You.

ZACHARIAH. What?

MORRIS. A letter. From Ethel. And you're not telling me about it. [*Pause.*] Okay. Two can play at this game, you know. Yes! Now that I come to think of it, I've also got a secret. And such a wicked secret! Hey! It's almost a sin! But I'm not going to tell somebody I know. . . . Oh no!

ZACHARIAH [*complacently*]. Good.

[*He continues eating, unaffected by Morris's manoeuvre. Realizing his tactics have failed, Morris tries another approach, hiding his impatience and curiosity behind a mask of indifference.*]

MORRIS [*joining Zachariah at the table*]. It's good value for a tuppenny stamp, all right. Hey, Zach?

ZACHARIAH [*cautiously*]. What?

MORRIS. Postage. Your letters, getting safely to Oudtshoorn, and in only a couple of days, and finding the right person at the other end . . . for only tuppence! Tell me that's not a bargain. That's the really big thing about pen-pals, I think.

A man's letters have got somewhere to go, and he gets a couple himself from time to time . . . like you, today. Come now, Zach. You did, didn't you?

ZACHARIAH [*after thought*]. Ja.

MORRIS. That's all I'm saying. Some more bread? [*He offers Zachariah a slice. He takes it.*] Same sort as usual? [*Zachariah looks at Morris.*] The letter. [*Zachariah puts down his bread and thinks. Morris seizes his opportunity.*] Didn't you notice? Hell, Zach! You surprise me.

ZACHARIAH. What do you mean: the same sort?

MORRIS [*simulated shock*]. Zach!

ZACHARIAH. So I'm asking you what you mean.

MORRIS. Well I never! To begin with there's the . . . envelope. Is it the same colour, or isn't it? I can see that somebody didn't take a good look, did he? [*Reluctantly Zachariah takes the letter out of his inside pocket.*] She's changed her colours! They used to be blue. What about inside?

ZACHARIAH. I'm not ready for that yet.

MORRIS. Okay. All I'm saying is . . . I don't care.

ZACHARIAH [*studying the envelope*]. I see they got animals on stamps nowadays.

MORRIS [*his patience wearing thin*]. You mean to tell me you only see that now?

ZACHARIAH. The donkeys with stripes.

MORRIS. Zebras.

ZACHARIAH. . . . with stripes.

MORRIS. That's not the point about a letter, Zach.

ZACHARIAH. What?

MORRIS. The stamps. You're wasting your time with the stamps. It's what's inside that you got to read.

ZACHARIAH. You're in a hurry, Morrie.

MORRIS. Who?

ZACHARIAH. You.

MORRIS. Look, I told you that all I'm saying is . . . I don't care and the stamps don't count. Other than that, have your fun. Go ahead. It means nothing to me.

ZACHARIAH. And my name on the envelope. How do you like that, hey?

MORRIS. *Your* name?

ZACHARIAH. *Ja.* My name.

MORRIS. Oh.

ZACHARIAH. Now what do you mean, with an 'Oh' like that?

MORRIS. What makes you so sure that that is your name? [*Zachariah is trapped.*] How do you spell your name, Zach? Come on, let's hear.

ZACHARIAH [*after a long struggle*]. Zach . . . ah . . . ri . . . yah.

MORRIS. Oh, no, you don't! That's no spelling. That's a pronounciation. A b c d e . . . that's the alphabet. [*After a moment's hesitation Zachariah holds up the letter so that Morris can see the address.*]

ZACHARIAH. Is it for me, Morrie?

MORRIS. I'm not sure.

ZACHARIAH. Mr. Zachariah Pietersen.

MORRIS. I know your name. It's for one Z. Pietersen.

ZACHARIAH. Well, that's okay then.

MORRIS. Is it?

ZACHARIAH. Isn't it?

MORRIS. Since when are you the only thing that begins with a Z? And how many Pietersens didn't we know as boys, right here in this very selfsame Korsten?

[*Zachariah keeps the letter for a few more seconds, then hands it to Morris.*]

ZACHARIAH. You win. Read it.

MORRIS. I win! [*Laughs happily.*] Good old Zach! I win! I'll sit down to this. [*Nudging Zachariah.*] It pays to have a brother who can read, hey? [*Opens the letter.*] Ready? 'Dear Zach, How's things? I'm okay, today, again. I got your letter. Lucy had a laugh at you. . . .'

ZACHARIAH. What's that?

MORRIS. 'Lucy had a laugh at you. . . .' I think she means a smile.

ZACHARIAH. What's funny?

MORRIS. Not that sort of smile, Zach. I'm sure she means the kind sort. [*Zachariah is not convinced.*] Look at me. [*He smiles at Zachariah.*] Is there anything funny? Of course not. Only you. I was feeling sympathy, not funny. [*Continues his reading.*] 'Lucy had a laugh at you, but my brother is not so sure.' [*Pause.*] That's something. That, I feel, means something. What does it do to you?

ZACHARIAH. Nothing.

MORRIS. Remember his boots.

ZACHARIAH. No. Nothing.

MORRIS. Not even a little bit of fear? [*He reads on.*] 'I'm looking forward to a ride in your car. . . .' They believed it, Zach! [*Zachariah smiles.*] They believed our cock-and-bull about the car.

ZACHARIAH [*laughing*]. I told you.

MORRIS. 'I'm looking forward to a ride in your car . . . and what about Lucy? Can she come?'

[*Their amusement knows no bounds.*]

ZACHARIAH. You must come too, Morrie. You and Lucy! Hey? We'll take them at ninety.

MORRIS. To hell and gone. [*Reads on through his laughter.*] 'We're coming down for a holiday in June, so where . . . can we . . . meet you?' [*Long pause. He reads again.*] 'We're coming down for a holiday in June so where can we meet you?'

ZACHARIAH. Ethel . . . ?

MORRIS. Is coming here. [*Puts down the letter and stands up. A false yawn and stretch before going to the window.*] I've noticed that hardly any moths. . . .

ZACHARIAH. Coming here!

MORRIS. As I was saying. Hardly any moths I've noticed have. . . .

ZACHARIAH. Ethel!

[*Morris abandons his thoughts about the moths.*]

MORRIS. I warned you, didn't I? I said: I have a feeling about this business. I remember my words; and wise ones they turn out to be. Because now you've got it! I told you to leave it alone. Hands off! Don't touch! Not for you! I know these things I said. But oh no, Mr. Z. Pietersen was clever. He knew how to handle it. Well, handle this, will you please.

ZACHARIAH [*dumbly*]. What else does she say?

MORRIS [*brutally*]. I'm not going to read it. You want to know why? Because it doesn't matter. The game's up, man. Nothing else matters now except: I'm coming down in June so where can we meet you? That is what Mr. Z. Pietersen had better start thinking about . . . and quick!

ZACHARIAH. When's June?

MORRIS. Soon.

ZACHARIAH. How soon?

MORRIS. Look. Are you trying to make me out a liar? [*Ticking them off on his fingers*.] January, February, March, April, May, June, July, August, September, October, November, December! Satisfied?

[*Another long pause. Morris goes back to the window.*]

ZACHARIAH. So?

MORRIS [*to the table, where he reads further into the letter*]. 'I'll be staying with my uncle at Kensington.' [*Little laugh.*] Kensington! Near enough for you? About five minutes walking from here, hey? And notice . . . with my uncle. Uncle! [*Another laugh.*] That's a ugly word, when you get to know its meanings. Oom Jakob! Do you hear it? Hairy wrists in khaki sleeves with thick fingers. When they curled up, that fist was as big as my head!

[*Back to the window. Zachariah is frightened.*]

ZACHARIAH. Morrie, I know. I'll tell her I can't see her.

MORRIS. She will want to know why.

ZACHARIAH. It's because I'm sick, with my heart.

MORRIS. And if she feels sorry and comes to comfort you?

ZACHARIAH [*growing desperation*]. But I'm going away.

MORRIS. When?

ZACHARIAH. Soon. June.

MORRIS. And what about where, and why and what, if she says she'll wait until you come back?

57

ZACHARIAH. Then I'll tell her. . . . [*Pause. He can think of nothing else to say.*]

MORRIS. What? No, Zach. You can't even tell her you're dead. You see, I happen to know. There is no whitewashing away a man's . . . facts. They'll speak for themselves at first sight, if you don't say it.

ZACHARIAH. Say what?

MORRIS. The truth. You know it.

ZACHARIAH. I don't. I don't know nothing.

MORRIS. Then listen, because *I* know it. 'Dear Ethel, forgive me, but I was born a dark sort of boy who wanted to play with whiteness. . . .'

ZACHARIAH [*rebelling*]. No!

MORRIS. '. . . and that's the truth, so help me God, help me!'

ZACHARIAH. I say no!

MORRIS. Then tell me what else you can say. Come on. Let's hear it. What is there a man can say or pray that will change the colour of his skin or blind them to it?

ZACHARIAH. There must be something.

MORRIS. I'm telling you there's nothing. When it's a question of smiles, and whispers, and thoughts in strange eyes . . . there is only the truth and. . . . [*He pauses.*]

ZACHARIAH. And then what?

MORRIS. And then to make a run for it. Yes. They don't like these games with their whiteness. You've heard them. 'How would you like your daughter to correspond with a black man?' Ethel's got a policeman brother and an uncle and *your* address.

ZACHARIAH. What have I done, hey? I done nothing.

MORRIS. What have you thought? That's the question. That's the crime. I seem to remember somebody saying: 'I like the thought of this little white girl.' And what about your dreams? They've kept me awake these past few nights, Zach. I've heard them, mumbling and moaning away in the darkness. They'll hear them quick enough. When they get their hands on a dark-born boy playing with a white idea, you think they don't find out what he's been dreaming at night? They have ways and means, my friend. Mean ways. Like confinement, in a cell, on bread and water, for days without end. They sit outside with their ears to the keyhole and wait . . . and wait. They got time. You'll get tired. So they wait. And soon you do, and no matter how you fight, your eyeballs start rolling round and . . . around and then, before you know it, maybe while you're still praying, before you can cry, or scream for help . . . you fall asleep and dream! All they need for evidence is a man's dreams. Not so much his hate. They say they can live with that. It's his dreams that they drag off to judgment, shouting: 'Silence! He's been caught! With convictions? He's pleading! He's guilty! Take him away.' [*Pause.*] Where? You ask where with your eyes, I see. You know where, Zach. You've seen them, in the streets, carrying their spades and the man with his gun. Bald heads, short trousers, and that ugly jersey with the red, painful red stripes around the body. [*Morris goes back to the window.*] I miss the moths. They made the night a friendly sort of place. [*Turning to Zachariah.*] What are you going to do about it, Zach?

ZACHARIAH. I'm thinking about it.

MORRIS. What are you thinking about it?

ZACHARIAH. What am I going to do?

MORRIS. Better be quick.

ZACHARIAH. Help me, Morrie.

MORRIS. Are you serious?

ZACHARIAH. I'm not smiling.

MORRIS. Dead serious?

ZACHARIAH. God.

MORRIS. Good. Then let's go. Begin at the beginning. Give me the first fact.

ZACHARIAH [*severe and bitter*]. Ethel is white. I am black.

MORRIS. That's a very good beginning, Zach.

ZACHARIAH. If she sees me. . . .

MORRIS. Keep it up.

ZACHARIAH. . . . she'll be surprised.

MORRIS. Harder, Zach.

ZACHARIAH. She'll laugh.

MORRIS. Let it hurt, man!

ZACHARIAH. She'll swear!

MORRIS. Now make it loud!

ZACHARIAH. She'll scream!

MORRIS. Good! Now for yourself. [*Pause.*] She's surprised, remember?

ZACHARIAH. I'm not strange.

MORRIS. And when she laughs?

ZACHARIAH. I'm not funny.

MORRIS. When she swears?

ZACHARIAH. I'm no dog.

MORRIS. She screams!

ZACHARIAH. I just wanted to smell you, lady!

MORRIS. Good, Zach. Very good. You're seeing it clearly, man. But, remember there is still the others.

ZACHARIAH. What others?

MORRIS. The uncles with fists and brothers in boots who come running when a lady screams.

ZACHARIAH. What about them?

MORRIS. They've come to ransack you.

ZACHARIAH. I'll say it wasn't me.

MORRIS. They won't believe you.

ZACHARIAH. Leave me alone!

MORRIS. They'll hit you for that.

ZACHARIAH. I'll fight.

MORRIS. There's too many for you.

ZACHARIAH. I'll call a policeman.

MORRIS. He's on their side.

ZACHARIAH. I'll run away!

MORRIS. That's better, and bitter of course. I realize that. You see, we're digging up the roots of what's the matter with you now. I know they're deep; that's why it hurts. But we must get them out. Once the roots are out, this thing will die and never grow again. I'm telling you I know. So we've got to get them out, right out. You're lucky, Zach.

ZACHARIAH. Me?

MORRIS. Yes, you. I think, for a man like you, there shouldn't be too much discomfort in pulling it right out.

ZACHARIAH. Just show me how!

MORRIS. Go back to the beginning. Give me again that first fact. [*Pause.*] It started with Ethel, remember. Ethel. . . .

ZACHARIAH. . . . is white.

MORRIS. That's it. And. . . .

ZACHARIAH. . . . and I am black.

MORRIS. You've got it.

ZACHARIAH. Ethel is white and I am black.

MORRIS. Now take a good grip.

ZACHARIAH. Ethel is so . . . so . . . snow white.

MORRIS. Hold it! Grab it all!

ZACHARIAH. And I am too . . . truly . . . too black.

MORRIS. Now, this is the hard part, Zach, so be prepared, hey? Be broad in the shoulder. Be a man and brace yourself to take the strain. Some men I know couldn't, and sustained eternal injuries. Now, get ready, I'll urge you on, keep steady, I'm with you all the way remember . . . and pull! With all your might and all your woe, heave, harder, still harder, Zach! Let it hurt, man! It has to hurt a man to do him good because once bitten twice shy, just this one cry and then never again; just this once, try to think of it as one of those bitter pills that pull a man through to better days and being himself again . . . at last and in peace, in one piece, because you'll mend you'll see, and, as they say, tomorrow is another, yet another day, and a man must carry on. Doesn't matter so much where; just on, just carry your load on somewhere and teach your lips to smile with your eyes closed, to say, lightheartedly if you can, with a laugh as if you didn't care, to say . . . let's hear it, Zach.

ZACHARIAH. I can never have her.

MORRIS. Never ever.

ZACHARIAH. She wouldn't want me anyway.

MORRIS. It's as simple as that.

ZACHARIAH. She's too white to want me anyway.

MORRIS. For better or for worse.

ZACHARIAH. So I won't want her any more.

MORRIS. Not in this life, or that one, if death us do part, that next one, God help us! For ever and ever no more, thank you!

ZACHARIAH. Please, no more.

MORRIS. We cry enough.

ZACHARIAH. I know now.

MORRIS. We do.

ZACHARIAH. Everything.

MORRIS. Every last little thing.

ZACHARIAH. From the beginning.

MORRIS. And then on without end.

ZACHARIAH. Why it was.

MORRIS. And will be.

ZACHARIAH. The lot in fact.

MORRIS. The human one.

ZACHARIAH. The whole, rotten, stinking lot is all because I'm black!

MORRIS. Yes. That explains it, clearly. Which is something. I mean when a man can see 'why?', quite clearly, it's something. Think of those who can't.

ZACHARIAH. I'm black all right. What is there as black as me?

MORRIS. To equal you? To match you? How about a dangerous night. Try that for the size and colour of its darkness. You go with it, Zach, as with certain smells and simple sorrows too. And what about the sadness of shoes without socks, or no shoes at all!

ZACHARIAH. I take it. I take them all. Black days, black ways, black things. They're me. I'm happy. Ha Ha Ha! Do you hear my black happiness?

MORRIS. Oh yes, Zach, I hear it, I promise you.

ZACHARIAH. Can you feel it?

MORRIS. I do. I do.

ZACHARIAH. And see it?

MORRIS. Midnight, man! Like the twelve strokes of midnight you stand before my wondering eyes.

ZACHARIAH. And my thoughts! What about my thoughts?

MORRIS. Let's hear it.

ZACHARIAH. I'm on my side, they're on theirs.

MORRIS. That's what they want.

ZACHARIAH. They'll get it.

MORRIS. You heard him.

ZACHARIAH. This time it's serious.

MORRIS. We warn you.

ZACHARIAH. Because from now on, I'll be what I am. They can be what they like. I don't care. I don't want to mix. It's bad for the blood and the poor babies. So I'll keep mine clean, and theirs I'll scrub off, afterwards, off my hands, my unskilled, my stained hands, and say I'm not sorry! The trembles you felt was something else. You see you were too white, so blindingly white that I couldn't see what I was doing.

MORRIS [*quietly, and with absolute sincerity*]. Zach! Oh Zach! When I hear that certainty about whys and wherefores, about how to live and what not to love, I wish, believe me, deep down in the bottom of my heart where my blood is as red as yours, I wish that old washerwoman had bruised me too at birth. I wish.... [*The alarm goes off. Morris looks up to find Zachariah staring strangely at him. Morris goes to the window to avoid Zachariah's eyes.*] Yes. I remember now. The moths. I was on the road somewhere and it got dark again. So I stopped at a petrol station and sat up with the night boy in his little room. An elderly *ou*. I asked his name. Kleinbooi. But he didn't ask mine. He wasn't sure, you see. So often in my life they haven't been sure, you see. We sat there on the floor and cars came a few times in the night, but mostly it was just Kleinbooi and me, dozing ... and, of course, the moths. Soft, dusty moths, flying in through the door to the lamp, or on the floor dragging their wings, or on their backs. I'm telling you there are millions of moths in this world, but only in summer; because where do they go when it's winter? I remember having a deep thought about moths that night, Zach. . . .

[*He turns from the window to find Zachariah still staring at him. Morris goes to the table to turn off the lamp.*]

ZACHARIAH. Morris!

MORRIS. Zachariah?

ZACHARIAH. Keep on the light.

MORRIS. Why?

ZACHARIAH. I saw something.

MORRIS. What?

ZACHARIAH. Your skin. How can I put it. It's. . . . [*Pause.*]

MORRIS [*easily*]. On the light side.

ZACHARIAH. *Ja.*

MORRIS [*very easily*]. One of those things. [*Another move to the lamp.*]

ZACHARIAH. Wait, Morrie!

MORRIS. It's late.

ZACHARIAH. I want to have a good look at you, man.

MORRIS. It's a bit late in the day to be seeing your brother for the first time. I been here a whole year now, you know.

ZACHARIAH. *Ja.* But after a whole life I only seen me properly tonight. You helped me. I'm grateful.

MORRIS. It was nothing. . . .

ZACHARIAH. No! I'm not a man that forgets a favour. I want to help you now.

MORRIS. I don't need any assistance, thank you.

ZACHARIAH. But you do. A man can't really see himself. Look at me. I had an odd look at me in the mirror—but so what? Did it make things clearer? No. Why? Because it's the others what does. They got sharper eyes. I want to give you the benefit of mine. Sit down. [*Morris sits.*] You're on the lighter side of life all right. You like that . . . all over? Your legs and things?

MORRIS. It's evenly spread.

ZACHARIAH. Not even a foot in the darker side, hey! I'd say you must be quite a bright boy with nothing on.

MORRIS. Please, Zach!

ZACHARIAH. You're shy! *Ja*. You always get undressed in the dark. Always well closed up, like a woman. Like Ethel. I bet she shines.

MORRIS. *Sis*, Zach!

ZACHARIAH. You know something. I bet if it was you she saw and not me she wouldn't say nothing. [*Morris closes his eyes and gives a light, nervous laugh. Zachariah also laughs, but hollowly.*] I'm sure she wouldn't be surprised, or laugh, or swear or scream. Nobody would come running. I bet you she would just say: How do you do, Mr Pietersen? [*Pause.*] There's a thought there, Morrie. You ever think it?

MORRIS. No.

ZACHARIAH. Not even a little bit of it? Like there, where you say: Hello, Ethel . . . and shake her hand. Then what do you do? Ah, yes! I see this thing very clear. You say: Would you like a walk with me? *Ja*. You'd manage all right, Morrie. One thing is for certain: you would look all right, with her, and that's the main thing, hey?

MORRIS. You're dreaming again, Zach.

ZACHARIAH. No, man! This is not my sort of dream. [*He laughs.*] My dream was different. I didn't shake her hands. You're the man for shaking hands, Morrie.

MORRIS. Finished, Zach?

ZACHARIAH. No. We're still coming to the big thought.

MORRIS. What is that?

ZACHARIAH. Why don't you meet her? [*Pause.*]

MORRIS. You want to know why?

ZACHARIAH. *Ja*.

MORRIS. You really want to know?

ZACHARIAH. I do.

MORRIS. She's not my pen-pal.

[*Morris moves to get up. Zachariah stops him.*]

ZACHARIAH. All right. Let's try it another way. Would you like to meet her?

MORRIS. Listen, Zach. I've told you before. Ethel is your. . . .

ZACHARIAH [*pained*]. Please, Morrie! Would—you—like—to—meet—her?

MORRIS. That's no sort of question.

ZACHARIAH. Why not?

MORRIS. Because all my life I've been interested in meeting people. Not just Ethel. Anybody. I'm telling you the question is meaningless.

ZACHARIAH. Okay, I'll put it this way. Would you like to see her, or hear her, or maybe touch her?

MORRIS. That still doesn't give the question any meaning! Look, you know me. Don't I like to touch . . . horses? Don't I like to hear . . . church bells? Don't I like to see anything that's nice to see? And anyway, Ethel is your pen-pal.

ZACHARIAH. Right. Wait! You can have her.

MORRIS. What's this now?

ZACHARIAH. She's yours. I'm giving her to you.

MORRIS [*angry*]. This is no game, Zach!

ZACHARIAH. But I mean it. Look. I can't use her. We seen that. She'll see it too. But why throw away a good pen-pal if somebody else can do it? You can. You're bright enough, Morrie. I don't know why I never seen it before, but you're pretty . . . a pretty white. I'm telling you now, as your brother, that when Ethel sees you all she will say is: How do you do, Mr. Pietersen? She'll never know otherwise.

MORRIS. You think so?

ZACHARIAH. You could fool me, Morrie, if I didn't know who you was.

MORRIS. You mean that, Zach?

ZACHARIAH. Cross my heart and hope to die. And the way you can talk! She'd be impressed.

MORRIS. That's true. I like to talk.

ZACHARIAH. No harm in it, man. A couple of words, a little walk, and a packet of monkey-nuts on the way.

MORRIS. Monkey-nuts?

ZACHARIAH. *Tickey* a packet. Something to chew.

MORRIS. Good God, Zach! You take a lady friend to tea, man!

ZACHARIAH. To tea, hey?

MORRIS. With buns, if she's hungry. Hot cross buns.

ZACHARIAH. Now, you see! I would have just bought monkey-nuts. She's definitely not for me.

MORRIS. Yes, to tea. A pot of afternoon tea. When she sits down, you pull out her chair . . . like this. [*He demonstrates.*]

ZACHARIAH. I think I seen that.

MORRIS. The woman pours the tea but the man butters the bun.

ZACHARIAH. Well, well, well.

MORRIS. Only two spoons of sugar, and don't drink out of the saucer.

ZACHARIAH. Very good.

MORRIS. Take it slow, chew it small, and swallow before you speak.

ZACHARIAH. What else?

MORRIS. If she wants to blow her nose, offer your hanky, which you keep in a breast pocket.

ZACHARIAH. Go on.

MORRIS [*waking up to reality*]. It's no good! [*Bitterly.*] You're wasting my time, talking like this! It's a lot of rot. I'm going to bed.

ZACHARIAH. But what's the matter, man? You were telling me everything so damn good. Come on. Tell me. [*Coaxing.*] Tell your brother what's the matter.

MORRIS. I haven't got a hanky.

ZACHARIAH. I think we can buy one. Couldn't we? I reckon for a meeting with Ethel we can manage a hanky all right.

MORRIS. And the breast pocket?

ZACHARIAH. What's the problem there? Let's also. . . .

MORRIS. Don't be a bloody fool! You got to buy a whole suit to get the breast pocket. And that's still not all. What about socks, decent shoes, a spotty tie, and a clean white shirt? How do you think a man steps out to meet a waiting lady? On his bare feet, wearing rags, and stinking because he hasn't had a bath? She'd even laugh and scream at me if I went like this. So I'm giving Ethel back to you. There's nothing I can do with her, thank you very much.

[*Morris to his bed. Zachariah thinks.*]

ZACHARIAH. Haven't we got enough money?

MORRIS. All I got left from the fish today is one shilling, and until you get paid. . . . What am I talking about! You know what a right sort of for-a-meeting-with-the-lady type of suit costs? Pounds and pounds and pounds. Shoes? Pounds and pounds. Shirt? Pounds. And then there's still two socks and a tie.

ZACHARIAH [*patiently*]. We got that sort of money.

MORRIS. Here it is. One shilling. Take it and go buy me a suit, please.

ZACHARIAH. Thank you. [*Takes the coin and throws it away without even looking at it.*] Where's the tin?

MORRIS. Tin?

ZACHARIAH. Round sort of tin.

MORRIS [*horror*]. Our tin?

ZACHARIAH. There was sweets in it at Christmas.

MORRIS. You mean, our future?

ZACHARIAH. That's the one. The future tin.

MORRIS. Our two-man farm?

ZACHARIAH. Where is it?

MORRIS. I won't tell you.

[*He runs and stands spread-eagled in front of the cupboard where the tin is hidden.*]

ZACHARIAH. Ah-ha!

MORRIS. No, Zach!

ZACHARIAH. Give it to me!

MORRIS. I won't! I won't! [*Grabs the tin and runs away. Zachariah lurches after him. Morris is quick and elusive.*]

ZACHARIAH. I'll catch you, Morrie, and when I do. . . .

MORRIS. Zach, please! Just stop! Please! Just stand still and listen to me. Everything . . . everything we got, the most precious thing a man can have, a future, is in here. You've worked hard, I've done the saving.

ZACHARIAH. We'll start again.

MORRIS. It will take too long.

ZACHARIAH. I'll work overtime.

MORRIS. It won't be the same.

[*Zachariah lunges suddenly, but Morris escapes.*]

ZACHARIAH. *Bliksem!* Wait, Morrie! Wait! Fair is fair. Now this time you stand still . . . and think. Ethel. . . .

MORRIS. I won't.

ZACHARIAH. Yes you will, because Ethel is coming and you want to meet her. But like you say, not like any *ou hotnot* in the street, but smartly. Now this is it. You're wearing a pretty smart for-a-meeting-with-the-lady type of suit. [*Morris, clutching the tin to his chest, closes his eyes. Zachariah creeps closer.*] Shiny shoes, white socks, a good shirt, and a spotty tie. And the people watch you go by and say: Hey! Hey! Just come and look, man. Will you please just come and look at that! . . . Who's you . . . ? There goes something! And Ethel says: Who's this coming? Could it be my friend, Mr. Pietersen? And you say: Good day to you, Miss Ethel. May I shake your white hands with my white hands? Of course, Mr. Pietersen. [*Zachariah has reached Morris. He takes the tin.*] Thank you, Morrie.

[*Morris doesn't move. Zachariah opens the tin, takes out the money, and then callously throws the tin away. He takes the money to the table, where he counts it.*]

MORRIS. Why are you doing this to me?

ZACHARIAH. Aren't we brothers?

[*Pause.*]

MORRIS. Where was I? Yes. At a garage, on the floor, with Kleinbooi and there were moths. Then I had that deep thought. You see they were flying in out of the darkness, out of the black, lonely night . . . to the lamp . . . into the flame. Always to light, I thought. Everything always flying, or growing, or turning, or crying for the whiteness of light. Birds following the sun when winter comes; trees and things standing, begging for it; moths hunting it; Man wanting it. All of us, always, out of darkness and into light.

ZACHARIAH. What sort of suit? And what about the shoes.

MORRIS. Go to a good shop. Ask for the outfit, for a gentleman.

SCENE FIVE

The next day.

   Morris is lying on his bed, staring up at the ceiling. There is a knock at the door. Morris rises slowly on his bed.

MORRIS. Who is there? [*The knock is heard again.*] Speak up. I can't hear. [*Silence. Morris's fear is now apparent. He waits until the knock is heard a third time.*] Ethel . . . I mean, madam . . . no, no! . . . I mean to say Miss Ethel Lange, could that be you? [*In reply there is a raucous burst of laughter, unmistakably Zachariah's.*] What's this? [*Silence.*] What's the meaning of this? [*Morris rushes to his bed and looks at the alarm-clock.*] This is all wrong, Zach! It's still only the middle of the day.

ZACHARIAH [*outside*]. I know.

MORRIS. Go back to work! At once!

ZACHARIAH. I can't.

MORRIS. Why not?

ZACHARIAH. I took some leave, Morris, and left. Let me in.

MORRIS. What's the matter with you? The door's not locked.

ZACHARIAH. My hands are full. [*Pause.*] I been shopping, Morrie. [*Morris rushes to the door, but collects himself before opening it. Zachariah comes in, his arms piled high with parcels. He smiles slyly at Morris who has assumed a pose of indifference.*]

ZACHARIAH. Oh no you don't, this time! I heard you run. So you thought it was maybe our little Miss Ethel, and a bit scared too at that thought, I think I heard? Well, don't worry no more, Morrie, because you know what these is? Your outfit! Number one, and what do we have? A wonderful hat . . . sir. [*Takes it out and holds it up for approval. His manner is exaggerated and suggestive of the shopkeeper who sold him the clothing.*] . . . which is guaranteed to protect the head on Sundays and rainy days. Because! Think for a moment! Who ever knows what the weather will be? It's been bad before. Number two is the shirt, and a grey tie, which is much better taste. Spots are too loud for a gentleman. Next we have—two grey socks, left and right, and a hanky to blow her nose. [*Next parcel.*] Aha! We've come to the suit.

71

Now before I show you the suit, my friend, I want to ask you, what does a man really look for in a good suit? A good cloth. Isn't that so?

MORRIS. What are you talking about?

ZACHARIAH. That's what he said. The fashion might be a season old, but will you please feel the difference. It's lasted for years already. All I can say is, take it or leave it. But remember, only a fool would leave it at that price. So I took it. [*Next parcel.*] Here we have a real ostrich wallet.

MORRIS. What for?

ZACHARIAH. Your inside pocket. *Ja*! You forgot about the inside pocket, he said. A gentleman always got a wallet for the inside pocket. [*Next parcel.*] And a cigarette lighter, and a cigarette case for the outside pocket. Chramonium!

MORRIS. Since when do I smoke?

ZACHARIAH. I know. But Ethel might, he said.

MORRIS [*fear*]. You told him?

ZACHARIAH. Don't worry. I just said there was a lady who someone was going to meet. He winked at me and said it was a good thing, now and then, and reminded me that ladies like presents. [*Holds up a scarf.*] A pretty *doek* in case the wind blows her hair away, he said. Here we got a umbrella in case it's sopping wet. And over here. . . . [*Last parcel.*] . . . Guess! Come on, Morrie. Guess what's in this box. I'll shake it. Listen.

MORRIS. Shoes.

ZACHARIAH [*triumphantly*]. No! It's boots! I got you boots. Ha ha! *Ja.* [*Watching Morris's reaction.*] They frighten a *ou*, don't they? [*Happy.*] Satisfied?

MORRIS [*looking at the pile of clothing*]. It seems all right.

ZACHARIAH. It wasn't easy. At the first shop, when I asked for the outfit for a gentleman, they said I was a agitator and was going to call the police. I had to get out, man . . . quick! Even this fellow . . . Mr. Moses . . . 'Come again, my friend' . . . 'You're drunk,' he said. But when I showed him our future he sobered up. You know what he said? Guess.

MORRIS. No.

ZACHARIAH. He said, 'Are you the gentleman?' Me! He did. So I said, 'Do I look like a gentleman, Mr. Moses?' He said, 'My friend, it takes all sorts of different sorts to make this world.' 'I'm the black sort,' I said. So he said, 'You don't say.' He also said to mention his name and the fair deal to any other gentlemen wanting reasonable outfits. Go ahead, Morrie. [*The clothing.*] Let's see the gentle sort of man.

MORRIS. Okay. Okay. Don't rush me. [*Moves cautiously to the pile of clothing. Flicks an imaginary speck of dust off the hat. Zachariah is waiting.*] Well?

ZACHARIAH. Well, I'm waiting.

MORRIS. Give me time.

ZACHARIAH. What for? You got the clothes.

MORRIS. For God's sake, Zach! This is deep water. I'm not just going to jump right in. Men drown that way. You must paddle around first.

ZACHARIAH. Paddle around?

MORRIS. Try it out!

ZACHARIAH [*offering him the hat*]. Try it on.

MORRIS. The idea, man. I got to try it out. There's more to wearing a white skin than just putting on a hat. You've seen white men before without hats, but they're still white men, aren't they?

ZACHARIAH. *Ja.*

MORRIS. And without suits or socks, or shoes. . . .

ZACHARIAH. No, Morrie. Never without socks and shoes. Never a barefoot white man.

MORRIS. Well, the suit then. Look, Zach, what I'm trying to say is this. The clothes will help, but only help. They don't maketh the white man. It's that white something inside you, that special meaning and manner of whiteness that I got to find. I know what I'm talking about because . . . I'll be honest with you now, Zach . . . I've thought about it for a long time. Why do you think I really read the Bible, hey? What do you think I'm thinking about when I'm not saying something? I'm being critical of colour, and the first-fruit

73

of my thought is that this whiteness of theirs is not just in the skin, otherwise . . . well, I mean . . . I'd be one of them, wouldn't I? Because, let me tell you, I seen them that's darker than me. Yes. Really dark, man. Only they had that something I'm telling you about. That's what I got to pin down in here.

ZACHARIAH. What?

MORRIS. White living, man! Like . . . like . . . like let's take looking at things. Haven't you noticed it? They look at things differently. Haven't you seen their eyes when they look at you? [*Pause.*] That snapshot of Ethel. See how she stands there against that brick wall, facing the camera without fear. They're born with that sort of courage. Just suppose, when I'm taking her away to afternoon tea, a man jumps out and points a camera at me! I'm telling you, my first thought will be to run like hell, to protect my face! It's not that I'm a coward. It's what they call instinct, and I was born with it, and now I got to learn to conquer it. Because if I don't, you think that Ethel won't know what it means? I'll be done for, man! . . . again. How else did they know? Because we agree that I'm just as white as some of them. It all boils down to this different thing they got, and, let me tell you, it's even in their way of walking. Something happened to me once which proves it. It was on the road. The first time I had started going.

ZACHARIAH. Where?

MORRIS. Just places. I've got to explain something, Zach, otherwise you won't feel what I mean. A road, Zach, is not a street. It's not just that there isn't houses, or lamp-posts, or hasn't got a name. It's that it doesn't stop. The road goes on and on, passing all the time through nothing. And when a man, a city man, a man used to streets and things, walks out onto it . . . he just doesn't know what he's walking into. You see, you're used to people . . . but there's no people there! You're used to a roof . . . where there is only a sky . . . silence instead of sound. I'm telling you, man, it was nothing instead of something, some any old thing like a donkey, or a dog, or children kicking an empty tin . . . there was nothing, and it was the first time. This is no place for me, I thought, this emptiness! Not even trees, Zach. Only small, dry, little brittle bushes and flat hills in the distance. That, and the road running straight. God, that hurts the eyeball! That straight, never-stopping road! You've reached the end you think, you come to the top, and there ... t-h-e-r-e it goes again. So the bushes and the hills and the road and nothing else ... or maybe just a car running away in the dust ... but only a few of them, and far between, a long way between each one. You see, they never stopped. So all of that and me, there, in the middle for the first time. It hits you when the sun goes. That's when you really know why men build homes, and the meaning of that word 'home', because the veld's gone grey and cold with a blind, bad feeling about you being there. [*Pause.*] So there I was on the road. I'd been watching him all day.

ZACHARIAH. Who?

MORRIS. The man ahead of me.

ZACHARIAH. I thought you was alone.

MORRIS. I was feeling alone, but there was this man ahead of me. At first it was enough just to see him there, a spot in the dusty distance. A man! Another man! There was one other man on that road with me, going my way! But then the time came for the sun to drop, and I found myself walking through the shadows of those white stones on the side of the way. When a man sees shadows he thinks of night, doesn't he? I did. So I began to walk a little faster. I think he began to walk a little slower. I'm sure he also saw the shadows. Now comes the point. The more I walked a little bit faster and faster each time, the more I began to worry. About what, you ask? About him. There was something about him, about the way he walked, the way he went to the top when the road had a hill and stood there against the sky and looked back at me, and then walked on again. And all the time, with this worry in my heart, the loneliness was creeping across the veld and I was hurrying a bit more. In fact, I was going quite quick by then. When the sun went at last, I was trotting you might say, and worried, Zach, really worried, man, because I could see the warm glow of his fire as I ran that last little bit through the dark.

When I was even nearer he saw me coming and stood up, but when he saw me clearer he picked up a stick and held it like a hitting stick, stepping back for safety and a good aim . . . so what could I do but pass peacefully. [*Pause.*] Because he was white, Zach. I had been right all along . . . the road . . . since midday. That's what I mean, you see. It's in the way they walk as well.

ZACHARIAH. So you must learn to walk properly then.

MORRIS. Yes.

ZACHARIAH. And to look right at things.

MORRIS. Yes.

ZACHARIAH. And to sound right.

MORRIS. Yes! There's that, as well. The sound of it.

ZACHARIAH. So go on. [*Again offering the hat.*] Try it. For size. Just for the sake of the size. [*Morris takes the hat, plays with it for a few seconds, then impulsively puts it on.*] Ha!

MORRIS. Yes?

ZACHARIAH. Aha!

MORRIS [*whipping off the hat in embarrassment*]. No.

ZACHARIAH. Yes.

MORRIS [*shaking his head*]. Uhuh!

ZACHARIAH. Come.

MORRIS. No, man.

ZACHARIAH. Please, man.

MORRIS. You're teasing.

ZACHARIAH. No, man. I like the look of that on your head.

MORRIS. Really?

ZACHARIAH. 'Strue's God.

MORRIS. It looked right?

ZACHARIAH. I'm telling you.

MORRIS. It seemed to fit.

ZACHARIAH. It did, I know.

MORRIS [*using this as an excuse to get it back on his head*]. The brim was just right on the brow . . . and with plenty of room for the brain! I'll try it again, shall I? Just for size.

ZACHARIAH. Just for size. [*Morris puts it on.*] Ja. A good fit.

MORRIS. A very good fit, in fact. [*Lifting the hat.*] Good morning!

ZACHARIAH. Very good.

MORRIS. Did it look right? [*Again.*] Good morning . . . Miss Ethel Lange! [*Looks quickly to see Zachariah's reaction. He betrays nothing.*]

ZACHARIAH. Maybe a little bit higher.

MORRIS [*again*]. Good morning. . . . [*A flourish.*] . . . and how do you do today, Miss Ethel Lange! [*Laughing with delight.*] How about the jacket?

ZACHARIAH. Okay. [*Hands him the jacket. Morris puts it on.*]

MORRIS [*preening*]. How did you do it?

ZACHARIAH. I said, 'The gentleman is smaller than me, Mr. Moses.'

MORRIS. It's so smug. Look, Zach, I'm going to do that little bit again. Watch me careful. [*Once again lifting his hat.*] Good day, Miss Ethel Lange. . . . [*Pleading, servile.*] . . . I beg your pardon, but I do hope you wouldn't mind to take a little walk with. . . .

ZACHARIAH. Stop!

MORRIS. What's wrong?

ZACHARIAH. Your voice.

MORRIS. What's wrong with it?

ZACHARIAH. Too soft. They don't never sound like that.

MORRIS. To a lady they do! I admit, if it wasn't Ethel I was addressing, it would be different.

ZACHARIAH. Okay. Try me.

MORRIS. How?

ZACHARIAH. You're walking with Ethel. I'm selling monkey-nuts.

MORRIS. So?

ZACHARIAH. So you want some monkey-nuts.

MORRIS. That's a good idea. . . . [*His voice trails off.*]

ZACHARIAH. Go on. I'm selling monkey-nuts.

MORRIS [*after hesitation*]. I can't.

ZACHARIAH [*simulated shock*]. What!

MORRIS [*frightened*]. What I mean is . . . I don't want any monkey-nuts. I'm not hungry.

ZACHARIAH. Ethel wants some.

MORRIS. Ethel.

ZACHARIAH. *Ja*. And I'm selling them.

MORRIS. This is hard for me, Zach.

ZACHARIAH. You must learn your lesson, Morrie. You want to pass, don't you?

MORRIS [*steeling himself*]. Excuse me!

ZACHARIAH. I'll never hear that.

MORRIS. Hey!

ZACHARIAH. Or that.

MORRIS. Boy!

ZACHARIAH. I'm ignoring you, man. I'm a cheeky one.

MORRIS. You're asking for it, Zach!

ZACHARIAH. I am.

MORRIS. I warn you, I will!

ZACHARIAH. Go ahead.

MORRIS [*with brutality and coarseness*]. Hey, *Swartgat*! [*An immediate reaction from Zachariah. His head whips around. He stares at Morris in disbelief. Morris replies with a weak little laugh, which soon dies on his lips.*] Just a joke! [*Softly.*] Oh, my God! What did I do? Forgive me, Zach. Say it, please. Forgiveness. Don't look at me like that! [*A step to Zachariah who backs away.*] Say something. For God's sake, say anything! I didn't mean it now. I didn't do it then. Truly. I came back. I'm your brother.

ZACHARIAH [*disbelief*]. My brother?

MORRIS. Me, Zach, Morris!

ZACHARIAH. Morris?

[*Morris at last realizes what has happened. He tears off the jacket and hat in a frenzy.*]

MORRIS. Now do you see?

ZACHARIAH. It's you.

MORRIS. Yes!

ZACHARIAH. That's funny. I thought. . . .

MORRIS. I know. I saw it again.

ZACHARIAH. What?

MORRIS. The pain, man. The pity of it all and the pain in your eyes.

ZACHARIAH. I was looking, I thought, at a different sort of man.

MORRIS. But don't you see, Zach? It was me! That different sort of man you saw was me. It's happened, man! And I'll swear, I'll take God's name in vain that I no longer wanted it. That's why I came back. I didn't want it any more. I turned around on the road and came back here because I couldn't stand that look in your eyes any more. Those bright, brotherly eyes in my dreams at night, always wet with love, full of pity and pain . . . God, such lonely eyes they were! . . . watching and sad and asking me, why? softly, why? sorrowfully, why? . . . Why did I do it? . . . Why try to deny it? Because . . . because . . . I'll tell you the whole truth now. . . . Because I did try it! It didn't seem a sin. If a man was born with a chance at a change, why not take it, I thought . . . thinking of worms lying warm in their silk, to come out one day with wings and things! Why not a man? If his dreams are soft and keep him warm at night, why not stand up the next morning, Different . . . Beautiful! It's the natural law! The long arm of the real law frightened me—but I might have been lucky. We all know that some are not caught, so . . . so . . . so what was worrying me? You. Yes, in my dreams at night, there was you, as well. What about you? My own brother. What sort of a thing was that to do to a *ou*'s own flesh-and-blood brother? Because he is, you know. There was only one mother, and she's what counts. And watch out! She will, too, up in heaven, her two little chickens down here and find one missing. She'll know what you've done! If you don't mind about hell, all right, go ahead . . . but even so there was still you, because it wasn't that next life but this old, worn out, and wicked one, and I was tired because there was still you. Anywhere, any place or road, there was still you. So I came back. [*Pause.*] It's not been too hard. A little uneasy at times, but not too hard. And I've proved I'm no Judas. Gentle Jesus, meek and mild, I'm no Judas!

[*The alarm rings. Neither responds.*]

SCENE SIX

Night.

The two men are asleep. Silence. Suddenly Zachariah sits up in bed. Without looking at Morris he gets up, goes to the corner where the new suit of clothes is hanging, and puts on the suit and hat. The final effect is an absurdity bordering on the grotesque. The hat is too small and so is the jacket, which he has buttoned up incorrectly, while the trousers are too short. Zachariah stands barefooted, holding the umbrella, the hat pulled down low over his eyes so that his face is almost hidden.

ZACHARIAH. Ma. Ma! Mother! Hullo. How are you, old woman? What's that? You don't recognize me? Well, well, well. Take a guess. [*Shakes his head.*] No. [*Shakes his head.*] No. Try again. [*Shakes his head.*] What's the matter with you, Ma? Don't you recognize your own son? [*Shakes his head violently.*] No, no! Not him! It's me, Zach! [*Sweeps off the hat to show his face.*] *Ja.* Zach! Didn't think I could do it, did you? Well, to tell you the truth, the whole truth so help me God, I got sick of myself and made a change. Him? At home, Ma. *Ja.* A lonely boy, as you say. A sad story, as I will tell you. He went on the road, Ma, but strange to say, he came back quite white. No tan at all. I don't recognize him no more. [*He sits.*] I'll ask you again, how are you, old woman? I see some signs of wear and tear. [*Nodding his head.*] That's true . . . such sorrow . . . tomorrow. . . . *Ja* . . . it's cruel . . . it's callous . . . and your feet as well? Still a bad fit in the shoe? *Ai ai ai!* Me? [*Pause. He struggles.*] There's something I need to know, Ma. You see, we been talking, me and him . . . *ja*, I talk to him, he says it helps . . . and now we got to know. Whose mother were you really? At the bottom of your heart, where your blood is red with pain, tell me, whom did you really love? No evil feelings, Ma, but, I mean, a man's got to know. You see, he's been such a burden as a brother. [*Agitation.*] Don't be dumb! Don't cry! It was just a question! Look! I brought you a present, old soul. [*Holds out a hand with the fingers lightly closed.*] It's a butterfly. A real beauty butterfly. We were travelling fast, Ma. We hit them at ninety . . . a whole flock. But one was still alive, and made me think of . . . Mother. . . . So I caught it, myself, for you, remembering what I caught from you. This, old Ma of mine, is gratitude for you, and it proves it, doesn't it? Some things are only skin-deep, because I got it, here in my hand, I got beauty . . . too . . . haven't I?

SCENE SEVEN

The next evening.

  For the first time the room is untidy. The beds are not made, the table cluttered, the floor littered with the strings and wrappings of the parcels of the previous day. Morris is alone. He sits lifelessly at the table, his head fallen on his chest, his arms hanging limp at his sides. On the table is a small bundle. Then Zachariah comes in. He behaves normally, going straight to the bed and taking off his shoes. Only when this is done, does he realize something is wrong. The footbath hasn't been prepared.

ZACHARIAH. What's this? [*Looking around for the basin.*] Foot-salts finished? Hell, man! Couldn't you have seen? What must I do now? My feet are killing me again. I've been on them today, you know. [*Touching the toes.*] *Eina*! *Eina*! Forget the salts then. Just give me some hot. A soak will do them good. [*Morris doesn't move.*] Some hot, Morrie! Please! [*Nothing happens.*] What's the matter with you? Don't tell me the stove is buggered up! [*Goes to the stove and feels the kettle.*] *Ag*, no, man! What the hell's happened? A man works all day, his feet are killing him and he comes home and finds this [*The stove.*] . . . and this. [*The room.*] Floor not swept! Beds not made! [*Beginning to realize.*] There is something wrong in here. You say nothing. [*Morris struggles to find a word, but fails and drops his shoulders in a gesture of defeat and resignation.*] You mean. . . . [*Disbelief.*] . . . You mean you got nothing to say? [*A little laugh, but this quickly dies.*] No! It's not funny. Try to say something, Morrie. Please. [*Desperate.*] Try telling me what happened. *Ja*! What happened?

MORRIS. I've given up.

ZACHARIAH. What?

MORRIS. I mean, I can't carry on.

ZACHARIAH. Oh, so you've just stopped.

MORRIS. Yes.

ZACHARIAH. But that won't do! Emphatically not! A man can't just stop like that, like you. That's definitely no good, because. . . . You want to know why? Because a man must carry on. Most certainly. Otherwise who is going to sweep the floor? *Ja*. Ever think about that? If everybody just gave up, just sat down and couldn't carry on . . . me at the gate . . . you in here . . . why, nothing would happen. Isn't that so? One by one we would just topple over and nothing would happen. But we all know that *something* got to happen. So that proves it, doesn't it? We *must* carry on. Okay? Feeling better? [*Sees the bundle on the table for the first time.*] What's this bundle, Morrie?

MORRIS. My belongings.

ZACHARIAH. What's that?

MORRIS. My Bible, my other shirt, and my alarm-clock.

ZACHARIAH. And what would they be doing in here?

MORRIS. I was leaving, Zach.

ZACHARIAH. Leaving?

MORRIS. Going away.

ZACHARIAH. Where?

MORRIS. The road. Wherever it went.

ZACHARIAH. Oh! [*Pause.*] And what about me?

MORRIS. I know, I know.

ZACHARIAH. But you don't care, hey?

MORRIS. I do care, Zach!

ZACHARIAH [*ignoring the denial*]. That's a fine thought for a loving brother. I'm surprised at you. In fact, I'm shocked.

MORRIS. Stop it, Zach! I'm still here. I know I can't go. You see, this morning when you were at work, I thought it out. It's no use any more, I said. There's no future left for us now, in here. So I wrapped up my Bible and my clock in my shirt and wrote the farewell note. Four pages! I explained everything. I was ready to go, man . . . until I realized that you couldn't read. My God, that hurt! That cut me deep! Zach can't read without me! [*Pause.*] So you see, I know I can't go . . . but I've given up.

ZACHARIAH. Come on, cheer up. It's not so bad.

MORRIS. I can't, Zach. Honestly I can't any more.

ZACHARIAH. But I've got a surprise for you.

MORRIS. It will have to be damn good to make any difference.

ZACHARIAH. How good is a letter from Ethel?

MORRIS. No damn good! You've missed the point. Don't you see, man? She's to blame. [*Zachariah takes out the letter.*] I don't want it. Take it away.

ZACHARIAH [*putting the letter down on the table so that Morris can see it*]. It's not mine. I gave her to you.

MORRIS. Everything was fine until she came along.

ZACHARIAH. She hasn't yet.

MORRIS. What do you mean?

ZACHARIAH. Come along. You've missed the problem. Ethel coming along was the problem. She hasn't yet. But she might be on her way. I mean. . . . It could be June, couldn't it? Where's the moths? And she did say June. That's what I'm saying. She might be on the train, on her way right now, and one fine day, you know what? Guess.

MORRIS. What?

ZACHARIAH. Another knock at the door. But it won't be me. So, you see, if I was you, just for safety's sake, of course, I'd have a quick peep at that letter.

[*Zachariah goes to his bed. Morris hesitates for a second, then takes the letter, opens it, and reads in silence. When he has finished he puts it down and looks at Zachariah vacantly.*]

ZACHARIAH [*unable to contain himself any longer*]. She's coming! Let me guess. She's on the train, on her way, and it's June. When do you meet, man? What did she say? Tell me, Morrie.

MORRIS. No. She's not coming. Never. Prepare yourself for . . . good news. Ethel's gone and got engaged to get married, to Luckyman Stoffel.

ZACHARIAH. No.

MORRIS. Yes.

ZACHARIAH. No.

MORRIS. It's true.

ZACHARIAH. No!

MORRIS. Then listen. [*Reads.*] 'Dear Pen-pal, It's sad news for you but good news for me. I've decided to get married. Ma says it's Okay. The lucky man is Stoffel, who plays in my brother's team, full-back. It's a long story. Lucy thought she had him, but she didn't, so now we're not on talking terms no more. Stoffel works at Boetie's Garage and doesn't like competition so he says pen-pals is out if we're going to get married to each other. He's sitting here now and he says he wants to say this: Leave my woman alone if you know what's good for you. That was Stoffel. He's a one all right. Well, pal, that's all for now, for ever. Ethel.' [*Pause.*] Down here at the bottom she says: 'You can keep the snapshot for a keepsake.'

[*Morris looks vacantly at Zachariah, whose attitude has hardened with bitter disappointment.*]

ZACHARIAH. So?

MORRIS. So I think we can begin again.

ZACHARIAH. What?

MORRIS. That's a good question. [*Pause.*] Well, let's work it out. Where are we? Here. That's a good beginning. What is this? Our room. Me and you, Morrie and Zach . . . live here . . . in peace. Yes. It's coming now, Zach. I feel it. I'm filling up again with thoughts and things. We're living here in peace because the problem's gone . . . and got engaged to be married . . . and I'm Morrie . . . and I was going to go, but now I'm going to stay! [*With something of his old self Morrie goes to work. Opens his bundle and packs out his belongings.*] Hey, Zach! [*Holding up the clock.*] It's stopped. Like me. What time shall we make it? Supper?

ZACHARIAH. I'm not hungry.

MORRIS. Bedtime?

ZACHARIAH. I don't want to sleep.

MORRIS. Just after supper, then. We'll say we've eaten.

ZACHARIAH. You can say what you like!

MORRIS. What's the matter, Zach? I don't like to see you so . . . so . . . sort of. Come on now. Tell me what it is. I've helped you before, haven't I?

ZACHARIAH [*slowly*]. You aren't going to wear that suit any more?

MORRIS. I see. Zach, look at me now. Solemnly, on this Bible, I promise you I won't.

ZACHARIAH. That's it.

MORRIS. What?

ZACHARIAH [*slyly*]. You looked so damn smart in that suit, Morrie. It made me feel good.

MORRIS. You mean that!

ZACHARIAH. Cross my heart.

MORRIS. You mean you want to see me *in it*?

ZACHARIAH. I do.

MORRIS. Be honest now, Zach. Is what you are saying that you would like me to put that suit on?

ZACHARIAH [*emphatically*]. Now.

MORRIS. Now! This comes as a surprise, Zach. But if as you say it makes you feel better . . . well . . . that just about makes it my duty, doesn't it? [*Moving to the suit.*] It was a damn good buy, Ethel or no Ethel. I really am tempted.

ZACHARIAH. Then get in.

MORRIS. You'll have to help me. It's not so easy now . . . after yesterday. Say something to help me.

ZACHARIAH. Just for size. No harm done. We're brothers. She's gone for the good. We're only playing now.

MORRIS. Only playing! Of course! That does it.

[*With a laugh Morris puts on the suit. When he is dressed, he walks around the room in exaggerated style. Zachariah encourages him.*]

ZACHARIAH. *Ek sê*! Just look! *Hoe's dit vir 'n ding. Links draai, regs swaai. . . . Aitsa! Ou pellie*, you're stepping high tonight!

[*Morris stops, turns suddenly.*]

MORRIS. Hey, *Swartgat*! [*A second of silence, and then Zachariah laughs hollowly.*] No harm done now, hey, Zach?

ZACHARIAH. No pain.

MORRIS. That's the way to take a joke. [*Again.*] Hey, *Swartgat*!

ZACHARIAH [*playing along*]. *Ja, Baas*?

MORRIS. Who are you?

ZACHARIAH. I'm your boy Zach, *Baas*.

MORRIS. Who am I?

ZACHARIAH. *Baas* Morrie, *Baas*.

MORRIE. *Baas* Morrie and his boy, Zach! My God, you're comical! Where the hell you get that joke from, Zach?

ZACHARIAH. At the gate.

MORRIS. So that's what it's like.

ZACHARIAH. They're all dressed up smart like you, and go walking by. Go on. Try it.

MORRIS. What?

ZACHARIAH. Walk past.

MORRIS. You want to play it?

ZACHARIAH. Why not?

MORRIS. I haven't seen the gate before, Zach. It's difficult to play something you haven't seen.

ZACHARIAH. I'll show you. Here it is. [*Vague gesture.*] This here is the gate.

MORRIS. What's on the other side?

ZACHARIAH. Does it matter?

MORRIS. It does if we're going to play this thing right.

ZACHARIAH [*looking back*]. Trees.

MORRIS. Ah! Tall trees, with picnics in the shade.

ZACHARIAH. Grass.

MORRIS. Green, hey! We'll make it spring.

ZACHARIAH. Flowers with butterflies.

MORRIS. That's a good touch.

ZACHARIAH. And benches.

MORRIS. How thoughtful! I'll want to rest.

ZACHARIAH. And I'm squatting here.

MORRIS. Right. So you'll open the gate for me when I get there.

ZACHARIAH. No. It's open. I'll just watch your boots as you go by.

MORRIS. Then what's your job at the gate?

ZACHARIAH [*pause*]. They put me there to chase the black kids away. [*Morris hesitates.*]

MORRIS. Are you sure we should play this?

ZACHARIAH. It's only a game. Walk past.

[*Morris flourishes his umbrella and then saunters slowly towards Zachariah.*]

MORRIS. Shame! Look at that poor old boy. John? What are you doing . . . ?

ZACHARIAH [*cutting him*]. No, Morrie.

MORRIS. What's wrong?

ZACHARIAH. They never talk to me. Start again. [*Morris tries it again. This time he doesn't speak, but pretends to take a coin out of his pocket and tosses it to Zachariah.*] How much?

MORRIS. Half a crown.

ZACHARIAH. What!

MORRIS. Shilling.

ZACHARIAH. Too much.

MORRIS. Sixpence. [*Zachariah is still doubtful.*] All right then, a penny.

ZACHARIAH. That's a bit better, but. . . .

MORRIS. But what?

ZACHARIAH. You think you're the soft sort of white man, hey! Giving me a penny like that.

MORRIS. What's wrong with being the soft sort? You find them.

ZACHARIAH. I know. But not you. Not with boots, Morrie. Never with boots. That sort doesn't even see me. So don't stop. Just walk past.

[*The mime is repeated. This time Morris walks straight past.*]

MORRIS. Now what?

ZACHARIAH. I have a thought. I'm squatting here, watching you, and I think.

MORRIS. Okay.

ZACHARIAH. Bastard!

MORRIS [*sharply*]. Who?

ZACHARIAH. Don't spoil it, man! You don't hear me. It's a thought. [*Taps his forehead.*]

MORRIS [*looking away, frowning*]. Carry on.

ZACHARIAH. That's all.

MORRIS. Just . . . ?

ZACHARIAH. Just a bastard.

MORRIS. What happens now?

ZACHARIAH. I'm watching you, but you're looking up the trees, remember?

MORRIS. Yes, of course. It's a tall tree. I'm wondering if I've ever seen a tree as tall as this tree. There's also a great weight of birdies on the branches and ... actually I'm finding difficulty keeping my mind up the tree with you behind my back. I feel your presence. So I think, I'll move further on. You see, you bothered me as I passed. Moments of recognition, you know, at first sight, and all that. So I'll take this road. I mean ... I'll have to get away if I want to admire the beauty, won't I? Yes. It's a good road. It's going places, because ahead of me I see the sky. I see it through the trees ... so I'm climbing up the hill in this road, putting miles between us; and now, at last, there ahead of me is the sky, big blue; and I hurry on to the top where I turn against it and look back at you ... far behind me now, in the distance, outside the gate. Can you see me?

ZACHARIAH. A little.

MORRIS. What is it you see here, in the distance, beyond the trees, upon the hill, against the sky?

ZACHARIAH. Could it be a ... man?

MORRIS. A white man! Don't you see the way I stand? Didn't you see how I turned and looked back at you, at all that is past and forgotten? What do you think now?

ZACHARIAH. He's a bastard!

MORRIS [*reckless in his elation*]. Well, I don't care. It's too far away now for me to see your eyes. In fact, I'm almost free ... because downhill is always easier! I can run now! So I turn my back and away I go, laughing, over the green spring grass, into the flowers and among the butterflies. And what do I say? What do I shout? I've changed! Look at me, will you please! I too flew from darkness to light, but I didn't burn my wings. [*Pause.*] Now I'm tired. After so many years so much beauty is a burden. I need rest. [*Sits.*] Ah dearie, dearie me. [*Zachariah comes past, bent low, miming the picking up of litter in the park. One hand trails a sack, the other is stabbing with a stick at pieces of paper. Morris watches this with critical interest.*] What are you doing?

ZACHARIAH. Picking up rubbish. I got a stick with a nail on the end. Every afternoon, at four o'clock, I go through the trees and around the benches and pick up the papers and peels.

MORRIS. I thought I'd left you behind.

ZACHARIAH. I know.

MORRIS. The sight of you affects me, *Swartgat*.

ZACHARIAH [*continuing with his mime*]. I can feel it does.

MORRIS. It's interesting. Just looking at you, does it. I don't need the other senses. Just sight. Not even smell. Just the sight of you crawling around like some . . . some . . . thing . . . makes me want to bring up.

ZACHARIAH. Is that so?

MORRIS [*rising*]. In fact I'd like to. . . . [*Stops himself.*]

ZACHARIAH. Carry on.

MORRIS [*walking away*]. I can't.

ZACHARIAH. Try.

MORRIS. I'm telling you, I can't.

ZACHARIAH. Why?

MORRIS. Not with that old woman watching us. [*Zachariah stops and looks questioningly at Morris.*] Over there. [*Pointing.*]

ZACHARIAH. Old woman?

MORRIS. Horribly old.

ZACHARIAH. Alone?

MORRIS. All by her lonely self.

ZACHARIAH. And she's watching us?

MORRIS. All the time. [*Impatience.*] Can't you *see*? She's wearing a grey dress on Sunday.

ZACHARIAH [*recognition dawning*]. Soapsuds. . . .

MORRIS. . . . on brown hands.

ZACHARIAH. And sore feet! The toes are crooked, hey!

MORRIS. With sadness. She's been following me all day, all along the road, the long, unending road . . . begging!

ZACHARIAH. Call the police.

MORRIS. No, no. Not that.

ZACHARIAH. Then what will we do?

MORRIS. Let's work it out. We can't carry on with her watching us . . . behind that bush . . . like an old spy.

ZACHARIAH. So she must go.

MORRIS. I think so, too.. [*A step in the direction of the old woman.*] Go away.

ZACHARIAH. Is she moving?

MORRIS. No. [*Trying again.*] Go away, old one! Begat and be gone! Go home! [*Sigh.*] It's no use.

ZACHARIAH [*trying to scare her off*]. Hey!

MORRIS [*excited*]. She jumped! Ha ha. She jumped!

ZACHARIAH. *Voetsek!*

MORRIS. Another jump. [*Zachariah goes down on his hands and knees.*] What are you doing?

ZACHARIAH. Stones.

MORRIS. Hoooooo! She heard you. She's trotted off a little distance. But you're not really going to use them, are you?

ZACHARIAH. It's the only way. [*Throws.*]

MORRIS. Almost. [*Zachariah throws again.*] She jumped!

ZACHARIAH. *Voetsek!*

MORRIS. Yes. *Voetsek* off! We don't want you!

ZACHARIAH. Bugger off!

MORRIS. You old bitch! You made life unbearable!

ZACHARIAH [*starts throwing with renewed violence*]. *Hamba!*

MORRIS. She's running now.

ZACHARIAH. Get out!

MORRIS. *Kaffermeid!*

ZACHARIAH. *Ou hoer!*

MORRIS. *Luisgat!*

ZACHARIAH. *Swartgat!*

MORRIS. You've hit her! She's down. Look. . . . Look!

ZACHARIAH. Look at those old legs sticking up!

MORRIS. She's got no *broeks* on! [*Their derision rises to a climax, Morris shaking his umbrella, Zachariah his fists.*] That's the last of her, I think. By God, she ran! [*Pause while they get their breath.*] Where were we?

ZACHARIAH. It was four o'clock. I was collecting the rubbish. You wanted to do . . . something.

MORRIS. Yes. I remember now. I just wanted to . . . just wanted to. . . . Poke you with my umbrella. He-he-he! [*He attacks Zachariah savagely.*] Just wanted to poke you a little bit. That's all. He-he! What do you think umbrellas are for when it doesn't rain? Hey? [*Zachariah tries to escape, but Morris catches him with the crook of the umbrella.*] Wait, wait! Not so fast, John. I want to have a good look at you. My God! What sort of a mistake is this! A black man! All over, my boy?

ZACHARIAH. *Ja, Baas.*

MORRIS. Your pits and privates?

ZACHARIAH. *Ja, Baas.*

MORRIS. Nothing white?

ZACHARIAH. Forgive me please, my *Baas.*

MORRIS. You're horrible.

ZACHARIAH. Sorry, *Baas.*

MORRIS. You stink.

ZACHARIAH. Please, my *Baasie.* . . .

MORRIS. You don't use paper do you?

ZACHARIAH. . . . oh, my *Baasie*, my *Baasie*, my good little *Baasie.*

MORRIS. You know something? I hate you! What did you mean crawling around like that? Spoiling the view, spoiling my chances! What's your game, hey? Trying to be an embarrassment? Is that it? A two-legged embarrassment? Well, I hate you, do you hear! Hate! . . . Hate! . . . Hate! . . . [*He attacks Zachariah savagely with the umbrella. When his fury is spent he turns away and sits down.*] It was a good day. The sun shone. The sky was blue. I was happy. [*Smiling, released of all tensions.*] Not the sort of day to forget in a hurry. There's a spiny chill sprung up now, though. [*Shivering. Zachariah is moaning softly.*] Something sighing among the trees . . . must be the wind. Yes! There were the trees as well today. The tall trees. So much to remember! Still . . . [*Shivering.*] . . . it has got nippy . . . and I haven't got an overcoat . . . with me.

ZACHARIAH. Ding-dong . . . ong . . . ong . . . Ding-dong . . . ong . . . ong.

MORRIS. What is that sound I hear?

ZACHARIAH. The bells. They're closing up. Ding-dong . . . ong . . . ong.

MORRIS. I'd better hurry home. [*Stands.*] Yes, it was a good day . . . while it lasted.

ZACHARIAH. Ding-dong . . . ong . . . ong.

MORRIS. Ah, there's the gate.

ZACHARIAH. What's the matter with you?

MORRIS. What's the matter with me?

ZACHARIAH. Can't you see the gate is locked?

MORRIS. Is it? [*Tries the gate.*] It is.

ZACHARIAH. I locked it before I rang the bell.

MORRIS. Heavens above! Then I'd better climb over.

ZACHARIAH. Over those sharp pieces of glass they got on the top?

MORRIS. Then the fence.

ZACHARIAH. Barbed wire . . . very high. . . .

MORRIS. So what do I do?

ZACHARIAH. You might try calling.

MORRIS. Hello! Hello there! Hello, anybody there!!

ZACHARIAH. Nobody hears you, hey!

MORRIS. Now what?

ZACHARIAH. Now, you think you'll try the gate on the other side.

MORRIS [*alarm*]. All the way back?

ZACHARIAH. Ja. [*Moves quietly to the lamp on the table.*]

MORRIS. Through the trees?

ZACHARIAH. Looks like it.

MORRIS. But it's getting dark!

[*Zachariah is turning down the lamp.*]

ZACHARIAH. It happens, every day.

94

MORRIS. And cold . . . and I never did like shadows . . . and
. . . [*Pause.*] . . . where are you?

ZACHARIAH. Behind a tree.

MORRIS. But . . . but I thought you were the good sort of
boy?

ZACHARIAH. Me?

MORRIS. The simple, trustworthy type of John-boy. Weren't
you that?

ZACHARIAH. I've changed.

MORRIS. Who gave you the right?

ZACHARIAH. I took it!

MORRIS. That's illegal! They weren't yours! That's theft.
'Thou shalt not steal.' I arrest you in the name of God.
That's it! God! [*Looking around wildly.*] My prayers . . . please!
My last wish . . . is to say my prayers, please. You see . . . you
might hear them. [*Morris goes down on his knees. Zachariah begins
to move to him.*] Our Father, which art our Father in heaven,
because we never knew the other one; Forgive us this day
our trespassing; I couldn't help it; The gate was open, God,
your sun was too bright and blinded my eyes, so I didn't
see the notice prohibiting! And 'beware of the dog' was in
Bantu, so how was I to know, Oh Lord! My sins are not
that black. Furthermore, just some bread for the poor, daily,
and let Your Kingdom come as quick as it can, for Yours
is the power and the glory, but ours is the fear and the
judgment of eyes behind our back for the sins of our birth
and the man behind the tree in the darkness while I wait. . . .
Eina! [*Zachariah stands above Morris on the point of violence. The
alarm-clock rings. Morris crawls frantically away.*] Bedtime!
[*Morris jumps up, rushes to the table, and turns up the lamp. Zachariah
goes to his bed and sits. A long silence. They avoid each other's eyes.
Morris takes off the jacket. At the window.*] Wind's turning again.

ZACHARIAH. *Ja.* I got the whiff coming home.

MORRIS. Not a bird left now . . . to break the still hate of its
face.

ZACHARIAH [*moved to fear, as always, by these words*]. Hell!

MORRIS. Yes. I know what you mean . . . what you feel. The

waters are shivering, too. Always in a shiver when the wind blows. Have you noticed?

ZACHARIAH. No.

MORRIS. Yes. It's the mystery of my life, that lake. I mean. . . . It smells dead, doesn't it? If ever there was a piece of water that looks dead and done for, that's what I'm looking at now. And yet, who knows? Who really knows what's at the bottom?

ZACHARIAH. I knew him.

MORRIS. Who?

ZACHARIAH. At the bottom.

MORRIS [looking out of the window with added interest]. Yes!

ZACHARIAH. Went for a swim and drowned.

MORRIS. Didn't they get him out?

ZACHARIAH. Never found him.

MORRIS. That's a hell of a way to go! And not be found in the bargain! But it proves it, doesn't it? [Leaving the window.] We'll sleep well tonight, you'll see.

ZACHARIAH. Morris?

MORRIS. Yes?

ZACHARIAH. What happened?

MORRIS. You mean . . . ?

ZACHARIAH. Ja.

MORRIS. We were carried away, as they would say, by the game . . . quite far in fact. Mustn't get worried, though . . . I don't think. I mean, it was only a game . . . as long as we play in the right spirit . . . we'll be all right. I'll keep the clock winded, don't worry. One thing I'm certain is sure, it's a good thing we got the game. It will pass the time. Because we got a lot left, you know! [Little laugh.] Almost a whole life . . . stretching ahead . . . in here. . . . [Pause.] Yes. [Pause.] As I said . . . I'm not too worried at all. Not at all . . . too worried. I mean, other men get by without a future. In fact, I think there's quite a lot of people getting by without futures these days.

[Silence. Morris makes the last preparations for bed.]

ZACHARIAH. Morris?

MORRIS. Yes?

ZACHARIAH. What is it, Morrie? The two of us . . . you know . . . in here?

MORRIS. Home.

ZACHARIAH. Is there no other way?

MORRIS. No. You see, we're tied together, Zach. It's what they call the blood knot . . . the bond between brothers.

[*As Morris moves to his bed . . .*

CURTAIN

PEOPLE ARE LIVING THERE

A PLAY
IN TWO ACTS

CHARACTERS

MILLY, *a Johannesburg landlady*
DON, *one of her lodgers*
SHORTY, *another of her lodgers*
SISSY, *Shorty's wife*

PEOPLE ARE LIVING THERE was first publicly performed at the Hofmeyr Theatre, Cape Town, on 14 June 1969, with the following cast:

MILLY	Yvonne Bryceland
DON	Athol Fugard
SHORTY	Ken Leach
SISSY	Gillian Garlick

ACT ONE

The kitchen of an old, double-storeyed house in Braamfontein, Johannesburg.

Two doors—one leading to the back-yard and an outside room where Don lives, the other to a passageway and so to the rest of the house. There is also a window looking out onto a street. Centre stage is a kitchen table and chairs with an electric light hanging above them. For the rest we see, but not too clearly because the light is bad, the walls, a kitchen dresser, shelves and in one corner an old-fashioned gas stove.

Curtain-up—early on a cold winter's evening. The room is in darkness except for a little light from the street outside. It is a Saturday night but still too early for the rush of traffic to the city. Only occasionally does the window catch the movement of light as a car drives by.

A figure appears in the passage doorway. All we can see is the white blur of a dressing gown. The figure stands motionless, obviously listening, then calls out in a husky woman's voice:

Hullo! Anybody home? [*Pause.*] Help!

Silence. A sudden, determined move to the door leading to the back-yard. Halfway across the room this is stopped by the frail, silken chimes of a grandfather clock somewhere else in the house. The woman stops and listens. We hear the four sets of chimes preceding the hour, then silence. The woman turns and exits back into the passage from which comes the sound of a blow to the grandfather clock which now starts its belated chiming of the hour. At the fourth stroke the woman is back in the doorway. Three more. It is seven o'clock.

An arm comes up. The light goes on.

We see Milly. About fifty years old, dressed in an old candlewick dressing gown, her hair disordered, her face swollen with sleep. She waits expectantly, as if the light and chimes might evoke some response in the silent house.

MILLY. Shorty!
 [*Silence. She directs her attention very obviously to the ceiling and listens. Satisfied that there is no sound of life, Milly moves to the back door and opens it, shivering and clutching her gown against the cold night air.*]
Hey, Don. [*Louder*] Don! [*She waves*].
Jeez, it's cold hey!

VOICE. I'm busy.

MILLY. Winter all right. What are you doing?

VOICE. Leave me alone!

[*Pause. Milly shivers.*]

MILLY. Come on over and have some coffee. Warm you up.
That room of yours must be like a morgue.

VOICE. No. Go away.

MILLY. Suit yourself. Kettle's on all the same.

[*She closes the door with pretended indifference, then bends down and
peeps through the keyhole. Satisfied with what she sees, she straightens
up and goes around the kitchen, looking for a cigarette, picking up
and discarding several empty packets before she finds the right one.
She lights a cigarette and waits, watching the back door.* Don *comes
in and moves straight for the passage.*]

DON. Coming!

[*Exit. Milly goes on smoking. Lavatory flushes off—in the passage.
Don returns. Plain, almost featureless face with a sallow complexion.
Body and movements without virility. He is about twenty years old
and is wearing a nondescript grey suit, vaguely ill-fitting. Soft collared
shirt, no tie. He stands in the doorway frowning darkly at Milly.*]

What did it look like to you?

MILLY. What?

DON. Me.

MILLY. Bladder-bursting.

DON. No, no. In my room. What did you see?

MILLY. You, on your bed, on your back, looking up at the
ceiling.

DON. Nothing out of the ordinary?

MILLY. Hardly call that out of the ordinary.

DON. Purpose was dead in me. When I lay down at four o'clock
there were a hundred reasons why I should have got up. When
you saw me not one was left. I had systematically abandoned
the lot. Sartre calls it Anguish.

MILLY. Still looking for it are you?

DON. I've told you before the expression is 'finding oneself'.

MILLY. What's the difference?

DON. Nothing's lost in the way you make it sound.

MILLY. Well, according to the language I speak, when I want to find something I'm looking for it, and when I'm doing that I can be bloody certain I lost it to begin with.

DON. Well, I never had it to begin with, so I can't lose it.

MILLY. Good Lord!

DON. Look, this is beyond you.

MILLY. You're in trouble, my boy.

DON. Let's talk about something else please.

MILLY. What's all this got to do with Bachelor of Commerce anyway?

[*Don tries to ignore her.*]

Because quite frankly it doesn't sound like studying to me. For the sake of your poor parents I hope you are going to pass this time.

DON. It's my life.

MILLY. And their money.

DON. In any case I've decided to chuck it up.

MILLY. Just like that! What happened?

DON. Accountancy.

MILLY. Again. How many times does that make?

DON. Only two.

MILLY. I don't think you try hard enough.

DON. Why should I? What's bookkeeping got to do with the dilemma of our age? I need time. I've worked it out. Fifty pounds a month will keep body and soul together, leaving my mind free. The paper is full of jobs.

MILLY. That doesn't sound like a career to me.

DON. An Age of Crisis, and you talk about a career. You're as bad as my parents. You'll be on to pension funds next.

MILLY. Doesn't worry me what happens to you, my boy. As long as I get my rent the lot of you can go down the drain for all I care.

DON. Then it's settled. Where's that coffee?

MILLY [*yawning*]. I've just woken up. Where are the others?

DON. Shorty's at the gym.

MILLY. That's right. Saturday. I forgot. And him? [*She indicates the ceiling.*] You see him go out?

DON. No.

MILLY. All quiet on the Western Front. [*Another yawn.*] Hell, my heart is still asleep. Anyway, I think I'll pop out. What's on your programme for tonight?

DON. Nothing. And I want to keep it that way.

MILLY. Well, I want a change in scenery. Get dressed in a mo. Maybe a walk. Brisk walk. Bit of fresh air. You could do with some too. It's healthy. What about it?

DON. The air outside is not as fresh as you think.

MILLY. Better than the lot in here, thank you very much. You're going all pimply again.

DON. I never said I was good-looking.

MILLY. Maybe you eat too many sweets.

DON. Maybe I do.

MILLY. Well, there's something sickly somewhere.

DON. It's none of your business.

MILLY. Thank you.

DON. That coffee.

MILLY. I feel like a bit of excitement tonight. Movies or something. Been in all day.

DON. Where's that coffee?

MILLY. Coming. [*She doesn't move.*]

DON. So is Christmas.

MILLY [looking at the ceiling]. You sure you didn't see him go out?

DON. Why should I lie to you?

MILLY. To spite me. [*Don smiles.*] Yes! Don't think I don't know. There's a spiteful streak in you sometimes.

[*Returns her attention to the ceiling.*]

There's no sound of life.

DON. Maybe he's dead.

MILLY. Like hell.

DON. It was meant to be a joke.

MILLY. And I'm not laughing because it's not possible. Must

have made a run for it behind my back. He knew I was waiting. Kept to his room all day. Did you notice? Avoiding me. There's proof. Guilty conscience! And then as soon as I closed an eye—the getaway!

[*Stubs out her cigarette viciously and lights another, an automatic gesture.*]

I didn't mean to—close my eye, I mean. I was lying down in wait for him. You know, spring the surprise when he got to the door. But the last thing I remember is Sissy's radio going full blast. Blah-blah-blah! God! I hated it. Get up, Mildred, I said, get up and go up and grab it and chuck the bloody thing out! Blah-blah-blah! I must have dropped off then, because the next thing I knew it was cold and dark and ... I don't know. Empty! Waking up is a cold business in an empty house. Specially old houses. Wherever you look it's just walls. God, it's depressing! Put out the light and you're as good as in your grave.

[*Don takes out a pencil and makes a note on the back of one of the empty cigarette packets. Milly watches him.*]

What did I say?

DON. That bit about the walls. The featureless face of horror.

MILLY. I've got some pictures somewhere. We'll get them up. [*Breaking mood.*] Anyway ...

DON. Where's that coffee?

MILLY. Give me a chance to get my bearings!

DON [*looking at the stove*]. Isn't it on yet?

MILLY. I'll put it on in a minute.

DON. You told me the kettle was on.

MILLY. I did not.

DON. Milly you distinctly said 'Kettle's on'.

MILLY. Oh, you're a liar!

DON [*putting away his pencil*]. In that case....

MILLY. Give it a rest, man. You won't find yourself tonight.

DON. I came because you said the coffee was ready.

MILLY. Well, I'm going to put the kettle on right now. [*She stands.*]

DON. Call me when it's ready.

MILLY [*stopping his move to get up*]. Ssssssh! Activity!

[*Goes quickly to the door, where she listens.*]

It's him! Must have been in the bathroom. So! Togging himself up. Ever known him to have a bath on a Saturday? It's to spite me. God, I wish I knew where he was going!

[*She follows his movements in the room overhead.*]

Bed. Wardrobe. Dressing table. Putting on his hair oil. Ever seen that? If you want to lose your breakfast one morning go up and have a look. It's enough to make any decent person sick. He sort of washes those big paws of his in the stuff, smoothes down the few hairs left on his nut and then smiles at the result. It's revolting. Greenish. Looks like peppermint liqueur.

DON [*standing*]. If you decide to make that coffee, call me.

MILLY. I'm putting it on now—*now*—right this very minute. Satisfied?

[*She goes to the stove.*]

DON. Good. I'll be waiting.

MILLY. Sit down.

DON. Later.

MILLY. Sit down! I want to tell you something.

DON. I've heard enough.

MILLY. You don't know what I'm going to say, so please sit down.

DON. You've got one minute. Well?

MILLY [*looking at the ceiling*]. Him.

DON. I knew it!

MILLY. Do you know what he's done?

DON [*emphatically*]. Yes!

MILLY. After ten years, mark you. Ten years!

DON. I know.

MILLY. That's a good piece of anyone's life. Well? isn't it?

DON. It is.

MILLY. You bet it is. Give me back those ten years and he'd never get the smell of them again. [*Pause.*] I'm not finished! [*Pause*]. It was a custom, Don. Every Saturday night.

Regular as rent. Beer and sausages for two down at the
Phoenix. Until tonight.

DON. Are you finished now?

MILLY. Yes. *No!* Wait. I just want to ask you one question.
Is it right? Come on. Answer that. Smearing on his stinking
hair oil. Is it right?

DON. It isn't.

MILLY. Then go up and tell him. You call yourself a man,
don't you? Go up there and tell him it isn't right. And then
hit him. A lady's honour is at stake. Ten years of her life.
Hit him for it. [*With intensity.*] All that talk about meeting an
old friend from Germany! Old friend, my foot. Where does
he suddenly come from after ten years and a World War?
And last week that new suit. For an old friend? From
Germany? I wasn't born yesterday. I can also put one and
one together and get two evil-minded birds in the bush.

[Shorty Langeveld *appears in the passage doorway. He is short but
stockily built, about twenty-five years old. He is wearing the tunic
and trousers of a postman's uniform and carries a small bag and a
pair of boxing gloves.*]

SHORTY. Hey, Milly.

MILLY. Go to hell, I'm busy.

DON [*to Milly*]. Go on.

MILLY [*realizing she has gone too far*]. Oh! So now you're
interested.

DON. Two birds in the bush.

MILLY. I'll tell you some other time.

DON. Why not now?

MILLY. This is not the right moment.

SHORTY. Hey, chaps. Is Sissy gone?

MILLY. I'm not your wife's nursemaid. Damned good idea to
get her one. For both of you. Kids. Man and wife! [*To Don.*]
You ever heard such nonsense?

SHORTY. Why you in such a bad mood, Milly?

MILLY [*shaking a finger at him*]. Don't you get impertinent with
me, Shorty Langeveld! And take your togs out of here. I've
told you before the kitchen's not a boxing ring.

[*Exit Shorty with bag and gloves.*]

Gutless little whiner. He gets on my nerves.

[*Don, who has been worrying Milly with his intent stare, now laughs at her obvious discomfort.*]

What's so funny?

DON. I'll tell you some other time.

MILLY. Don't bother.

[*Milly lights another cigarette. Shorty returns.*]

SHORTY. What about some coffee to warm us up, Mill?

MILLY. Drop dead!

[*She moves to the door.*]

SHORTY [*in a whisper*]. What's wrong with her?

MILLY [*at the door*]. I heard that.

DON. How did the boxing go?

SHORTY. We was sparring today. Major Jeffries says my defence is weak, but I got a sledge-hammer left, if I try. He's going to pick a team to fight Railways and Harbours in Durban at Christmas.

DON. Think you'll make it?

SHORTY. Well, Don, I'll try my best. Only this afternoon a guy called Jacobs rocked me man. One-two, one-two, then Dwada! Straight left, straight through. If it was for real, I would be out for the count.

DON. Use that left next time.

SHORTY. Sledge-hammer, he says. If only I could get me a native for sparring partner it would be better. Specially Zulus. They is tough, man! You can't just knock them out, you know. Their heads are hard. That's what Toweel does. I asked Emily if she's got any brothers and she said she will look. What about it sometime, Don? Me and you. A few rounds.

DON. I'm a wrestler.

SHORTY. Judo-jitsu.

DON. Hari-kari, the lot.

SHORTY. You're bluffing! What you doing tonight?

DON. Nothing.

SHORTY. Same here. You seen Sissy? [*Takes out his pay-packet.*] Pay-day!

DON. You're in the money!

SHORTY [*laughing*]. Ja! There's a guy at work—George—in the Despatch Room. He says: Pay-days is happy days! We laugh at him, Don. He's always full of sports. But I got worries tonight. One pound ten from ten pound nineteen and six is nine pounds nine and six, right?

MILLY [*joining them at the table*]. And one week's bed and breakfast is four pound ten, please, plus six bob for washing.

SHORTY. Five bob.

MILLY. Six bob. There's a shilling fine. Emily says your socks were very smelly this week.

SHORTY. It's the walking, Milly. I sweat.

MILLY. Six bob!

SHORTY [*handing her the money*]. There's change.

MILLY. Are you accusing me of something?

VOICE [*suddenly and just beyond the passage doorway*]. Shorty!

SHORTY. Sissy!

VOICE. Shorty!

SHORTY. I'm in here, Sissy.

VOICE. Well, I'm waiting.

SHORTY. I'm coming. [*To Don.*] Here goes. Hold your thumbs for me, man. [*Hurries off.*] It was the trams, Siss. I waited . . .

VOICE. You said you would be home by seven. Where's the money?

[*Milly lays out two cups and saucers. Into each cup a teaspoon of instant coffee. Then condensed milk from a tin with two holes.*]

MILLY. She's a little bitch, that one. And he's a little fool.

DON. I have a feeling he knows.

MILLY. That makes it even more disgraceful. He should be ashamed.

DON. But he is.

MILLY. Then why doesn't he do something about it?

DON. Such as?

MILLY. I think that's perfectly obvious. To begin with, he could hit her.

DON. Violence won't solve his problem.

MILLY. Exactly. He's got no guts.

DON. Now there's a word I hate. What's guts?

MILLY. Guts? If you don't know what guts is, my boy, then I feel sorry for you.

[*She adds hot water and sugar to the cups and sits down.*]

'He's got guts.' Let's see. [*Pause.*]

> 'Then up he rose
> With an awful sound
> And smote the bastard down.'

[*Chuckles with deep satisfaction.*] God that's good! And smote the bastard down! Anyway, there you have it. That's guts. If you can't hit out once in a while, you might as well throw in the towel.

[*Don has in the meantime taken out a pipe—new—and is trying to smoke it.*
Voices of Sissy and Shorty off-stage.]

SHORTY. Sissy....

SISSY. No.

SHORTY. But....

SISSY. No!

SHORTY. Please, Sissy.

SISSY [*entering*]. I said *No*!

[*White-faced, about eighteen years old with straight, mouse-coloured hair. Dressed with cheap extravagance. She is barefoot, carrying her shoes and handbag.*]

I'm sick of you and those silkworms! Anyway you told me you threw them away.

SHORTY [*now also in the room*]. I did, Sissy. Those what you did prick and died.

SISSY. Oh! Hiding the others, are you? From who? From me? That's not very nice, is it? They're mine, you know. Jossie gave them to me.

SHORTY. You didn't want them. You never fed them.

SISSY. I want them now. Where are they? [*Pause.*] Shorty Langeveld, where are my silkworms? [*He doesn't move.*] You know what you are? A bad boy.

SHORTY. If you bring some beetroot leaves for them to eat, I'll....

SISSY [*stamping her foot*]. I said N—O spells No! Beetroot leaves! Ask some old Coolie shop for beetroot leaves? On a Saturday night? Are you mad?

SHORTY [*holding out a brown paper bag*]. Only a few, Siss. If you put them in here nobody will see.

SISSY. And what will that make me look like? Going to the movies with a brown paper bag! Full of beetroot leaves. What will Billy think? 'Beetroot leaves, Billy. For Shorty.' Yes. That's what I will say. 'Shorty eats beetroot leaves, Billy.' He'll laugh at you, you know. He'll tell me again I'm married to a poep.

SHORTY [*prepared to suffer this*]. Okay.

SISSY. Ag! Why do I talk to you?

[*Sissy turns away in disgust and goes to the stove where she collects a pair of stockings that have been hanging up to dry. Milly and Don are drinking their coffee, watching the scene between the other two with detached interest.*]

MILLY. Since when is my stove your washing line?

SISSY. They got wet. I only got one pair. He's to blame. [*Pointing to Shorty.*] Blame him. He's supposed to earn the living. [*Speaking to Shorty again.*] Jossie's got five pairs, you know. Five. And she hasn't even got a husband.

[*On the point of putting on the stockings she turns to Shorty, who has been standing abashed, watching her.*]

Where's your respect? Look the other way!

[*Shorty turns his back.*]

What I would like to ask you, Shorty Langeveld, is what use is a husband that don't even bring home the living what he's supposed to earn?

SHORTY [*his back turned*]. Please, Sissy.

SISSY. What sort of postman loses his letters! That's what I'd like to know.

SHORTY. Sissy!

SISSY. Ashamed of yourself, I hope. [*To Don and Milly.*] I don't suppose he told you. One pound ten taken off because he lost letters again. It's not the first time. There he is. Ask him. You told Ma you could earn me a living. This is no married life.

[*She is finished with her stockings.*]

You can look now!

[*Sissy puts on her shoes, then takes out lipstick, mirror, and powder-compact.*]

You know what I warned you! Well, I mean it. Once more, oh boy! Just you come home once more with your pay short and I'll do it. I swear to God I'll do it. And it won't do you any good to cry.

SHORTY. Stop now, Siss!

SISSY. Yes, he cried. This big boy cried. Whaaa ... whaa ... whaa. Real tears. 'Don't, Sissy! Please, Sissy! I promise, Sissy!'

[*Shorty has not yet turned to face her.*]

I said you can look now. Turn around!

[*He does so. The sight of him provokes her still more.*]

Come here. Let's make you pretty.

SHORTY [*covering his mouth with his hands*]. No, no.

SISSY. Tell Milly and Don what a pretty boy we make you in the room. Red lips, rosy cheeks. [*To Don and Milly.*] He lets me do it upstairs. [*To Shorty.*] Didn't you tell them? You don't seem to tell your friends anything about what goes on. You know what you are?

[*Sissy leans forward suddenly and writes on his forehead with her lipstick.*]

That's what you are!

[*Picks up her bag and flounces out of the room. Shorty stands hanging his head. Milly and Don watch him.*]

MILLY. Shorty! Come here.

[*He moves to Milly. She examines his forehead.*]

'Bad boy.'

[*Don also examines it and then writes on the back of his cigarette packet.*]

Why didn't you hit her? You're a boxer. Why didn't you give her one good wallop?

DON. Who's Billy?

MILLY. She says he's her cousin. Know what I mean?

DON [to Shorty]. You know him?

SHORTY. Sort of.

DON. Have you actually met him?

MILLY. Answer the man!

SHORTY. No.

MILLY. You idiot! Go on. Go and wash your face.

[Exit Shorty.]

Satisfied? If that wasn't taking it lying down then I'd like to know what is. And let me assure you that's the only lying down she lets him do when she's around. You heard him. When a woman is stingy that way then she's really stingy. Dammit all, old Shorty's entitled to it.

DON [looking up from his notes]. The aggressive female and the submissive male. The loss of male virility and the woman's rebellion. The neurosis of our time.

MILLY. Who?

DON. Shorty and Sissy.

MILLY [amazed]. When?

DON. Now. Right here under our nose.

MILLY. This tiff? Come off it.

DON. Undercurrents, Milly. Undercurrents. Didn't you feel them? This room was like a dynamo. I couldn't have taken it much longer.

MILLY. What was going on? In plain language, please.

DON. She was trying to arouse Shorty.

MILLY. Nonsense. It's Billy she's after. I've seen it happen before. Shorty's just too dumb to see it.

DON. He knows all about it.

MILLY. Then why doesn't he do something?

DON. Because the thought of Billy and Sissy arouses him.

MILLY. Where in God's name do you get this rubbish from? Honestly, sometimes you can talk the biggest lot of . . . .

DON. I'm not finished. There's something else. She knew I was watching. She was trying to arouse me as well.

MILLY. You sure?

DON. I should know.

MILLY. She's a little bitch, all right.

DON. I wanted to hit her.

MILLY. And where it hurts, I hope.

DON. She aroused a tremendous urge in me to grab hold of her and hit her. The way she put on her stockings? Did you catch that? I saw the suspenders, you know. I think that was deliberate.

MILLY. I seem to have missed a hell of a lot.

DON. There's material here.

[*Turns back to his notes. Shorty returns, his face washed, carrying a large pair of black shoes. From a shelf at the back he collects a box containing polish, brush, etc., then settles down on a chair to clean the shoes.*]

MILLY [*to Don*]. Work it out and let me know. There's obviously something going on and I don't know if I like it. I warn you, any high jinks and the lot of you get notice. I won't have it under my roof.

[*She stares idly at Shorty.*]

SHORTY. Spit and polish! Army style.

MILLY [*with sudden suspicion*]. Let me see those?

[*Shorty hands her the shoes.*]

Twelves!

SHORTY. Mr. Ahlers. He wants to see his face in them.

MILLY. You're helping him?

SHORTY [*still unsuspecting*]. He's going out so he asked me to do him a little favour and give his shoes a good shine. He's wearing his new suit.

MILLY. And you're going to? Help my worst enemy?

SHORTY. It's only a little favour.

MILLY. So whose side are you on?

SHORTY. Yours.

MILLY. Sneaking away behind my back to do *him* a little favour! That makes you the enemy.

SHORTY. I didn't know there was anything wrong.

MILLY. The impudence! To sit in front of me, in *my* kitchen, and clean *his* shoes. And think you can get away with it! Wait, my boy. Zero hour is on its way...with no holds barred.

[*Milly leaves the table indignantly, but remains in the room.*]

SHORTY [*to Don*]. You think I should polish?

DON. Go ahead. Don't let her bully you.

SHORTY [*polishing*]. It's hell tonight, hey! And I'm trying to say the right things. You know, Don...Girls? I give up. What do they want? You try your best but they is still unhappy. Like Sissy. She's unhappy, I know. But what must I do? There's always struggles in life, isn't that so? I tell her. Sissy, I say, there's always struggles in life.

DON. What does she say?

SHORTY. 'Well, struggle harder!' Hey? And I sweat, Don. On my rounds. And at Christmas, when it's three rounds and also parcels. Boy, then I sweat! You know what I think it is? Love takes a long time for a woman. You just got to keep your trap shut and wait.

MILLY [*moving to Shorty at the table*]. Does he look frightened? Ahlers?

SHORTY. No.

MILLY. Well, he'd better be. And when you take back those shoes you can tell him I said so. Before he leaves this house tonight, I want a straight answer to a few simple questions.

SHORTY. I'll tell him, Milly.

[*She moves away again.*]

DON. How long have you been married?

SHORTY. Going on for six months. I met her down by Booysens. Her Ma's place. Forty-nine Vereeniging Road. I was still a telegram boy then. Her Oupa died you see. So I gave her Ma the telegram and when she reads it she cries, Don! Hell, man, that old woman cries there on the back stoep. Sissy was in the yard. They got an old tyre hanging from a tree there... for a swing, you know. She was swinging. Anyway, her Ma was crying there and Sissy calls out: 'What's wrong, Ma?' So I take off my cap and I go over and tell her. She asked my name. That's how we got friends with each other.

[*He is polishing the shoes all the time.*]

We went like that for maybe six months. Then I reckoned we were ready. I spoke to Sissy and she said it was okay. She wanted to get married for a change. Her Ma asked me if I was making enough money and I said yes. So she said it was certainly okay by her and may God help me.

[*Pause. He puts down the shoes.*]

But there's one thing, Don. We wasn't married in a church. It was by Special Licence. She was in a hurry, you see. The man in charge said it was okay and we could now go ahead. Because it's legal, you see. I got the certificate. But it was so quick! Just like seeing somebody for a job. You put on your suit, you get your papers, and your Ma and your Pa, and the bride-to-be. Then there's some questions and more papers... and then you got it, you think. But when we got home—we had our honeymoon in the Shamley Boarding House in De Korte Street—well, when we got there, we wasn't so sure we got it. That's the trouble, Don. I think Sissy is still not so sure we got it. She gets scared.

DON. How long do you give yourself?

SHORTY. What?

DON. Your marriage. How long do you think it will last?

SHORTY. For ever.

DON. In the face of all this ...! [*Turns to his notes.*]

SHORTY. We do love each other.

DON. Let's discuss this objectively. What do you think love means?

SHORTY. Well, I say to love something is to like it a lot, and more than anything else. And you?

DON. Suppose I say sex.

SHORTY. You mean...?

DON. Yes. I put it to you that the heart of love throbs below the belt. Very good! [*Makes a note.*] Yes?

SHORTY [*strongly*]. No!

MILLY [*back at the table*]. For one thing there's that little matter of the fifty pounds which he's so conveniently forgotten about. Well, I haven't. And if he walks through that door

tonight I want it back, cash, plus ten years' interest. You can tell him that, too.
Did he say where he was going?

SHORTY. No.

MILLY. Don't just say no! Think.

SHORTY. He just said he was going out.

[*Milly resumes her pacing.*]

[*To Don.*] I would love Sissy even if she only had one leg and eye!

DON. You sure? Picture it.

SHORTY. Yes! Shame, Don!

DON. Aha! Pity. That's something else. It's no good, Shorty, there's only one way out. The womb! A man called Freud discovered it. Do you dream?

SHORTY. Yes.

DON. Give me one.

SHORTY. Well, these days I'm in this building with this letter to deliver. And it's registered, which makes it worse. My bag is weighing like lead. Hell, it's heavy, man! But there's hundreds of postboxes and I can't find the right one and somebody is shouting: 'Hurry up, man! It's urgent!' And I'm looking and sweating and that bag is heavy and then I wake up.

DON. Do you ever find the right box?

SHORTY. No.

DON. Who's the letter addressed to?

SHORTY. I'll look next time.

DON. It's as clear as daylight. The registered letter is phallic, the boxes are female, the bag is your conscience. That's why it's heavy. Mark my words, one night you'll open it and find Sissy inside.

[*A thoughtful Milly is again at the table.*]

MILLY. Shorty. Do you want to wipe out the past with a favour?

SHORTY. Anything, Mill.

MILLY. I want you to do something for me when you take back those shoes. So make them shine! We'll use them as bait. I think I've got it, Don. [*To Shorty.*] But you must be careful.

SHORTY [*polishing industriously*]. Okay.

MILLY. Very careful!

SHORTY [*uneasy*]. What is it?

MILLY. Shorty, my darling, it's a trap.

SHORTY [*now nervous*]. I don't know if I can do that.

MILLY. Of course you can. Polish! I've definitely got it, Don! Now we'll see who gets the last laugh. [*To Shorty.*] Now listen. You're going to take back those shoes. Right?

SHORTY. Right.

MILLY. When you give them back start talking.

SHORTY. About what?

MILLY. Anything. You were talking to him about something this morning.

SHORTY. Mario Lanza.

MILLY. So talk about him again, or the shoes, or anything —just get him talking. Then you ask casually: 'Where are you going, Mr. Ahlers?' You got that?

SHORTY. Yes.

MILLY. Casually, you understand. Get his answer, then hightail it back here.

[*Shorty hesitates.*]

You said you would do me a favour. Anything. Didn't he say anything, Don?

DON. He did.

MILLY. Thank you. Well?

SHORTY. Start talking.

MILLY. Casually.

SHORTY. Where are you going, Mr. Ahlers?

MILLY. But for God's sake casually or else he'll smell a rat. Well, go on!

[*Exit a worried Shorty.*]

MILLY. We've got him, Don. We've got him. Stand by for action.

DON. I haven't volunteered.

MILLY. You'd better, before all hell breaks loose.

DON. I'll stay neutral. Every fight needs a ref.

MILLY. Not this one. It's going to be foul. There's a month's free bed and breakfast in it for you.

DON. What do I have to do?

MILLY. The plan is as follows. Shorty tells us where he is going. Our first move is to get dressed. We tog up to kill the cats. My white costume with matching gloves! You'll see something tonight, my boy. That done we then descend on the enemy. Ha! That will be triumph. He's sitting there, you see, with his so-called friend from Germany, and in we march, sit down and have a good time of our own! And right under his nose where he can see us. Then when he comes crawling to ask if he can join in, I'll have him arrested for molesting.

[*Shorty appears timidly in the doorway.*]

SHORTY. Milly....

MILLY [*eagerly*]. Well?

SHORTY. I tried, but he just said thank you and closed the door.

MILLY [*hissing*]. Then go back there and knock!

SHORTY [*hissing back*]. You didn't say nothing about knock, Milly. Hey, Don? You just said....

MILLY. Then listen. Knock! Say you want to borrow a razor blade or something, then Mario Lanza, then where are you going, Mr. Ahlers? But casually!

SHORTY. Where are you going...? [*Exit.*]

MILLY [*with a premonition of disaster*]. I'll murder that little runt if he makes a mess of this.

DON. Suppose it's that place he goes to sometimes...the German Club. You've got to be a member.

MILLY. We'll gatecrash. And if they chuck us out, then we'll do it on the pavement outside.

DON. What?

MILLY. Laugh and sing and be happy. So will you. Yes! You're coming! You'll tell me jokes and make me laugh, loudly, so that he can hear.

DON. I've never faced a prospect like this in all my life.

MILLY. You'll survive. It's him I'm after.

[*Shorty is back in the doorway, obviously frightened of Milly. He moves so as to keep the kitchen table between them.*]

SHORTY. I did like you said, Milly.

MILLY. And?

SHORTY [*faltering*]. And...Mr. Ahlers...he said....

DON. Thank God!

MILLY. Go on.

SHORTY. ...to tell you that he knows I don't shave and...

MILLY. Yes?

SHORTY. ...and that he is going out to dinner with an old friend from Germany.

MILLY [*quietly*]. Come here, Shorty.

SHORTY. No.

MILLY. Will you kindly come here.

SHORTY. I did it just the way you said, Milly.

MILLY [*now impotent with anger*]. Shorty Langeveld, come here this very minute.

SHORTY. What are you going to do?

MILLY. I don't know yet....

SHORTY. I'll ask him again.

MILLY [*stops and listens*]. Sssssh! [*Moving to the door.*] It's him! [*To Shorty.*] Sit down! [*She lights a cigarette.*] Sit down, I said.

SHORTY. You're not cross with me no more?

MILLY. Sit down. Talk to Don. Pretend nothing's happened. It's him all right.

[*She goes to the door and takes up a pose of studied indifference, her arms folded, smoking. In a loud voice, and heavily sarcastic to start with.*]

As I was saying, chaps, fine feathers making fine birds is one thing but a bald head that can't even speak the English language properly is another. There's not a hope in hell for you know who, even in a new suit. So it's no good anybody trying to get classy ideas around here, because we know all about it! [*Now speaking directly to Ahlers, who is in the passage.*] Enjoy yourself...with your old friend from Germany. And please don't worry about me. I'll just sit here in the kitchen and twiddle my thumbs. After all, it was only ten years. Why worry about them! [*Her anger and resentment beginning to break through.*] Well, you'd better, because they were mine. Those were ten years of my life and you had them cheap. Just don't think that means I'm hard-up for you. Because I've got a surprise for you, Mr. Big Shot. I'm also going to have a good time tonight. You bet. I'm going to have the best good time of my life. And it won't be beer and sausages at the Phoenix! Put that where the monkey puts his nuts. And when you come home I'll be out and there'll be an account for fifty pounds in your bed. [*Now shouting and gradually moving out of sight into the passage.*] Because if you think this is the end of me you've got another guess coming. I've only started.

[*Front door slams.*]

Yes, go on! Go on, get the hell out of here, you rotten stinking thief. *Thief!*

[*Silence. The clock chimes, then one stroke. The sound of a vicious blow. The clock strikes seven more times. It is eight o'clock. The window reflects heavy traffic in the street outside. Shorty and Don wait. Milly appears quietly in the doorway, standing there for a few seconds before moving to the table for a cigarette.*]

You heard that, I hope? [*Shorty and Don nod.*] Good! I'm glad. I wanted to humiliate him in public, and I think I succeeded. You should have seen him. He crawled through that door like a dog with his tail between his legs. [*Pause. With an edge of suspicion.*] What did you hear?

SHORTY. You told him, Milly.

MILLY. Where to get off! Didn't I?

SHORTY. To get out!

DON. And go to hell.

MILLY. Thank you. Enough! Let's leave it at that. Because I meant it. Every solitary syllable. I *am* going out and I *am* going to have a good time. Because, just between you and me, the old Phoenix was a bit of a flop the last couple of times. Strictly speaking, that makes this a stroke of luck. A chance to really enjoy myself for a change. In fact why not the three of us? There's an idea! Let's make it a trio.

SHORTY. What, Mill?

MILLY. Anything. You're invited.

SHORTY. I'm game.

MILLY. Settled. I'll get dressed. [*She sits.*] Where are we going?

DON. Nowhere.

MILLY. You promised.

DON. I did not.

MILLY. I'm ignoring you. [*To Shorty.*] Your turn. Think. Give us a bright idea.

SHORTY. There's still time for the second session.

MILLY. The movies?

SHORTY. At the Roxy....

MILLY. Seen it.

SHORTY. What about the Plaza? They is showing....

MILLY. Seen that, too.

SHORTY. I'll get the paper.

MILLY. I've seen them all. The movies! Who the hell wants to go to the movies?

SHORTY. You said....

MILLY. I said, think of a bright idea for a good time. Don't you understand the English language? A good time!

DON. The movies are all right, Mill.

MILLY. 'The movies are all right, Mill.' [*Turns to the window.*] Look out there. Go on, look! Thousands of them. Millions. Where are they going? They're going to have a good time. Every Saturday night they drive past on their way to have a good time. And don't try to tell me they're going to the movies! So what I want to know is, where is it?

[*Shorty smiles.*]

Don't just sit there grinning like an ape. Go out and ask them.

[*Shorty laughs with embarrassment.*]

What are you laughing at? Go out and ask them.

SHORTY. No, Milly.

MILLY. Yes, Milly! Go out there and stop one of those cars and say 'Milly wants to know where is it? Where do you get this good time every Saturday night? She's stuck in her kitchen with two good-for-nothing nitwits, so can she come?'

DON [*tapping out his pipe*]. You're not going to like this, Milly, but I feel I've got to tell you. Your good time is an illusion.

MILLY. Listen to him!

DON. It doesn't exist.

MILLY. You haven't even looked for it, so stop talking.

DON. Because I know I won't find it. It's not there. It's a hoax.

MILLY. Why don't you dry up! I've had them—good times! And when I walk out of here now, in ten minutes' time, I'll find another.

DON. It's like the sandwiches I took to school. Polony or jam. In a toffee tin. Somebody else had the toffees.

MILLY. What the hell are you talking about now?

DON. Life with a capital F. There's no mystery, Milly. That's what you want to believe. Romance around every corner. Adventure at the bottom of the street. The classic lower-middle-class illusion. I'm telling you it's polony or jam. Will you believe it that in my twenty years I have never yet once been surprised?

MILLY. Well, you had better start! Because it's not like that. [*Indignant.*] There's a hell of a lot of mystery, my boy. Going on all the time. And surprises. Oh yes! I could tell you a thing or two that would surprise you.

DON. Impossible. What?

MILLY. Aha! About me for example. [*Don laughs.*] You think you know all the answers? Well, you don't. Because I could tell you something about me that would make your hair stand on edge.

[*Shorty is busy at a shelf behind Milly's back.*]

DON. Go ahead.

MILLY. It happens to be a secret.

[*Shorty knocks over a pot.*]

What are you doing there?

SHORTY. Nothing.

MILLY. Liar! Come here.

SHORTY [*a shoe-box in his hands*]. Just my silkworms.

MILLY [*in horror*]. And where have you been keeping them?

SHORTY. Sissy doesn't . . . .

MILLY. Well, neither do I!

SHORTY. Just that old pot what you never use, Mill.

MILLY. Suppose they escape and crawl into the food?

SHORTY. They was in our room, Milly, but Sissy sticks pins in them. They don't do nothing. They are nearly all in the silk already.

MILLY [*vaguely interested*]. Let me see?

DON. Is it something you did?

MILLY. What?

DON. Your secret.

MILLY. I'm not telling.

DON. Something that was done to you?

MILLY. Try again.

[*Shorty puts the shoe-box on the table in front of Milly.*]

SHORTY. I was feeding them. Beetroot leaves.

MILLY [*examining the contents of the box*]. Well, I'll be . . . ! Just look at that, will you. You seen this, Don?

SHORTY. They was just so small when Jossie gave them to me.

MILLY. Cosy, isn't it. Sort of a pod. Nature is damn marvellous when you come to think of it.

DON. Simple! An accident of birth.

[*Milly looks at him.*]
Your secret.

MILLY. There were no accidents. I arrived on the dot, head first, six pounds four ounces with everything where it should be. They say I hardly cried.

DON. I mean something before birth. Like your father being the Prince of Wales.

MILLY. There's good blood. But I wouldn't go as far as that. Jenkins is an old Port Elizabeth name.

DON. Then there's nothing. There's no secret. You're just making it up.

MILLY [*with a superior smile*]. Suit yourself. I'm saying nothing.

[*Don is still intrigued. Milly returns her attention to the silkworms.*]

So this is silk. And to think worms do it! Do they...how do they do it?

SHORTY. From the back.

MILLY. Their bowels?

SHORTY. Yes.

MILLY [*highly indignant*]. No, they don't! Don, where does the silk come from?

DON. Two glands in the head.

MILLY. That's better. [*To Shorty.*] How could it be precious if you were right?

[*Don now also examines the worms.*]

MILLY [*to Shorty*]. That's all. [*Shorty smiles.*] You can go now!

[*Shorty moves to one side with his shoe-box.*]

DON. Let's get back to your secret.

MILLY [*delighted*]. Got you guessing, have I? Thought you knew everything.

DON. Be honest with me, Milly. Is there definitely a secret?

MILLY [*simply, convincingly*]. Yes, it's there all right. Something happened. I feel it, Don. Nowadays more and more. It gets so bad sometimes I don't want to look or listen any more. Honestly. Because when I do...I don't know....

DON. Something sad.

MILLY. Sort of.

DON. Pain.

MILLY. It hurts.

DON. You cried.

MILLY. I'll confess to a tear or two, on occasions.

DON. If I said Horror would that be going too far?

MILLY. Horror? Maybe. Horrible? Could be.

DON. Horror, pain, sadness, and you were young.

MILLY. Christ, what a life!

DON. I've got it! You were raped.

MILLY [*indignant*]. By whom?

DON. Wait! Let me give you the picture. I'm good at this. You were on your way to school, a sweet little girl in her gym slip and black stockings...garters!...when you met this man who'd been hiding behind a tree. You're innocent, you see. So when he offered you toffees you ate one. Then came the suggestions. When you resisted, he forced you down....

MILLY. I'd like to see anyone try!

DON. It happens every day.

MILLY. Mind you, there was that old le Roux once, when me and Beryl Conwright were on the swings. But hell! You could hardly call that rape. No! Try again.

DON. What about your mother? She was raped and you're the result.

MILLY. Mommy! I'd have liked to see someone try something with her. She was as strong as an ox.

DON. There's still your father. Why do you never mention him?

MILLY [*promptly*]. Alfred Jenkins, storeman, grade one, on the South African Railways. Retired on pension. You won't find anything there.

DON. Not so fast, not so fast. Let's probe.

MILLY. Dig as deep as you like. Southend Cemetery, if you want to know. Him and Mommy. Side by side. There's an angel pointing upwards.

DON. Little girls and their daddies! Psychology's got a word for it.

MILLY. What are you getting at?

DON. The realm of the subconscious, Milly. Where lusts and libidos writhe like tormented serpents.

MILLY. Good God!

DON. Yes! So let's have a look at Alfred. Did he drink?

MILLY. Daddy had his pots on a Saturday night with the other ex-servicemen.

DON. That's enough. Too much is anaesthetic. Too little leaves the inhibitions intact.

MILLY. Hurry up! I haven't got all night.

DON. Here's the picture. It's a Saturday night. The pubs have closed. You're in your room, in bed...in the dark! Your mother is asleep. She's the ailing sort—psychosomatic. The front door opens and closes. Silence. You think: that must be

Daddy. You lie and listen. The footsteps hesitate then lurch towards *your* room. The door opens, the door closes, and you know he's in the room. You can hear him breathing heavily. Daddy, you say. Silence. Then a few more steps. He's at your bed now. You can smell brandy fumes....

MILLY. Stop! [*Don laughs.*] It's disgusting.

DON. Watch it, Milly. Guilt!

MILLY. Alfred Jenkins was a good man. If he could hear what you've just said he'd turn in his grave. And Mommy, too.

DON. It's good enough for a trauma.

MILLY. Well, you're wrong. You're on the wrong track altogether.

DON. Give me a clue.

MILLY. I'll tell you when you get hot.

[*Lights a cigarette, now thoroughly absorbed in the game.*]

DON. Was it something sudden?

MILLY. Give me the picture.

DON. There you are, a young girl in a white dress, full of hope....

MILLY. You're getting warm.

DON. Life is peaceful. You are happy. Until suddenly, like a bolt from the blue, it happens. The dream is shattered and you are set on your hopeless journey through dark and dusty rooms. How's that?

MILLY [*emphatic*]. No! It wasn't like that at all.

DON [*still under the momentum of his thought*]. An early marriage!

MILLY. No.

DON. A death? A suicide?

MILLY. No.

DON. Then life. Birth! What about a baby?

MILLY [*with sudden vehemence*]. *No!* There was no baby. And I don't care, because I don't want babies. Understood? Finished. Settled. Next one.

DON. So then it took its time.

MILLY. Come again?

DON. Whatever happened to the young girl in the white dress, happened slowly.

MILLY. 'It took its time.' My time . . . bit by bit . . . yes! That sounds better. Slow, and sly. What I mean is I try to remember when. The Moment When—the way they say: 'And from then on so and so' . . . and so on. But I can't. There doesn't seem to be a day or a date. Once upon a time it wasn't, now it is, but when or where . . . ? It's not easy to pin down. Believe me, I've tried.

DON. Milly, do *you* know what it is? [*She smokes.*] You mean you *don't* know?

MILLY [*irritably*]. Wouldn't be much of a secret if I knew, would it?

DON. Just as I thought. You're making it up.

MILLY. I'm not.

DON. This secret is a figment of your imagination. In my opinion you're compensating for a colourless existence by inventing . . . .

MILLY. Sometimes I could brain you! What do you know about it?

DON. Apparently as much as you. Nothing. Which most likely means there is nothing.

MILLY. Nothing! I said it hurts, didn't I? Can nothing hurt? I'll say it again, as God is my witness, it hurts. And it took its time. Mine. And once upon that time there was a little girl in a white dress, full of hope, and she was happy. But now she's not any more. Is that my imagination? Those are facts.

DON. But not scientific facts. I can't measure them. You tell me it hurts. But what can a scientist do with that? Unless you can be more specific give it up and suffer in silence.

MILLY. You mean the details?

DON. Call them what you like.

MILLY [*stalling*]. You're asking for the details?

DON. Yes.

MILLY. Okay.

DON. I'm waiting.

MILLY. Let's see . . . it hurts.

DON. Where?

MILLY. All over.

DON. I give up.

MILLY. Hold your horses. We'll try again. It hurts. An ache. A sort of dull ache.

DON. Go on.

MILLY. Yes, it's coming now. It hurts. There's pain. Sometimes...sometimes it's in the colour of things. They go grey. Yes. I'm on to it! Things go grey. Know what I mean? Dull. Dreary. For days on end. And the days too. Sunday, Monday, even Someday...all grey. Faces, and calendars and the right time when I look at the kitchen clock and then the taste of the next cigarette—all of them seem to lose their colour. It's enough to make me sick. If you're looking for symptoms, there's one. I get sick. In the afternoons, when I look at the clock and I see it's some old time again, I could vomit. And the way things can suddenly... [*looking for words*] ...Be! You know, there It Is. Let's just say things get me down.

DON. Don't stop now!

MILLY. Well, I walk into a room—I'm by myself because he's at work and you're somewhere else and it's all quiet so I'm alone—then I walk into a room and I stand still and think about something to do. I look around, you see, for a little task to while away the time. And then it comes. I begin to notice. It's like a plug has been pulled out and something's drained away down a big, black hole, leaving everything stranded. Things stand too still. Chairs and tables. All empty and still...and stupid. That's the word! Stupid. Like that chair. I know what it is. I look at it and I say Chair. But it doesn't help. It goes on being empty and useless. Once it got so bad I said: Well, I'll prove it. So I sat down. But that made it even worse.

DON [*eagerly*]. Because then *you* felt stupid!

MILLY. Exactly.

DON. You saw yourself—an object called Milly in an object called chair—but knowing the names didn't help because everything went on being useless, including yourself.

MILLY. You've got it.

DON [*excited*]. For God's sake, Milly, that's Anguish!

MILLY. Let's move on.

DON. Wait! We've got a situation here. You're in that chair and you think: Enough! Move! or Get Up!...one of the commands. But nothing happens. You think about it, but the reasons for moving break like bad string when you try to pull out of your inertia....

MILLY. We've already had that!

DON. This is a development. Now you're conscious of what is happening.

MILLY. Well, let's cut it short. I'm conscious. Now I move.

DON. Right. You stand up.

MILLY. That's better. Erect! I walk again.

DON. Walking consists of picking up one foot, swinging it forward, and putting it down. For a fraction of a second you stand precariously on one leg. Then you remember the other one so up it comes, and again forward and down. While this is going on there's the problem of your arms at your sides, your heart is beating, your chest rising and falling with breathing, your eyeballs swivelling in their sockets....

MILLY. Is it as bad as that?

DON. I have a dream. Music is playing, and I'm in a corner and so far no one has seen me. I think it's a party because there's a lot of people, and...well, all I know about them really is the noise, because I'm not watching. I'm holding my breath. But the noise is a hubbub—talking and jokes and one very loud voice laughing heartily. Then the music stops. I can't tell you how terrible that is. Just stops. Silence. And sweat. Because I know, I just know that that means *it's my turn*. Don't ask me what. That's the thought. *It's your turn now!* I feel their eyes. Without looking up I know they are staring and waiting and that it is my turn and I must do something. So I move. I walk. One foot up, a second on one leg, then down. Two or three steps, in this silence, safely. Then things start to go wrong. I begin to wobble during that second on one leg, my arms start swinging wildly. There's a feeling that I've got five elbows and they're all sticking out. I'm knocking glasses into people's laps, falling over their legs....

MILLY. Wake up!

DON. I always do. The trouble is I wake up too soon. I never reach the end. The terror, you see. My mind protecting itself.

MILLY. It's only a dream. You said so yourself.

DON. But don't you also feel it? How can I put it? The fit.
A feeling that things don't fit. Either life is sizes too big or
you're too small. Something's wrong somewhere and maybe
that is why people stare.

MILLY. At what?

DON. You haven't reached the stage where they stare?

MILLY. At what?

DON. You.

MILLY. No.

DON. It will come. A feeling of being watched, of people
waiting, because it's *your* turn. Some pull it off of course.
Others make a mess of it, like my dream, and have to leave
the party. The failures. You've seen them, those old sticks of
skin and bone sitting at the edge of oblivion on park benches.
It's happened.

MILLY. Hold on.

DON. Decrepit, decaying ....

MILLY. Wait!

DON. Neglecting themselves, neglected by others, forgotten ....

MILLY. *What?*

DON. They've been forgotten. It happens long before you are
dead.

MILLY. What do you mean, forgotten?

DON. You lose your place in the mind of man. With a bit of
luck once or twice in your life you have it. That warm nest in
another mind where 'You' is all wrapped up in their thinking
and feeling and worrying about 'You'. But even if you are one
of the lucky ones, sooner or later you end up in the cold again.
Nothing is for ever. They die, or you get divorced. One way
or another they go, they forget, and you end up in your little
room with your old age pension and a blind bitch for friendship. From then on it's just a matter of days. When they're
good, the two of you crawl out to a bench in the sun where
she can hate the pigeons and you can hate the people. When
it gets dark, you crawl back to the room. Until one day, one

more sunny day with the pigeons flocking and the people passing, you're not there. But who misses you? Who's to know that inside a room, finally, forgotten by the world . . . .

MILLY. Rubbish. That's absolute rubbish. Morbid muck.

DON. Read the papers. There are cases every day.

MILLY. For God's sake, man! This is a civilized country. Nobody gets forgotten like that. One thing I can assure you, it's not happening to me. Oh no! There are limits. [*Pause.*] What were the cases?

DON. A few days ago. An old woman. They had to break down the door. She was found . . . .

MILLY. I don't want to hear!

DON. Suit yourself. But it's happening . . . .

MILLY. I said . . . .

DON. Here! Tonight!

MILLY. Who?

DON. You. Him. Me. [*With sudden violence.*] Are you blind? It Happens! Who remembers us? At this moment? Ahlers? Is he thinking about you? With his old friend from Germany? [*Turning to Shorty, who has been following the argument for several minutes.*] Or Sissy? Billy-boy has just made her laugh. She's enjoying herself. She's forgotten she's got a husband, who he is, where he is. And you're waiting. You are waiting for her to remember you, to come back. And when they do, when they walk in and find us again, it will be the way you find something old and forgotten and almost useless. Something in a corner, put away a long time ago, and now there it is again, too broken to mend but too much trouble to throw away. So back it goes, because maybe one day . . . . That's us! We're hanging on by a maybe in somebody else's mind. [*Pause.*] I'm finished. [*He sits down and smokes his pipe.*]

SHORTY [*to Milly*]. What's going on?

MILLY. Shut up.

SHORTY [*to Don*]. Sissy misses me. She does, Don. She always comes home.

MILLY. I said shut up! [*Tries to light a cigarette.*] Is it my imagination or is it cold in here? My hands are like ice.

[*Exit Shorty.*]

So who cares?

DON. That's another way of putting it. Who cares?

MILLY. I mean *me*—about *him*. Because it so happens I'm not hard up, you see. You forgot about that. In fact I forget him sometimes. For hours on end. Pottering around in here, I forget him completely. The other day, playing patience, it was quite a surprise when he walked in because he was clean out of my mind. And tonight. If you think I'm going to spend my night thinking about him you've got another guess coming. I've got plans which will take my mind right off the subject.

[*Shorty returns with his pair of boxing gloves which he offers to Milly.*]

What's this?

SHORTY. You said your hands were cold.

MILLY. But boxing gloves!

SHORTY. They are warm.

MILLY. Oh well. Try anything once. But only for a second you understand. [*She is putting them on.*] I've got to get dressed in a mo. Sssssh!

[*Inside the house the clock begins to chime. They listen. The sixteen chimes end. The clock strikes three.*]

SHORTY. Three o'clock.

MILLY. Go and hit it.

[*Exit Shorty. A timid blow. Silence.*]

I said, hit it! Imagine it's Sissy.

[*A second blow. The clock continues its striking. Milly is obviously counting. After the sixth stroke she relaxes. But the clock strikes once more.*]

Can't be.

DON. What?

MILLY. Ten o'clock. I counted nine and then it struck again.

DON. Then it's ten o'clock.

MILLY. No. Don.

DON. All right, so it's eleven.

MILLY. No, no! It's nine o'clock.

DON. Never.

MILLY. The last time that clock struck it was eight.

DON. We must have been talking and didn't hear it.

MILLY. Nonsense. Shorty!

DON. Why get so agitated. Nine, ten, eleven, twelve....

MILLY. Shorty!

DON. Yesterday, tomorrow...

MILLY [*violently*]. *Shorty!*

SHORTY [*off-stage*]. I'm in here!

[*Exit Milly hurriedly into the passage. Don waits, smoking his pipe. Milly returns slowly.*]

DON. Well? [*Milly says nothing.*] It's ten o'clock. I told you. Two left. So much for today.

MILLY. What do you mean by that?

DON. It's ten o'clock, which, when you work it out, means that there are two hours left of today.

MILLY [*in growing agitation*]. So do you think I can't add?

DON. Correction. It's a subtraction sum. A taking away. [*Watching Milly closely.*] More and more. [*Pause.*] Until you've had the lot and then you're dead. Adding never comes into it.

MILLY. Well, just remember, Mr. Donovan Big-brain, it's also happening to you.

DON [*tapping on the table with his pipe*]. The passing seconds. Stop them. [*He taps.*] Go on! The sound of doom, Milly. Seconds becoming minutes, minutes becoming hours, days, months, years....

MILLY. All right!

DON. You said ten, didn't you?

MILLY. What?

DON. Years. With Ahlers. That makes a total of three thousand six hundred and fifty-two days, allowing for leap years. Do you want the other statistics?

MILLY. Let's hear them.

DON [*picking up his pencil*]. Was it beer and sausages every Saturday night?

MILLY. Without fail.

DON. How many sausages?

MILLY. Two fat frankfritters each.

DON. One thousand and forty sausages. Beer?

MILLY. Also two bottles each.

DON. Say they hold a pint—exactly one hundred and thirty gallons of beer.

MILLY. Come again?

DON. One thousand and forty sausages and one hundred and thirty gallons of beer, to the nearest belch.

MILLY. Both of us, or just my share?

DON. Just your share.

MILLY [*emphatically, after a moment's reflection*]. It is *not* a lot. Not for ten years, Don. It only sounds a lot. There were three thousand six hundred and fifty-two days remember!

DON. I can give it to you in hours.

MILLY. Yes! Let's hear that one.

DON [*A pause while he works it out. Shorty returns to the room*]. Eighty-seven thousand six hundred odd.

MILLY. *What!*

DON. Eighty-seven thousand....

MILLY. Stop! I don't want to hear. [*Trembling with emotion.*] Jesus Christ, I wish I'd known that when he went out.

DON. For the sake of accuracy we'd better subtract sleeping time. The human being sleeps an average....

MILLY. What do you mean subtract? He got that as well. All right! So I've said it. He got the lot. Body and Soul. And me? A pile of sausages and a barrel of beer! You call that a bargain? [*Her mounting anger starts her pacing. She is still wearing the boxing gloves and will keep them on until, as indicated, after the bout with Shorty.*] I must have been off my mind! There he stood ten years ago, on my threshold, with his suitcase of artificial roses—and I could have slammed the door in his face! I only bought a bunch out of pity. He gave me the old song and dance. Down and out, no friends, where's the next meal, and all of this on the verge of tears. So open went the big heart and out came the helping hand. I'm telling you it was pity. That's the only reason why I went out with him to begin

with. He looked lonely and as it so happened it was the end
of his first week under my roof. 'Dress up', he said. 'Ve mus
haf a celebrashin.' And then they appeared! Those leather
shorts with the bells and braces! Oh, my God! I nearly died
of embarrassment. It was his legs! 'You can't', I said. 'I'm
wearing white. They'll stare.' 'But ve ver dem in da mountince.' That was him. Da mountince!

SHORTY. Switzerland.

MILLY. He's a German.

SHORTY. No. Milly....

MILLY. I'm telling you he's a German. Look what they did to
the Jews.

SHORTY. Mr. Ahlers says....

MILLY. Mister? He's just plain Ahlers in this house and what
he says doesn't count because he's a liar, so shut up. Mister!
[Outraged.] Listen, he was a hobo, an immigrant. He had
nothing. If it wasn't for me he still wouldn't have a penny to
scratch his backside with. I put the firm of Ahlers Artificial
Flowers on its two flat feet that only had one pair of socks
when they walked into my life. I typed the letters to the
undertakers, and I'll give him notice.

DON. Tonight? When he comes home?

MILLY. Tonight.

DON. Want to bet?

SHORTY. What are you betting?

DON. Beer and sausages at the Phoenix.

[Shorty thinks this is very funny.]

MILLY. When you're finished laughing, nitwit, I'd just like to
remind you two what I said about somebody being the land-
lord around here and getting slowly sick to death. Think about
it.

DON [to Shorty]. She's threatening us.

MILLY. I assure you it wouldn't break my heart.

SHORTY. What?

MILLY. To kick you out! A change in the faces around here
would be as good as a holiday. Quite frankly, I'd rather do
away with myself than carry on like this.

DON [*picking up his pencil*]. How?

MILLY. Quick, because this is not worth it any more. How many times have I laughed today? Not once. Not even a chuckle. And all the two of you can do is sit there and watch. Look at you now! For God's Sake Do Something!

SHORTY [*Moving across to Milly where he adopts a boxer's stance*]. Put them up. I'll teach you to box.

[*Milly stares at him silently for a few seconds then lets loose a vicious swipe at his head. He dodges it easily.*]

That's it! Come on

[*He is now feinting and weaving. Milly tries a second swipe with the full intention of hitting him.*]

No good!

MILLY. I'm warning you.

SHORTY. Okay.

MILLY. I'll knock you out!

SHORTY. Try. Come on. Try!

[*Milly goes after Shorty, swinging wildly. Shorty puts up a great show. Soon Milly is enjoying herself immensely.*]

MILLY. I'll get you. Take that! And that! And that! Wait! Stand still, you little bugger . . . [*etc.*].

[*Eventually Shorty deliberately lets Milly connect. He goes down.*]

You're down! I told you!

[*Laughing freely she turns to Don. The look on his face stops her laughter abruptly. She turns sharply on Shorty who is still lying on the floor.*]

You trying to make me happy?

SHORTY. You was laughing.

MILLY. It was a trick. [*Tearing off the gloves.*] Take them.

SHORTY. Once more.

MILLY. Go to hell.

SHORTY. You did forget your troubles, Mill.

MILLY. Well, I don't want to forget. Not that way! It was ten years. You think it's quits because you make me laugh for ten seconds. Ten years! That's what criminals get.

DON. Not again, Milly! . . .

MILLY. Yes, again! And again and again. And you're going to listen. You're also on the face of this bloody earth. I'll make you listen. I'll make you say it's all wrong and he's bad and it isn't fair, because that's what it is.

Go on. Look! You. That. [*Indicating Shorty.*] This. [*Indicating the room.*] And me here in the middle of the mess while he's out there spending the profits I helped him earn on some cheap Jo'burg bitch.

DON. That's right.

MILLY [*outraged*]. Right?

DON. He's having a good time and you're forgotten. I told you that five minutes ago.

MILLY. So?

DON. So full stop. Finished. The end of a sad story.

MILLY. You mean he's going to get away with it?

DON. Why not? He hasn't broken the law. You're not married. He pays his rent. In the eyes of the law he's an innocent law-abiding citizen having what you call a good time.

MILLY. And in mine he's a low-down, rotten, stinking bastard, who has done something dirty and must be punished. And if nobody else is going to do it, I will. Tonight I will take my revenge.

DON. You tried once before and it didn't work.

MILLY. This time it will. We'll join forces. [*To Shorty.*] Think!

SHORTY. What?

MILLY. Our plan for revenge.

SHORTY. I don't....

MILLY. Don't you want Sissy to be sorry she left you in the lurch?

SHORTY. Yes—

MILLY. And to promise she won't go out with other men?

SHORTY. Yes.

MILLY. Then shut up, and think.

SHORTY. Listen, chaps. I think I'll go to bed.

MILLY. Stay where you are! You're in this too. Let's work it out. At this moment...come on, help me!

DON. You're forgotten.

MILLY. Right.

DON. They're laughing.

MILLY. Right.

DON. They're having a wonderful time and you're....

MILLY. All right! We've got the picture. Let's move on. They're going to come home. Expecting to find us at their mercy.

DON. Most likely.

MILLY. Waiting patiently.

DON. Willingly.

MILLY. Ready to crawl.

DON. Content with the crumbs.

MILLY. And that is when we strike. Because instead....

DON. Aha!

MILLY. And much to their surprise....

DON. It's coming!

MILLY. Much to their surprise, I repeat....

DON. Wait for it!

MILLY. I've got it! *They're* forgotten because *we* are having a good time. How's that? They walk in to find that we've forgotten all about them because we are laughing and singing and having a good time.

SHORTY [*with pleasure*]. Hey!

MILLY [*warming to her idea*]. Because guess what's going full swing when they walk in through that front door? A party!

SHORTY. That don't sound so bad, Milly.

MILLY. What do you say, Don?

DON. You've forgotten one thing. The party. Where does that come from?

MILLY. Us!

DON. You mean you, him, and me....

MILLY. Are going to have a party! Let me give you the picture this time. Half a bottle of Muscatel at the bottom of my wardrobe gets the ball rolling. We buy a cake, hang up some decorations. I've got all that stuff left over from Christmas. Let's be carefree, man! Laughing and singing until the cows come home. And them upstairs having to endure it all the time. Let's drive them mad. What do you say, chaps?

SHORTY. That don't sound so bad at all, Mill. I'm game.

DON [*with signs of nervous wariness*]. You can't produce a party just like that, at this hour of the night, and out of thin air.

MILLY. I said we are going to have a party!

DON. To spite them?

MILLY. Yes.

DON. Well, it won't work. Nobody has a party to spite some-body else. Take my advice and drop the idea.

MILLY. *No.*

DON. For God's sake, Milly. Can't you see it? The three of us trying to be happy? We haven't got a reason. Try something else.

MILLY. You want a reason?

DON. Yes. Give me one good reason why the three of us . . . .

MILLY. It's my birthday.

[*Pause.*]

DON. I don't believe it.

MILLY. That amounts to calling me a liar.

DON. Let's just say you've made a mistake.

MILLY. And if I prove it? [*Pause.*] If I prove it the party's on. Right?

DON. I'm not saying anything.

MILLY. Well, I'm saying it's my birthday and that I'm going to prove it . . . .

DON. I'll buy you a present on Monday.

MILLY. We are going to celebrate my birthday with a party.

DON. Suppose it doesn't work? Suppose we don't have a good time?

MILLY. Leave that side of it to me.

DON. I've tried before.

MILLY. What's the matter with you, for God's sake? We're not going to try to do a miracle. A party! What are you scared of?

DON. I'm not scared of anything.

MILLY. You're trying to get out of it.

DON. Yes!

MILLY. Well, you can't

DON. There's no law which says I have to, you know. Well, is there? Let's just say I'm not in a party mood tonight. And anyway I'm no good at laughing or singing . . . you won't miss me.

[*Pause. Growing embarrassment.*]

Tell you what, I'll watch.

SHORTY. Hell, Don!

DOŇ. Look, why am I so important? You two go ahead and . . . .

MILLY. So this is the thanks I get.

SHORTY. There's nothing wrong with a party, Don.

MILLY. After all the friendship and encouragement I've given you.

SHORTY. Come on, man! Say yes. For her sake.

DON. All right!

SHORTY. Yes?

DON. Yes. But I want it noted that I warned you.

[*He sits.*]

MILLY. It's on. Anybody who backs out now is a deserter. And at the front line you get shot for that. [*To Shorty.*] Get my bag. It's on my bed.

[*Exit Shorty.*]

She who laughs last, laughs longest, and tonight I'll also make it loudest. I'll have him down here, on his knees, begging for mercy before the cock crows thrice. That's my vow. So help me God.

[*Shorty returns with the bag. Milly takes out her purse.*]

Take that . . . [*in a sudden fit of extravagance*] take the lot. Get us a cake. The best. Something mouth-watering. Cool-drinks, peanuts and raisins . . . .

SHORTY. Potato crisps?

MILLY. The lot. It's got to look good. Well? What are you

waiting for? Action stations.

[*Shorty and Milly move to the door, leaving Don at the table.*]

CURTAIN

ACT TWO

The room is 'decorated', the table has a cloth, plates, glasses, etc. In the centre of the table is a candle stuck into a bottle.

Curtain goes up to the sound of Milly and Don arguing off-stage. Don is the first to appear.

DON. No.

MILLY [*close on his heels, carrying a long evening gown on a hanger*]. But it's an occasion.

DON. I prefer the one you're wearing.

MILLY. Are you trying to be funny?

DON. Then let's just say the colour doesn't suit you.

MILLY. Apricot.

DON. It's not in the spectrum.

MILLY. Look at the sequins.

DON. Save up and buy a new one.

MILLY. What do you mean? I've only worn this twice.

DON. So now it's out of fashion.

MILLY. Since when?

DON. Donkey's years.

MILLY. Listen to him!

DON. If you want my opinion....

MILLY. I don't.

DON. ...and you did ask for it, that garment is old-fashioned.

MILLY. And I'm telling you it is not!

DON. They stopped wearing those before the war.

MILLY. When you weren't even born yet, hey? [*Derisive laughter.*]

DON. Exactly! My mother had one just like it.

MILLY [*laying it on thick*]. When you weren't even born yet! Ha, ha! So kindly....

DON. I warn you if you wear that somebody will laugh.

MILLY [*unable to keep up the act*]. So kindly shut up!

DON. I've said what I wanted to. [*His pipe.*]

MILLY. *Shut up!* [*Exit with dress; returns immediately.*] I hope

143

you took the hint and are going to do something about your appearance. You look a disgrace.

[*Exit.*]

DON [*shouting*]. If Shorty doesn't come back soon you had better forget about a birthday party and call it a midnight supper!

[*Milly appears quietly in the doorway. Don doesn't see her. He shouts again.*]

I said if Shorty doesn't return....

MILLY. I heard you! [*Pause.*] We've still got half an hour. As long as we start before twelve it's valid. [*Pause.*] Worse comes to the worst we can start without him. So get ready.

DON. Just the two of us? Are you mad?

[*Pause. Milly stands quite still. So does Don.*]

MILLY. If he gets back too late I'll kill him. This is a hell of an end to my year. I won't scream, but I think I'm losing my hold.

[*Front door opens. Shorty rushes breathless into the room.*]

SHORTY. I've got everything Mill. Hey, this looks good!

MILLY. You know how close you've brought us to disaster?

SHORTY. Disaster?

MILLY. Stop wasting time and give me the grub. Hurry up. It's touch and go now.

[*Shorty puts on the lights, Milly blows out the candle and then sorts out the parcels Shorty has brought back. Out of one she takes a bunch of beetroot leaves.*]

What's this? [*Shorty laughs.*] I'm asking you what is this?

SHORTY. Beetroot leaves, for the silkies. That's why I took a little bit long, Mill. I went to that shop....

MILLY. Right! We'll settle that with this.

[*She slaps Shorty's face and then throws the leaves out of the window.*]

SHORTY. Why did you do that?

MILLY. Never you mind why. It helped. [*Turning back to the parcels.*] Where's the cake?

[*Shorty hands her a parcel which she opens.*]

And this?

[*She holds up a slab cake.*]

SHORTY. Cake.

MILLY. But it's slab-cake!

[*Shorty examines his purchase.*]

I didn't ask for slab-cake, idiot.

SHORTY. He said it's fruitcake.

MILLY. I wanted a round cake.

SHORTY. You didn't say nothing to me about a round cake, Milly. Did she, Don?

MILLY. Who the hell ever heard of a birthday party with slab-cake? What can I do with this? A few crumby slices. It's supposed to be wedges with icing. [*Throwing the cake onto the table.*] No! That does it.

[*Walks away and lights a cigarette.*]

DON. So what is happening?

SHORTY. Slap me again. Hard as you like.

DON. Are you calling it off?

MILLY [*turning back to the table*]. Now listen! Both of you! Just once more, you understand. So help me God, either of you just once more and you'll regret the day you were born. [*To Shorty.*] Get a plate. Come on, move! [*Indicating the half-bottle of muscatel.*] There's only one tot each so don't make pigs of yourselves. Sip it.

DON. I want it noted that I am going into this under protest.

MILLY. And without any improvement in your appearance! [*To Shorty.*] Put off the light.

[*He does so after she has lit the candle.*]

Ready?

[*Each of them is standing behind a chair.*]

All together!

[*They sit.*]

No, wait! Stand.

DON. Make up your mind.

[*They stand. Milly exits hurriedly and returns with a few paper hats.*]

MILLY. Last Christmas, but he'll never remember. Take one.

DON. Is this compulsory?

MILLY. Yes.

SHORTY [*singing*]. For she's a jolly good fellow, for she's a jolly good fellow, for she's a jolly good fellow, and so say all of us.

MILLY. All right. Sit. Together.

[*They sit.*]

SHORTY. To Milly, and may she live happily ever after.

[*Glasses are touched, they drink. Pause.*]

MILLY. And now?

DON. You're supposed to make a speech.

MILLY. No.

SHORTY. You must make a speech on your birthday, Milly.

MILLY. A few words then, but no speech. [*She stands.*] Well... [*Pause.*] No. [*She sits.*]

SHORTY. Come on, Mill.

DON. Reply to the toast.

MILLY. All right. I'm prepared to do that. I'll reply to the toast. [*Stands again.*] God, I feel a fool! [*Pulling herself together.*] Anyway, I'm happy—no, let's not exaggerate—I'm pleased to be here with you. Or rather, to have you here with me. It's my house, remember. It's also my birthday. I'm not an old woman by any manner of means. But I've seen a lot of life. Just don't get any ideas, because there's plenty left. The spirit is willing even though the flesh be weak. I'm not talking about Sin. I mean life, and it's taken its toll. Somebody once said you start to die the moment you are born. The fact remains however that the best years are the middle years, somebody else said. I side with him. Because the spirit *is* willing even ...though...back to the beginning! Bit of a knot. Anyway, I hope you know what I mean. Which is, there are plenty of kicks left in the old girl!

So what else? No one could call me mean. Share and share alike has always been my motto. I've never begrudged you second helpings or clean sheets. I've tried to make this a home for you boys.

Furthermore, Shorty, I don't hate you. But you do get on my nerves sometimes, quite honestly. Try and behave yourself

more. I'm not strict, but I hate fools. Really I do. As for
you, Don, for God's sake, man, buck up your ideas a little. Do
something. Get a girl or see a skin specialist but do something.
I also hate layabouts.

That seems to cover everything. No! One more thing. Let's
try and be more cheerful in future. What do you say? Postboxes and pimples aren't the end of the world, chaps. So let's
brighten up with a few more smiles. Let's make that the
resolution.

[*Milly sits. Applause from Shorty and Don.*]

SHORTY. Very good, Mill! Very good!

MILLY. Thank you.

SHORTY. Hip hip hooray! [*Still clapping.*] Blow, man! Blow!
It's your birthday.

[*Carried away by the flush of success Milly leans forward and blows
out the candle, plunging them in darkness. Silence.*]

MILLY. That wasn't very clever of you, was it? [*Pause.*] So
find the matches!

[*Fumbling in the dark. A bottle is knocked over, something falls to
the floor.*]

Watch out, you clumsy ape!

SHORTY. I got them.

[*Match flares, the candle is lit. Milly examines the table.*]

MILLY. Just look at this mess! No. We'll start again.

DON. Another speech?

MILLY. From scratch.

DON. But the booze is finished. We can't toast you with cool-
drink. For better or worse, we've reached the cutting of the
cake.

MILLY. Let's at least tidy up.

[*The table is tidied.*]

DON. Cut the cake. I'm hungry.

SHORTY. Same here.

[*Milly cuts the slab of fruitcake, putting a slice on each plate. They
begin to eat and drink. Apart from an occasional grunt of satisfaction,
not a word is spoken. Milly eats slowly, with affectation. Don and
Shorty pile in. They quickly finish their first slice. Milly cuts again.*]

The cool-drinks are opened, the potato crisps disappear, then the pea-nuts. Not a word is spoken. Don and Shorty hold out their plates for more cake.]

MILLY. Not so fast!

DON. I'm peckish.

MILLY. Youre wolfing.

[*She cuts two more slices. Don and Shorty continue eating. Milly now begins to realize something is going wrong. She eats slower and slower, eventually stopping altogether to watch the other two with growing frustration and disgust. When just about everything has been eaten, Don pushes back his chair and belches.*]

DON. An old Arab custom which means Thank you.

SHORTY. Hear, hear.

MILLY. You mean!

DON. The party. Wasn't as bad as I expected quite frankly.

MILLY. It's finished? It's over.

DON. Isn't it?

MILLY. No it's not. We haven't even started.

DON. What's left? We've eaten the cake....

SHORTY. There's still some cheese-tips here.

MILLY. The fun, for God's sake!

DON. Fun?

MILLY. Don't pretend you know nothing about it. [*Pause. She looks at them.*] The sound of merry laughter.

DON. In here? Us?

MILLY. That was the agreement.

DON. I thought it was too good to be true.

SHORTY. I think we had some fun, Milly.

MILLY. Merry laughter!

SHORTY. I laughed. Ask Don.

MILLY. You smirked once with shame because I caught you with your gob stuffed full of food.

DON [*wearily*]. So there hasn't been any fun. So what!

MILLY. Well, there's going to be. That's what. I'm throwing this party because I want to laugh. Understand? He's going to hear me laughing when he comes back. So this party is not yet over. Nobody goes to bed until I've laughed!

[*She lights a cigarette and smokes.*]

SHORTY. I've got a joke.

DON. No. Don't let's start that.

MILLY. Tell it.

DON. This is courting disaster, Milly. Believe me. Jokes....

MILLY. Tell it!

SHORTY. It's rude.

MILLY. We're not babies.

SHORTY. What's the difference between an ostrich egg and an ordinary egg?

MILLY. That's not a joke.

SHORTY. George called it a joke.

MILLY. It's a riddle, you idiot. A riddle doesn't make you laugh.

DON. What's the answer?

SHORTY. An arse-stretch.

MILLY. Apologize! Apologize for that immediately!

SHORTY. Sorry.

DON. Satisfied?

MILLY. Will you stop trying to make me satisfied with nothing.

DON. I think we had a fair run for our money.

MILLY. We've had one dirty riddle, and the spectacle of you gutsing yourself on *my* money.

DON. If I pay you back my share will you call it quits?

MILLY. You'll pay me back your share by making me laugh.

DON. Milly, please! I'm being serious.

MILLY. That makes two of us.

DON. I know, and that's why I'm nervous. It won't work. Take my advice and call it a day. Nothing's happened yet....

MILLY. Exactly!

DON [*trying to ignore her*] We're intact, in shape. We can still retire with grace. But beyond this lies the point of no return.

MILLY. Good! I've always hated going back.

DON. For the last time I'm warning you—this is getting dangerous.

MILLY. Coward!

DON. All right.

MILLY. Yellow belly!

DON [*standing*]. If that's the way you feel about it, I'll leave the two of you . . . .

MILLY. Just you try! [*Don stops.*] Just you try!

SHORTY [*trying to pour oil on troubled waters*]. Please, chaps.

MILLY [*to Don*]. So sit down and shut up, because here we go. [*With growing aggression.*] To start off with, there'll be a sing-song.

DON. I flatly refuse.

SHORTY. Don, please, man!

MILLY. We'll start the ball rolling with a sing-song. [*Stubs out her cigarette and lights another. She is now grimly determined.*] What songs do you know, Shorty?

SHORTY. 'Pack up your troubles in your old kit-bag and Smile, Smile, Smile.'

MILLY. One, two, three! [*Singing.*] 'Pack up your troubles in your old kit-bag and smile boys, that's the stuff . . . [*Shorty joins in.*]
What's the use of wor-ree-ying,
It only gets you down,
Sooo—pack up your troubles in your old kit-bag and
Smile, Smile, Smile.'

SHORTY. We did sing that in the lorry going to Military Camp, Mill!

MILLY. Next one, 'Roll out the barrel.' Sing! [*Shorty and Milly sing.*]
'Roll out the barrel
We'll have a barrel of fun
Roll out the barrel
Ta ta, te ta ta, tum tum . . . .' I forget the words.

SHORTY. Same here.

MILLY. 'Jerusalem!' [*Singing.*] 'Ja-roo-sa-lem . . .'

SHORTY. I don't know that one, Mill!

MILLY. What about 'When Irish eyes are smiling'?

SHORTY. I'll try. Come on, Don! [*Shorty and Milly sing.*] 'Sure the world seems bright and gay...for when Irish eyes are smiling....'

[*Don, who has sat tensed through the foregoing, making no attempt to help the other two, now jumps to his feet. Milly, blinded by determination, does not see the impending catastrophe. There is from this point on, a growing momentum to the final chaos, with everybody cutting into or talking over someone else's words.*]

DON. This is a fiasco!

MILLY. Almost, chaps. Almost!

DON. Officially....

MILLY. We're nearly there!

SHORTY. Mario Lanza!

DON. Officially this is now a fiasco....

MILLY. Once more and we'll make it!

DON. I can't stand it any longer.

MILLY. Then sit down and sing!

DON. There are fates worse than death.

MILLY [*closing her eyes*]. 'Smiling Through!'

SHORTY. But you isn't even trying, Don.

DON. Because I don't want to.

SHORTY. No, Don. You must sing.

DON. Are you deaf? I Don't Want To...!

SHORTY. Shame on you, Don! It's her birthday.

MILLY [*her eyes still closed*]. I said 'Smiling Through'. On your marks, get set, GO. [*Singing.*] There's a little grey road winding over the hill, to a little white house by the sea...' [*etc.*]

[*Don and Shorty continue their argument over this.*]

DON. Well, she can have it. Just leave me....

SHORTY. No, Don.

DON. Leave me out of it.

SHORTY. No, Don, that's not fair.

DON. I don't care if it's not!

SHORTY. I say you must sing, because....

DON. And I'm saying ....

[*Don and Shorty erupt simultaneously into protestations and accusations. Milly is still singing her song, in her loudest voice, with her eyes tightly closed. Bedlam. At the height of the racket she picks up a spoon and starts banging on the table.*]

MILLY. Order! Order!

[*The argument continues; Milly hammers away.*]

Order, I say!

DON. I warned you this was going to happen. I refuse to take the blame for this fiasco.

SHORTY. Well, it wasn't me, because I was singing.

MILLY. You're out of order. Both of you come to order at once!

[*Silence.*]

We won't get anywhere by shouting. [*She is speaking with a supreme effort at control and deliberation.*]

I know it's serious, but we must keep calm if we hope to get to the bottom of ... this .... In fact I think we're already there. Speaking from experience, I'd say this was rock bottom. I've never known it harder. Keep cool. I'm coming to the point. Hidden in all this confusion is a Crime—a serious criminal offence. I demand Justice! [*Pause.*] I can't show you blood or bruises. The victim isn't even dead. But that won't stop me now from looking at you, and you, and pronouncing you two bastards Guilty!

DON [*held by the accusation*]. And you?

MILLY. Your victim.

SHORTY. What we done this time, Milly?

MILLY. Tonight.

DON. And you're accusing *us*?

MILLY. Yes.

DON. *We're* to blame?

MILLY. I want to say it again....

DON. No.

MILLY. Guilty!

DON. No! I tried to stop you. I warned you—every inch of the way. But you wouldn't listen. *You* wanted a party.

MILLY. Yes. A bit of mirth. Sing out the old and laugh in the new. A few chuckles. Is that making impossible demands? This was my birthday.

SHORTY. But what was wrong with it?

MILLY. What do you call this? Slab-cake and pimples, cigarette butts and silkworms, and nothing to do?

SHORTY. It wasn't so bad, Mill.

MILLY. Is this all you want?

SHORTY. I'm happy.

MILLY. You're not.

SHORTY. But I am.

MILLY. Well, you've got no right to be. And if you're too stupid to see why, I'll tell you. And to start off with let me tell you to your face that I don't like you. As true as God is my witness, looking at you now I can say I don't like the sight of you. You nauseate me. He teases you. He's teasing you all the time, and I'm disgusted.

SHORTY. I don't mind a few jokes.

MILLY. There's only one. You. You're the joke. Sissy was right. You're ugly and a joke and I'm filled with shame to find you doing all this to mankind under my roof. Do you understand now. Must I say it again? We find you revolting. Ask him.

[*She smokes violently.*]

SHORTY [*to Don*]. She's joking.

MILLY [*to Don*]. Tell him. [*Pause.*] Coward! Funk!

DON. What do you hope to gain from all this?

MILLY. The truth. I want you down here—rock bottom— where you belong. Are you scared?

DON. No.

MILLY Well, he's waiting to hear it.

DON. I study you, Shorty.

MILLY. He thinks you're a curiosity.

DON. It's in the interest of Science.

MILLY. Get to the point.

DON. You see, you're what they mean by simple-minded.

MILLY. He once called you a perfect specimen of a retarded

poor white.

DON. Overseas you'd be a labourer—digging up the streets in London.

MILLY. No you don't! You said he'd be emptying the dirtbins in Birmingham.

DON. Here we have Natives to do the dirty work. You're saved by your white skin. Because examine the facts. You can just about read and write. You can't carry out the simple duties of a postman. I don't think you could do anything complicated. You blunder on from day to day with a weak defence— yet you survive. You even have a wife.

MILLY. Aha!

DON. I'm amazed at your survival. According to Darwin you should be dead. That's all.

MILLY. No, it's not. You've left out the best bit of the lot. Sissy. Tell him what we whisper.

DON. I don't think she's properly your wife.

MILLY. Don't be clever. He's a simple-minded poor white, remember.

DON. I don't think you know how.

MILLY [to Shorty]. Do you understand? He doesn't think you know how to do it. I think you do, but that Sissy doesn't want it from you, because we *both* think that Billy knows how.

[*They watch Shorty intently.*]

SHORTY. I'll hit you, Don.

MILLY. Bravo!

SHORTY. 'S true's there's a God, I'll hit you.

MILLY. And me? What will you do to me?

SHORTY. If you was a man I'd hit you too.

MILLY. And Billy?

SHORTY. I'll bugger up the lot of you.

MILLY. Now we're getting somewhere. The rock-bottom boxing match! Get out your gloves and hit! But first!...let's tell him if he wants to see a real psychological curiosity to have a good look in the mirror next time he squeezes his pimples. That's why no decent, clean-living girl will ever stomach the sight of you. Furthermore, you also blow your nose on the

sheets, I've seen you use the washbasin in the bathroom as a
W.C., and I've a strong suspicion that, as regards positively
filthy habits, that is still not the worst. Sometimes when I
think of your hands I want to vomit.

And he's looking for himself! Take my advice—don't! You'll
be disgusted when you find it. Who do you think you're
fooling? Calling him a freak? You're a washout.

DON. You finished?

MILLY. If you've hit the bottom with a bump—yes.

DON. Because there's a few things that could be said about you.

MILLY. Go ahead. It's a free-for-all.

DON [to Shorty]. Come on. Let's tell her.

MILLY. Christ, you're yellow.

DON. You've started to get old woman odours. You should use
scent. It's unpleasant being near you at times. That's why
I've got no appetite left. And maybe that's why Ahlers doesn't
want to marry you. Yes! You're also not fooling anybody.
I guessed it long ago. And quite frankly I don't blame him.
Because the thought of living intimately with you for the rest
of my life, in the same room . . . !

MILLY. So I'm also ugly. What does that prove?

DON. As much as you've proved against us. Nothing.

MILLY. But I'm accusing you of desertion. That's my charge.
That in the hour of need, in the thick of the fight, you deserted
a fellow human being who had her back to the wall in a
tight corner. Because I'll say it again . . . I tried!

DON. You won't get a medal for that. I also got out of bed.
I also breathed, and walked and scratched myself . . . and all
the other heroisms. Shorty, too. We suffered the same fate.
We're also victims.

MILLY. Then prove it.

DON. How?

MILLY. By crying. Come on. Shed one tear and I'll believe you.

DON. Have you?

MILLY. Yes! Twice today I went to the W.C., pulled the
chain so nobody would hear, and wept! But you two?
[Mimicking them.] 'It's not so bad, Mill.' 'Let's call it a day.'

Is this all we get?

DON [*with sudden vehemence*]. Yes! It's all you get. And what's more you've had it. It's nearly twelve o'clock and then you're a year older. And there's not many more left where that one came from. You're in the home stretch, Milly!

MILLY [*summoning up all her control to ask the question for the last time*]. You are telling me this is all I get?

DON. Yes!

MILLY [*almost a cry*]. Then somebody's a bloody liar. Because there were promises. The agreement was that it would be worth it. Well, it isn't. I've been cheated. The whole thing was just a trick to get me to go on. Otherwise who would? Who wants to get up tomorrow if this is it? If this is all? Fifty years! That's a lot of patience. Nobody's so well off that fifty years doesn't leave him hard up for what's left. I am. I'm broke. So I want what I'm owed. Pay up or be damned.
[*Pause. Shorty and Don stare at Milly. Her resolution has reached its climax and now begins to ebb.*]

Why? That's it! That's all. I just want to know why. It's not a silly question. When you lie in the dark and ask, and listen, it sounds like sense, like there should be an answer. Why? Why me? Why this?

[*Don and Shorty are still staring at her.*]

Go on, they said. It's good for you. Go on. Grow up! They all seemed happy with it back in old Pringle Street. So I believed them. I was young. And .... [*Pause, after which she continues softly, her voice charged with amazement.*] I was young! Yes. Come to think of it. Me. Once ... Pringle Street. Number nineteen, near the top. And a time, so young! A day, one special day that was eleven years old in one-way Pringle Street.

It was dark. It was Sunday night and getting dark and Basil my best friend was stamping cockroaches under the lamp-post. So I said, 'Shame on you, Basil!' But he said they didn't feel because there wasn't any blood. I was sitting on our wall singing, 'When you wish upon a star, makes no matter what you are.' Usually there was something sad about Sundays because of Monday and School. But this time it was holidays and altogether different. I was thinking about this and then slowly I began to grow happy. The darker it got the happier I grew. So I sang my song again and wanted to cry it was so big. And that night for the first time I beat Basil to the lamp-post when the light went on. He was so busy stamping cock-roaches he didn't see. So I ran and touched it first and shouted 'My Wish! My Wish!' Basil got jealous and said wishes didn't come true. But I just laughed at him. Because you know what I wished? Happiness! All those holidays it kept coming. You were right about the dress, Don—white. But you forgot the bell. There was a bell once. It was after Sunday School and I was running home singing 'All things bright and beauti-ful...' and there was this bell. Oh, my God! This bell was ringing, chaps! And I was running in that sun shining the way it should singing, 'All things bright and beautiful, all creatures great and small'! How's that for faith? With all the heart of eleven years old I believed it, that it was mine, and for ever. Because I wished. Every time, every chance—falling stars, black cats, white horses—every wish was Happiness!... I had it. That night I mean... Happiness. It felt like I was holding it so tight it was for ever and ever. But my hands!

Mildred Constance Jenkins. Fifty years old.... I'm not a woman any more... he says. I never thought of it like that, but he says I'm not a woman any more. Last week it was, one night. He was eating liver sausage in bed and I just told him, you know, in case he started wondering. Then he said, matter-of-fact I'll admit, not meaning to hurt, that therefore strictly speaking I'm not a woman any more. It sounded logical the way he put it. To do with function. The function of a thing, and being a woman, that meant babies. And you see, suddenly he sat up and said he wanted a family! Because of the business and Ahlers being a good name to keep alive through the ages. We better stop now, he said. But we can still be friends.

So you see it's gone. Or just about. A little left but mostly in the way of time. The rest just gone. Not broken, or stolen, or violated—which might make it sound like there's been no crime, I know. But I did have it and now it's gone and nobody ever gets it back so don't tell me that doesn't make us victims. Don't ask me how! Somehow! Victims of some-thing. Look at us. All flesh and bone, with one face hanging onto your neck until you're dead!

[*Inside the house the clock begins to chime. They listen in silence for a few seconds, then* . . . .]

Ignore that! Where were we? Today! What was I saying? Today . . . today . . . . Hold on! This one I won't let go! Today, today . . . . All right! You win, damn you. Yesterday!

[*The clock mechanism is again at fault. It chimes on and on and on. Exit Shorty. A blow off-stage stops the chiming.*]

MILLY [*softly*]. Mildred Jenkins, you are still alive!

[*Shorty returns.*]

SHORTY. Sunday!

MILLY. So let's sort it out. To begin with don't take what I said too seriously. I got excited—flushed—if you really want to know. Hot and bothered. It's a symptom. We'll survive. Also, if anyone asks, meaning you know who, let's all say we had a good time in the form of a quiet gathering. [*Pause.*] That's all.

[*Shorty goes up to Milly.*]

Well?

SHORTY. You said you hate me.

MILLY. I exaggerated.

SHORTY. So you like me?

MILLY. No need to go to the other extreme. Let's just say you're also human and leave it at that. 'Bury the hatchet on Sunday, dig it up on Monday.'

SHORTY. So we're all friends again. Okay, Don?

DON. Okay, Shorty.

SHORTY. Shake. [*They shake.*] Milly, I got an idea.

MILLY. You keep trying, I'll say that for you.

SHORTY. The zoo.

MILLY. It's cruel to keep living things behind bars.

SHORTY. What about us going tomorrow? It will be fun, man, George says there's a baboon with a blue bum who hates us.

MILLY. I think I remember him.

SHORTY. Everybody laughs, and then he gets cross.

MILLY [*in indignation*]. Do you blame him? No, really! I think that's going too far.

SHORTY. What?

MILLY. For God's sake! Blue? How would you feel? Honestly, sometimes, some of the shapes . . . ! I wonder if creation knows what it's up to. I'll have a good look at that poor bastard tomorrow.

DON [*quoting the hymn*]. 'All creatures great and small
                  The Lord God made them all.'

MILLY. But bright and beautiful! That's how the hymn starts. Blue might be bright, but it's not beautiful *there*. Oh no.

SHORTY. We'll have a good look, Milly.

MILLY. God help you if you laugh.

SHORTY. I won't, I promise.

MILLY. Because it's not funny.

SHORTY. So can I get my leaves?

MILLY. It's pathetic.

SHORTY. Leaves, Milly!

MILLY. Leaves? What leaves? It's winter.

SHORTY. To feed my silkies. You threw them away.

MILLY. So I did. Feed them by all means. I hope they're crisp.

SHORTY. They're still on the pavement. I seen them.
  [*Exit.*]

MILLY [*to Don*]. He means well. The heart's good. It's the mentality that's weak.

DON [*standing*]. To bed, to sleep, perchance no dreams.

MILLY. Not yet. Coffee. Drown our sorrows in the dregs.

DON [*sitting*]. Here we go again.

MILLY [*laughing*]. Into the Valley of Death! Know that one?

DON. 'The Lord is my shepherd. Yea though I walk.'

MILLY. Never! The Charge of the Light Brigade. 'Into the Valley of Death rode the gallant four hundred'.

DON. It's the same valley.
  [*Shorty returns and goes to a shelf at the back.*]

SHORTY [*going to the table with his shoe-box*]. Guess what, chaps? They're all in silk. I don't need the leaves now, Milly. Look! One is still spinning.

MILLY [*looking at the shoe-box*]. So that's how they do it! Congratulations, Shorty. Well done! What happens now?

SHORTY. Now?

MILLY. With them.

[*Shorty looks to Don for guidance.*]

The next step.

SHORTY. I don't know. Nothing.

MILLY. But the moths. Moths are going to come out. Isn't that so, Don?

SHORTY. I don't want moths.

MILLY. Well, that's just too bad, because you're going to get them.

SHORTY. Nobody keeps the moths.

MILLY. So tell me what happens to them!

SHORTY. I don't know.

DON. Don't start again.

MILLY. Don, what happens to the moths?

DON. We've had enough questions for one night, Milly!

MILLY. Will somebody kindly tell me what happens to the moths?

DON [*at breaking-point*]. I don't know and I don't care and as far as I am concerned ....

MILLY [*with mounting indignation*]. Now just hang on! There's something wrong here. I smell that rat again. [*To Shorty.*] Why have you been feeding them?

SHORTY. It was Jossie who ....

MILLY. Why Have You Kept Them Alive?

SHORTY. To see them spin. To see the silk.

MILLY. And now that they've done it, they've had it. Is that it?

SHORTY [*desperate*]. I don't know all about this, Milly!

MILLY. You're going to chuck them away.

SHORTY. Okay. I'll keep them and watch the moths.

MILLY. To starve! To die!

DON [*unable to take any more*]. For Christ's sake what do you want?

MILLY [*with equal violence*]. Some other way! Don't you? Must it always be the muck-heap? Isn't there another solution?

DON. Then find it!

MILLY. I will.

SHORTY. Hang on, Don. Look, Milly . . . . As God is my witness I'll feed them. They'll get fat.

[*Don gets up. Thinking he is making a move to his room, Milly jumps in front of the back-door and stands there spread-eagled, blocking his exit.*]

MILLY. Where do you think you're going?

DON. Come with. You can hold my hand. Come!

[*Exit into the passage where the lavatory door slams. Milly rushes to the doorway and shouts after him.*]

MILLY. You've got a dirty brain, Donovan Bradshaw!

MILLY [*turning back into the room she finds Shorty staring at her*]. Feed them!

[*She starts to clear the table. The front door opens. A disconsolate Sissy appears in the passage doorway.*]

SHORTY. Hello, Siss.

SISSY [*noticing the decorations*]. What's going on here?

SHORTY. We had a party.

SISSY. With dancing?

MILLY [*before Shorty can reply*]. Singing, dancing, drinking. The lot.

SISSY. Is it finished?

MILLY. Yes! We had a good time and it's finished. So you missed it.

[*Exit.*]

SISSY. You didn't say nothing to me about a party!

SHORTY. It was a surprise party. Even we didn't know. It was Milly's birthday. Say Happy Birthday when she comes back.

SISSY. No.

SHORTY. It's sad, Siss. She's unhappy.

SISSY. Well, so am I.

SHORTY. Wasn't it a good picture?

sissy. Who all was at the party?

shorty. Just us. Me and Don and Milly.

sissy. That doesn't sound so hot.

shorty. It was okay. But... [*Whispering.*] we didn't dance. [*Pause.*] We discussed. [*Pause.*] Sissy, I don't want you to see Billy any more.

sissy. Same here.

shorty. Why?

sissy. You men are all the same.

shorty. But I'm your husband.

sissy. That's your look-out.

shorty [*pointing to the shoe-box on the table*]. They're all in silk now, Sissy.

sissy. What do I care?

shorty. I'll wait for the moths.

sissy. I don't want moths in the room. They'll eat my clothes. I only got a few, for your information.

shorty. I'll keep them here in the kitchen. Milly likes moths.

sissy. God help you if you bring them into the room.

shorty. I won't, I promise.

sissy. You always promise but nothing comes true. We been married six months now and just look. You're lucky I didn't know.

shorty. Don't say that, Siss.

sissy. Well then, do something!

shorty [*really desperate*]. But what? What must a guy do? I slog.

sissy. Let's go away from here.

shorty. Aren't we happy here?

sissy. I'm not. They don't like me. You don't protect me, you know. You let them scandal about me.

shorty. Where do you want to go?

sissy. How must I know? [*Pause.*] Somewhere nice.

shorty. Shamley Boarding House?

sissy. Back there! Are you mad? [*Pause.*] Cape Town.

SHORTY. Cape Town? *Cape Town.*

SISSY. You asked me, so I'm telling you.

SHORTY. But what about my job?

SISSY. Ask them to transfer you.

SHORTY [*with finality*]. I know nothing about transfers, Sissy.

SISSY. Well, ask them. Ask George.

SHORTY. But I don't know the streets down there, Siss! I'll never get the letters right. Please, not Cape Town.

SISSY. So must it be Braamfontein all my life?

SHORTY. Sissy.... [*Pause.*]

SISSY. Hurry up. I haven't got all night.

SHORTY. Don't be unhappy, because...something happens.

SISSY. What?

SHORTY. It's to do with getting old.

SISSY. So?

SHORTY. We get old.

SISSY. What are you talking about?

SHORTY. I don't know. I'm all mixed up. But it was so clear.

SISSY. You're mad.

SHORTY. No. Ask Milly. She told us. Promises don't come true....

SISSY. That's not news to me with you around.

SHORTY. And we get old.

SISSY. You've already said that.

SHORTY. But we're young.

SISSY. So what?

SHORTY. You musn't be frightened. S'true's God, I'm your husband.

SISSY. All right!

SHORTY. So let's go to bed.

SISSY. I'm tired.

SHORTY. Okay. Come.

SISSY. I'm very tired tonight.

SHORTY. But we got it, Sissy. Truly. By Special Licence. It's okay. They all say it's as good as in a church.

SISSY. Have you been discussing my private life in public?

SHORTY. I just want you to be brave. Let's go.

SISSY. Just remember I'm tired. I want to go to sleep. Understand?

SHORTY. Come.

SISSY. Do you understand?

SHORTY. I'm also tired.

SISSY. Do You Understand? [*Pause.*]

SHORTY [*defeated*]. Yes.

SISSY. Because I'm warning you. If you do I'll call for help again.

[*She moves to the door, Shorty following. Before they reach it they are stopped by Milly's voice, loud and urgent.*]

MILLY [*off-stage, hammering on the lavatory door*]. Don! Hurry up! All hands on deck. You've got five seconds at the most!

[*She now enters the room highly excited, and finds Shorty and Sissy near the door.*]

Get back! Sit down!

SHORTY. What's going on, Mill?

MILLY. Sit down, I say!

[*A few seconds of furious activity, during which she piles empty bottles and plates on the table, rushes out for something and then grabs a glass and fills it up with cool-drink. In between all this she forces Sissy and Shorty into chairs, urging them to 'Smile'—'Grab a glass'—'Look Happy', etc. Don appears in the doorway.*]

DON. What's happened?

MILLY. Ahlers! He's coming up the road. Sit down. Now, all together . . . .

DON. No.

MILLY. Laugh!

DON. For heaven's sake, Milly!

MILLY. My sake, damn you! Sit down. Laugh you bas—

[*The front door opens.*]

Ha ha ha ha ha! [*Hissing.*] Come on! [*Shorty tries to help.*] Ha ha ha ha ha! Very good! Drink up, chaps! Empty the bottles. Polish off those savouries. Ha ha ha! My God, that's a killer! Ostrich eggs! One of the best jokes I've heard in years! [*Drifting towards the door. Then when she gets there she holds up her hand for silence as if the party was an uproar of merriment and noise.*] Hang on, chaps! Hang on! Come and see what the cat's dragged in. If you asked me, I'd say that a certain old friend from the Fatherland turned out to be a bit of a flop. [*Now speaking directly to Ahlers in the passage.*] What happened? She say you were too old for her? You are, you know. Just don't think that means you can come crawling back to me. Because I had a damn good time without you. Didn't we, boys?

[*Ahlers is now moving up the stairs. Milly shifts her position.*]

So don't start banging on the floor at four o'clock if we're still going strong. This happens to be my house! Let's get that straight. And don't bother to ask if you can join in, because you can't.

[*Milly moves out of sight into the passage.*]

And finally, let me tell you nothing is finished. I've proved it. You never had anything to do with it anyway. You're not God. You're a parasite. A bloodsucking Hitler!

[*A door slams.*]

That's right, shut your door. But you'll still hear me! [*She is back in the kitchen now and shouting up at the ceiling.*] If it's the last thing I do, I'll make you hear me! [*To the others.*] Sing! Come on! [*Singing.*] 'Why was she born so ....' *Come on!*

[*Shorty is again the only one who tries to help.*]

'Why was she born so beautiful, Why was she born at all!' [*Silence. Milly lights a cigarette and takes a few draws. To Shorty and Sissy.*] Party's over. Bugger off. [*To Don.*] Not you.

[*Exit Shorty and Sissy.*]

You think he believed it?

DON. Do you want my honest opinion?

MILLY. No! But I bet you anything you like there's doubt. That's even worse. I just hope it gnaws.

DON. You didn't give him notice.

MILLY. I will.

DON. You said tonight. We took a bet.

MILLY. Play my trump card just like that! Don't be a fool!

DON. Milly....

MILLY. If you were up in the trenches would you blast off all your ammo at one go?

DON. Milly! Milly! There aren't any trenches. This is Hospital Hill, Braamfontein.

MILLY. Well, if these aren't hostilities, I'd like to know what are.

DON. It can't last for ever, Milly.

MILLY. What?

DON. You and him.

MILLY. For ever! Who said anything about that? I'm halfway there anyway.

DON. So what do you hope to win?

MILLY. Tomorrow.

[*Pause.*]

DON [*helplessly*]. I don't know.

MILLY. That's right.

DON. I'm tired. Declare an armistice.

MILLY. What for?

DON. Then we can sleep in peace tonight.

MILLY. Peace! You can talk about peace in times like these? Are you mad? Some nights when I lie in bed and those ambulances go screaming past and I think: More casualties! ...I can just about smell the cannon smoke. Anyway, I couldn't sleep with him still stomping around. Last eye open in an old house...that's me!

DON. Suppose his doubt gnaws away all night?

MILLY. If that happens, I'm a happy woman.

DON. But if he doesn't go to bed?

MILLY. We hang on. Keep the fort. It's worth waiting for.

DON. We?

MILLY. You're in this up to your neck.

DON. I know. I'm drowning.

MILLY. Then call for help. That'll keep you awake if the coffee doesn't work. No point in going under half asleep.

DON. I can't, Milly.

MILLY. What?

DON. Call for help.

MILLY [*briskly*]. Go on! [*She moves, but stops after a few steps to stare at Don.*] What's this now?

DON. I'm dumb. When things happen, I watch. Even when it's to myself...all I do is watch. I used to think the right word for me was Numb...that there wasn't even Feeling. But I think that's wrong. I'm sure if I loved something, and then lost it, or it was killed...one of the tragedies...I know this is only probability, but I'm sure I would feel. My trouble is I wouldn't protest. [*Pause.*] I'm not too worried. Look at it soberly. Forgetting for the moment my face...the damage is not too extensive. The sexual urge is intact; like everyone else I eat, I sleep, my fingernails grow. The framework is still sound. If it comes to the worst I could always get a job in the Civil Service. The worst that can happen to me is that I'll be forgotten a bit before my time.

MILLY. You still believe that.

DON. If I were to sit down somewhere, unseen, and was quiet for a very long time, and the instinct to return to the herd petered out. All you need is four walls, and a lid.

MILLY [*looking around*]. In here?

DON. It's a likely spot. It's got the feel.

MILLY. But there's a street outside there, Don! All the people! Rush-hour traffic. Right outside that front door!

DON. Yes. But you've got to open it, Milly. [*Pause.*] Did you, today?

MILLY [*suddenly conscious of herself and her predicament*]. I'm still in my nightie. I haven't got dressed...yet.

DON. Exactly.

MILLY. You mean...it can happen like this? In a dressing gown?

DON. More ways than one.

[*Pause.*]

MILLY. There must be something we can do! Make a noise!...
Lest they forget, as the monument says. I can still do that.

I'll make it loud, make them stop in the street, make them say: People are living there! I'll remind them. Tomorrow. [*Looking at the ceiling.*] And he's gone to sleep. It's always easier when he's asleep, even when I was up there with him. I think calmly. Quite honestly, I saw it coming. I still hate him of course. [*Takes out another cigarette.*] Sit out this last fag with me and then you can go.

DON. Promise?

MILLY. Promise. It's hell, isn't it. Open your mouth and it starts again . . . the old song and dance.

[*Don is tearing off the backs of the cigarette boxes on which he made his notes during the course of the night. Milly watches him.*]

What's the score for tonight?

DON [*looking at his notes*]. On paper it looks like a draw. But I stopped halfway. It's a pity. You came out with some good things towards the end.

MILLY. I was on form.

DON [*examining his notes*]. Your secret? You and Ahlers?

MILLY. Meant to be. I suppose it's more of a mystery, really. Life.

DON. With a capital F. Remember that? I thought it was rather good.

MILLY. What else?

DON. Let's see. Yes . . . you said you would rather do away with yourself than carry on like this.

MILLY. Did I really?

DON. And quick. The simplest method of course is the brown paper bag. Just put it on and breathe.

MILLY. The old plunge. Head first.

DON. It's supposed to be painless. [*Looks at his notes again.*] Shorty said he'd love Sissy even if she only had one leg and one eye.

MILLY. That's big of him. She'd have to hop, wouldn't she? [*Small chuckle.*] I don't mean to be cruel, Don, but when it comes to sights and sore eyes! My God, you could do something with the lot of us in here if you had a sense of humour. Can you see it? You with your head in a brown paper bag, telling the world it's painless. Sissy jumping around on one leg like a whatsis-name . . . that thing with a pouch.

DON. Kangaroo.

MILLY. Chasing Shorty! And him wiping away his tears with his boxing gloves on.

DON. And you in the middle of the mess.

MILLY. As per usual!

DON. Trying not to laugh!

MILLY. Why?

DON. Because we've all got blue bums.

[*Milly's amusement breaks into laughter. Repeating random images from the picture just drawn—kangaroo, boxing gloves, blue bums, etc., etc.—her laughter grows enormous. At its height, and with Don watching her . . .*]

CURTAIN

HELLO AND GOODBYE

A PLAY
IN TWO ACTS

CHARACTERS

JOHNNIE SMIT
HESTER SMIT, *his sister*

HELLO AND GOODBYE was first produced at the Library Theatre, Johannesburg, directed by Barney Simon, on 26 October 1965, with the following cast:

HESTER	Molly Seftel
JOHNNIE	Athol Fugard

ACT ONE

A kitchen table and four chairs, lit by a solitary electric light hanging above.

On the table is a bottle of fruit squash, a jug of water, and a glass.

Slumped forward in one of the chairs is a man—his head resting face down on his arms on the table. He holds a spoon in one hand and is tapping it against the side of the glass.

About ten taps in silence, then. . . .

JOHNNIE [*counting as he taps*]. . . . fifty-five, fifty-six, fifty-seven, fifty-eight, fifty-nine, sixty!

[*Stops tapping.*]

Three hundred and. . . .

[*Pause.*]

Five minutes—become hours, become days . . . today! . . . Friday somethingth, nineteen . . . what? . . . sixty-three. One thousand nine hundred and sixty-three! Multiplied by twelve, by thirty, by twenty-four, by sixty . . .

[*Pause.*]

by sixty again! . . . gives you every second. Gee-sis! Millions.

[*Pause.*]

Yes, since Geesis.

[*He starts tapping again but stops after only a few.*]

No! I'm wrong. It's six. Sixty goes six times into three hundred and sixty. It's six minutes!

[*Looks around.*]

Walls. The table. Chairs—three empty, one . . . occupied. Here and now. Mine. No change. Yes there is! Me. I'm a fraction older. More memories. All the others! Same heres mostly. Here. Other nows. Then, and then when this happened and that happened. My milestones, in here mostly. 'And then one day, after a long illness, his. . . .'

[*Pause. Softly.*]

Which art now in heaven.

[*Pause.*]

Nearly. On the tip of my tongue that time. Just don't rush it. The shock to the nervous system has got to wear off!

[*Stands and exits. Returns a few seconds later and goes back to the table but doesn't sit. When he speaks this time it is in a loud, unnaturally matter-of-fact voice.*]

When the sun shines again. . . .

[*Pause.*]

Tomorrow! God willing, if it's a nice day I'll go to the beach. Bottle of beer and a packet of lemon creams. Make it an outing. Break the monotony. Open the door and leave the house. Walk down Upper Valley Road, then along the river to the bridge. There I'll catch the Summerstrand bus. Number six, and upstairs for the view. Sit on the rocks and watch the waves. Drink the beer and eat the biscuits. Breathe in the breeze. Come back in the twilight, refreshed. A day will have passed.

[*Pause. Softly.*]

How many now?

[*Loud again.*]

As I was saying, back in the twilight. Along the river with the frogs croaking. Back home. No place like here. That's a lie. What's the odds? Walk in, put on the light, have a look-see, look the same . . . NO!

[*Pause.*]

A day will have passed. Emptier. It will be . . . emptier. Somehow it's getting empty. But how? And what? And cold! When was it I went and came back and it was emptier and cold and every thing . . . so still!
Here it comes again! Quick. Something else.

[*He grabs the spoon on the table and starts tapping.*]

One two three four. . . .

[*Grabs the bottle.*]

Lemon squash! Ten tablespoons if there's a drop. Shake the bottle well before use! All the goodness sinks to the bottom! For quick relief of all, or eases, some say soothes. Depends on the pain. Change The Subject!

[*Notices there is some squash left in the glass.*]

Quench my thirst!

[*He drinks. Pause.*]

Am I going mad? No. This is not madness. Those who are, don't know they're mad. Whereas I know . . . I'm mad.

[*Pause.*]

Something wrong there. If you think you're mad you're not. That's it! Only when you think you aren't.

[*Exits and returns, but not to the table. He stops just inside the light.*]

It was the weight that shocked me. Suddenly so heavy! Why didn't I notice? All those times. My arms never ached. But they grunted. Sarel. The one called the other Sarel. 'Let's try it this way, Sarel,' he said. 'You go first.' One two three UP! In black suits with him weighing a weight that made them grunt and me . . . hanging around . . . my two helping hands useless and empty; all of me useless and big and getting in the way when they tried to get him through the door . . . excuse me try it again sorry am I in the way OOOOps gently does it don't drop it I beg your pardon your forgiveness your sorrow. . . . Suddenly they were out, going, and everybody on the pavement was staring at me. . . . Isn't there something to sign, I asked. A form to fill? We've got your name and address, he said. The office will contact you. So that was that. One two three UP! Picked up and carried out. Pushed in the back. Carried away. Bumping up and down because the road is bad. Finally just a thing. Horribly heavy. IT. Smothered by a sheet. Shoved in a hole. . . .

[*Desperate move to the table—grabs the spoon and starts tapping.*]

If this isn't madness it's a nervous breakdown. Think! Anything!

[*Tries to pour himself some squash.*]

Quick quench!

[*He can't get the stopper off the bottle fast enough.*]

Too late. HELP!

[*He grabs hold of the edge of the table, closes his eyes, and starts to speak at a very fast tempo—the first part of the speech is almost gabbled.*]

Queen Victoria's statue is on the square and during the day pigeons sit on it and do their business on it so looking up she

said thank god cows don't fly but we've heard that one before
and between shifts the bus conductors sit under it on benches
with little tin boxes waiting for their buses with boxes on
benches buses bunches of bosses all routes here we Go. . . .

[*Takes a deep breath.*]

Summerstrand Humewood Cadles Walmer Perridgevale
Newton Park Mount Pleasant Kensington Europeans only
and all classes double deckers with standing prohibited
spitting prosecuted and alighting while in motion is at your
own risk. . . .

[*Tempo gradually slowing down.*]

And sooner or later it starts to get dark in the square, the sun
sets, the last light goes riding away on the backs of the buses,
and then it's twilight with a sky stretching all the way down
Main Street and beyond who knows where, the ends of the
earth. . . . And all being well I'm in the gloom on Jetty Street
corner watching while it gathers, waiting for nothing in
particular with the City Hall clock telling the time, some time,
ding-dong, start to count forget to finish because it's all the
same . . . the cars get fewer, the newspaper boys stop calling
and count their pennies on the pavement while darkness is
coming it seems from the sea up Jetty Street. . . . Bringing
peace, the end of the day, my moment, everybody hurrying
away from it, leaving it, for me, just me, there in the
shadows and no questions asked, for once enough, ME is
enough, need nothing, whisper my name without shame. . . .
Until the lights go on. . . . Suddenly like a small fright, ON,
which is my sign to think of going. . . . Which I do. . . . I pull
up my roots as the saying goes and go. . . . Down Baakens
Street past the police station where the bars on the windows
and the pick-up vans give me the creeps. . . . To Baakens
Bridge. . . . And near the bus-sheds there, one night . . . I
saw a bus-conductor off duty pressing a girl against the wall
in a dark corner and he was smiling and holding his time-
sheet and she looked sly and then he kissed her. . . . Black
water was under the bridge running the wrong way because
of the sea. . . . While he kissed her and smiled and she was
sly. . . . While he held his time-sheet. . . .

[*Speaking now at an even tempo—each image distinct.*]

And not far away from there I will hear the frogs, without fail, the frogs never fail. In the meantime I hear trains shunting and try not to remember something; with the sky getting darker all this time and an old woman sitting with oranges under a lamp-post not selling any. . . . And me, me, walking, pressing on, I'm. . . .

[*Long pause. He opens his eyes.*]

Safe. Yes. Sure enough. Safe and sound. Firm ground. That was close. Like a hole, black and deep, among all the little thoughts. Suddenly there's nothing, and I'm falling! These are dangerous days. Safety first. Arrive in peace not in pieces. Bloody good!

[*Exits and returns.*]

So he kissed her. Just like that. And I thought, there are things to think about, which I did and still do, things to happen which hadn't and don't seem to. Other things happen to me. I am not complaining. I'm happy with my lot.

[*Pause.*]

My little.

So where were we?

[*Vigorous and clear, as if directing a stranger.*]

After the bridge turn sharp right. Carry on along the foot of the cliff until you come to a fork. Take the bottom prong. Then third to your left. It's on the left-hand side about half-way up. Fifty-seven A. You can't miss it. Green windows and a door . . .

. . . a door I never knock. Because it's my door. Open it with . . . some sort of heart and my right hand, close it with my left hand, behind me. Stand and listen. What sort of heart? Beating loud. Listening.

Stop! Just stop. Easy does it. Count the chairs. One two three four chairs. Table. One man. Friday somethingth. Move. Keep moving. Look for light entertainment.

[*Exits left and returns almost immediately with a comic.*]

Seen like that life's amazing!

[*He sits and reads the comic.*]

[*A woman appears up stage and walks slowly into the light. She is*] *wearing a coat and carrying a large and battered suitcase. This is* Hester. *Johnnie looks up from his comic and watches her.*]

HESTER [*putting down the suitcase*]. Hello.

JOHNNIE. Hello.

HESTER. Didn't you hear me calling?

JOHNNIE. No.

HESTER. Well I did!

JOHNNIE. I'm not arguing.

HESTER. I thought nobody was home.

JOHNNIE. No. I've been sitting here, minding my own business. . . .

HESTER. Well then listen next time, for God's sake. First the taxi hooted. But he was in a hurry so I told him to drop me. I could see the light was on.

JOHNNIE. I've been reading. . . .

HESTER. I even started to wonder if it was the right place.

JOHNNIE. Fifty-seven A Valley Road. Smit's the name.

HESTER. You being funny? Anyway the door wasn't locked. So what you got to say for yourself?

JOHNNIE. Surprised of course. I mean, put yourself in my shoes. I'm sitting here, reading a comic, passing the time, and then you! Suddenly you're here too.

HESTER. Not even a word of welcome.

[*Pause.*]

JOHNNIE. Welcome.

HESTER. Don't kill yourself!

JOHNNIE. Make yourself at home!

HESTER. I will.

JOHNNIE. What else? HospitaliTEA! How about a nice cup of. . . . No. Milk's finished. Can I offer you a refreshing glass of lemon squash? It's preserved with Benzoic Acid.

HESTER. Later.

[*She moves right and stares off in that direction.*]

Sleeping?

JOHNNIE. Who?

HESTER. Who? Him! Is he sleeping? Hell, you just woken up or something?

JOHNNIE. Me? No. I've been sitting here, reading. . . .

HESTER. Okay, okay. How's things otherwise?

JOHNNIE. Just a comic, mind you. Not a book. I've run out of reading-matter.

HESTER. I didn't come a thousand miles to talk about comics.

JOHNNIE. So?

HESTER. So change the subject.

JOHNNIE. There's no law against reading a comic in my own home.

HESTER. All right.

JOHNNIE. I admitted it wasn't a book.

HESTER. All right I said.

JOHNNIE. But I'm not harming anyone.

HESTER. For God's sake, all right. Read your bloody comic. All I wanted was a word of welcome. Is that asking so much? Look, let's start again. Have a cigarette.

[*They light cigarettes.*]

I'm leaving it to you.

JOHNNIE. What?

HESTER. The questions.

JOHNNIE. What questions?

HESTER. Or news.

JOHNNIE. No news, good news.

HESTER. Who cares? Let's hear it.

JOHNNIE. What?

HESTER. Anything. Just talk!

JOHNNIE. Okay.

HESTER. Good.

JOHNNIE. Can I be frank?

HESTER. Go ahead.

JOHNNIE. What do you want?

HESTER. How the hell do you like that!

JOHNNIE. I'm not telling you to go. Stay as long as you like.

I admire your—what's the word?—pluck. I always admire people who pluck up courage and barge in. But still—you and your suitcase, out of the blue, the dark, on my doorstep and before I could blink an eye in my house! You follow? What's all this in aid of?

HESTER. Listen to him!

JOHNNIE. Look, I said you could stay. I'm just interested. . . .

HESTER. Are you mad?

JOHNNIE. See what I mean. Straight to the point. Anyway, me mad. I worked it out. I don't think I am, therefore. . . . No . . . those that think they are . . . to cut a long story short I'm not.

HESTER. Johnnie?

JOHNNIE. You even know my name.

HESTER. Am I hearing you right? Of course I know your name.

[*Pause.*]

I don't believe it.

JOHNNIE. Truth is stranger than fiction.

HESTER. You don't know who I am.

JOHNNIE. You got me guessing.

HESTER. Don't you recognize me at all?

JOHNNIE. I admit I haven't had a really good look yet. I start with the feet and work up.

HESTER. Shut up! So why did you just sit there? Why didn't you ask?

JOHNNIE. But I did. I asked you. . . .

HESTER. All right!

[*Pause.*]

I'm Hester. Your sister, Hester Smit.

[*Pause.*]

Didn't you get my letter?

JOHNNIE. What letter?

HESTER. I wrote. Fifty-seven A Valley Road, Port Elizabeth. Saying I was coming. I waited and waited for a reply. Didn't you get it?

JOHNNIE. No.

HESTER. Well, I'm Hester, and I come back to visit you, Johnnie, my brother. So what you waiting for? Don't you believe me?

JOHNNIE. Give me time.

HESTER. I'm Hester, I tell you!

JOHNNIE. Prove it.

HESTER. You got a sister called Hester, haven't you?

JOHNNIE. Yes.

HESTER. And she's been gone a long time.

JOHNNIE. Yes.

HESTER. Well, that's me.

JOHNNIE. So prove it.

HESTER. You got a birthmark there . . .

   [*Pointing.*]

. . . what looks like the map of Africa upside down; and on your leg, your left leg I think—yes it is!—there's an operation from that time you were playing with the Boer War bullet and it went off. Are you satisfied?

JOHNNIE. But all of that's me. I know I'm Johnnie. It's *you.* You say you're Hester. Prove it.

HESTER. I'll hit you.

JOHNNIE. No you won't.

HESTER. How the hell would I know all about you if I wasn't me? If I wasn't Hester? I came *here*, didn't I? I know the address, your name, about him. . . .

   [*Pointing off-right. Pointing off-left.*]

That was our room; this was a lounge-cum-kitchen but after Mommie died I went on growing which isn't good for little boys to see so you moved in here and then it was kitchen-cum-bedroom, which also didn't matter because mostly there was a row on the go and nobody was talking to anybody else. Right or wrong? And when you got big and Daddy got worse it was you used to look after him because I was working at the Astoria Café, and that's his room and his lying there with only one leg left because of the explosion; and all our life it was groaning and moaning and what the

Bible says and what God's going to do and I hated it!
Right or wrong? Right! And it was hell. I wanted to scream.
I got so sick of it I went away. What more do you want?
Must I vomit?

[*Pause.*]

Well, don't just stand there. Take a good look and see it's me.

[*Hester moves close to Johnnie—she sees him properly for the first time. When she speaks again it is with the pain of recognition—what is and what was.*]

Johnnie! It's been a long time, *boetie.*

[*A small impulsive gesture of tenderness—hand to his cheek?—which she breaks off abruptly. She moves away.*]

[*Flat, matter-of-fact voice.*]

Well, is it me?

JOHNNIE [*quiet certainty*]. Yes, it's you.

HESTER. You sure?

JOHNNIE. I'm certain.

HESTER. Hester Smit.

JOHNNIE. I remember. . . .

HESTER. My face hasn't changed?

JOHNNIE. . . . your hate! It hasn't changed. The sound of it.
Always so sudden, so loud, so late at night. Nobody else
could hate it the way you did.

HESTER [*weary scorn*]. This? Four walls that rattled and a roof
that leaked! What's there to hate?

JOHNNIE. Us.

HESTER. I've got better things to do with my hate.

JOHNNIE. You hated something. You said so yourself.

HESTER. All right, something. The way it was! All those years,
and all of us, in here.

JOHNNIE. Then why have you come back?

HESTER. That was fifteen years ago.

JOHNNIE. You don't hate it now?

HESTER. Now. What's now? I've just arrived.

JOHNNIE. Tonight.

HESTER. I'll tell you tomorrow. Let me look at it in the light.

JOHNNIE. How long will you be staying?

HESTER [*ignoring the question*]. *Ja*. Fifteen years ago next month. I worked it out in the train. I was twenty-two. Best thing I ever did getting out of here.

JOHNNIE. Then why have you come back?

HESTER. You got lots of questions all of a sudden!

JOHNNIE. You said. . . .

HESTER. To hell with what I said. I'm here.

[*Looking around.*]

Mind you it's easier than I thought.

JOHNNIE. I've noticed that. It's always easier than we think.

HESTER. I thought it would be hard, or hurt—something like that. But here I am and it isn't so bad.

JOHNNIE. It's never as bad as we think.

HESTER. Do you know what I'm talking about?

JOHNNIE. No.

HESTER. Then shut up and listen!

[*Pause.*]

I'm talking about coming back. You see I tried hell of a hard to remember. That was a mistake. I got frightened.

JOHNNIE. Of what?

HESTER. Not like that. Maybe frightened is wrong. Don't get any ideas I'm scared of you lot. Just because I come back doesn't mean I'm hard-up. But at Kommodagga there was a long stop—I started remembering and that made me. . . .

[*Groping for words.*]

. . . I think nerves is better. The whole business was getting on my nerves! The heat, sitting there sweating and waiting! I'm not one for waiting. It was the slow train, you see. All stops. And then also this old bitch in the compartment. I hate them when they're like that—fat and dressed in black like Bibles because somebody's dead, and calling me Ou Sister. I had her from Nooupoort and it was non-stop all the time about the Kingdom of Heaven was at hand and swimming on Sunday and all that rubbish.

Because I was remembering, you see! It wasn't that I couldn't. I could. It was seeing it again that worried me. The same.

Do you understand? Coming back and seeing it all still the same. I wasn't frightened of there being changes. I said to myself, I hope there is changes. Please let it be different, and strange, even if I get lost and got to ask my way. I won't mind. But to think of it all still the same, the way it was, and me coming back to find it like that . . . ! Sick! It made me sick on the stomach. There was fruit cake with the afternoon tea and I almost vomited.

And every time just when I'm ready to be brave Ou Sister starts again on the Kingdom and Jesus doesn't like lipstick. By then I had her in a big way. So when she asks me if I seen the light I said no because I preferred the dark! Just like that, and I went outside to stand in the gangway. But next stop I see it's still only Boesmanspoort and ninety miles to go so it all starts again. Only it's worse now, because I start remembering like never before.

Those windy days with nothing to do; the dust in the street! Even the colour of things—so clear, man, it could have been yesterday. The way the grass went grey around the laundry drain on the other side, the foam in the river, and inside those Indian women ironing white shirts. And the smell, that special ironing smell—warm and damp—with them talking funny Indian and looking sad. Smells! I could give you smells a mile long—backyard smells, Sunday smells, and what about the Chinaman shop on the corner! Is he still there? That did it. Don't ask me why—something to do with no pennies for sweets—but that did it. If it's still there I said, if there's still those sacks of beans and sugar and rice on the floor with everything smelling that special way when I walk past, I'll bring up on the spot like a dog, so help me God.

So then I said, No, this isn't wise. Get off at Coega and catch the next one back to Jo'burg. Send them a telegram, even if it's a lie—sick of something, which was almost true. I was ready to do it. 'Strue's God!

But the next stop was Sandflats and there suddenly I see it's sunset. Somebody in the gangway said we were two hours late and it will be dark when we get in. That will help me, won't it, I think to myself. And it did. Because it was—dark and me feeling like a stranger in the taxi.

All my life I been noticing this, the way night works, the

way it makes you feel home is somewhere else. Even with the lights on, like now, looking at this . . . I don't know. It is and it isn't. I'm not certain. It could be true. Tomorrow will tell. I never have doubts in daylight.

So that was that. Jo'burg to P.E. second class. Over to you.

JOHNNIE. Why have you come back?

[*Hester lights a cigarette, giving no sign of replying to the question.*]

That was a very good description. My journey to P.E. on the S.A.R. I'd give you eight out of ten.

[*Pause.*]

Why have you come back?

HESTER. It's also my home. I've got a right to come here if I want to. I'm still his daughter. How is he?

JOHNNIE. How long you staying?

HESTER. What you worried about? I'll buy my own food.

JOHNNIE. Is this a holiday? Back home for old times sake sort of thing. Two weeks annually.

HESTER. In here? I got better things to do with my holidays.

JOHNNIE. So why have you come?

HESTER. Look, stop worrying! I'm passing through. It's hello and goodbye. Maybe I'm gone tomorrow.

[*Looking off-right to father's room.*]

And him?

[*Johnnie stares at her.*]

Speak up! I don't care what you say.

[*Pause.*]

So he still hates me. I wasn't expecting miracles. Any case I also got a memory. Don't think I've forgotten some of the things that was said in here. It's my life and I'll do what I like.

JOHNNIE. Yes, he still hates you. He doesn't want to see you.

HESTER. So what? Just remember Mommie didn't hate me and half of this house was hers so I'm entitled to be here. You can tell him that from me.

JOHNNIE. He's sleeping.

HESTER. I heard he was in a bad way.

JOHNNIE. He's sleeping in there.

HESTER. I know he's sleeping in there! But I heard he was in a bad way.

[*Pause.*]

Well, is it true?

JOHNNIE. No.

HESTER. I met old Magda Swanepoel and she told me nobody ever sees him any more and that she heard he was in a bad way. Death's door. Those were her words.

JOHNNIE. NO!

HESTER. So then tell me what's happening.

JOHNNIE. He's recovering.

HESTER. Well, it can't last for ever.

JOHNNIE. He's making a splendid recovery! Improving day by day. I've got him on Wilson's Beef and Iron tonic—one tablespoon with water after every meal. It's working wonders. Building up his strength. . . .

HESTER. But he's still cripple.

JOHNNIE. Yes.

HESTER. Still in bed most of the time.

JOHNNIE. Yes.

HESTER. Don't tell him I'm here. I'll be quiet. I'm not scared of him! But I can't stay long. Maybe tomorrow. Like I said it's just hello and goodbye. Anyway, let's see. Yes.

[*To her suitcase, which she opens, taking out a small packet.*]

There's no hard feelings between us so I bought you a present. We got on well together, didn't we?

[*Hands it over to Johnnie.*]

Well, aren't you going to open it? What's the matter with you, man? You never used to be like this. It's a cigar called a cheroot. Put one in your mouth and let's see. Oh well. . . . What else?

[*Back to her suitcase, rummaging through its contents.*]

I had some tea left, and this tin of condensed milk. Jam. It all helps. You want a pot? Here. I'm damned if I was going to leave her anything.

JOHNNIE. Who?

HESTER. Mrs. Humphries. Trocadero Court. The landlady. As it is she gets . . . let's see. I'm paid up till the end of the month. Ten days! By rights she owes me.

[*Back to the suitcase.*]

My own knife and fork. Spoon. Plate. That's all.

[*Rummaging.*]

Just my clothes.

JOHNNIE [*watching her*]. You've come back for something, Hester.

HESTER. Have I?

JOHNNIE. What?

HESTER. I didn't say yes.

JOHNNIE. I say you've come back for something.

HESTER. You can say what you like, my boy.

JOHNNIE. I know you.

HESTER. You know me, do you? Ten minutes ago you were singing another song.

[*Standing.*]

I feel dirty. Still the old zinc bath from the yard and a kettle of hot?

JOHNNIE. Yes.

HESTER. *Ag*, it can wait. I'm too tired. I suppose you're in my room now?

JOHNNIE. You take it.

HESTER. I'll be all right in here.

JOHNNIE. No! You take the bed. He needs me. He calls.

[*Pause.*]

HESTER. Yes. I remember that too. Late . . . *late* at night, when everybody was in bed, groaning or calling softly, on and on. . . .

JOHNNIE. He never called for you!

HESTER. I heard him all the same. Don't you hate it?

JOHNNIE. I don't know . . . NO! I don't hate it. I don't think about it. He's my father.

[*Hester breaks off staring at Johnnie and struggles off-left with her suitcase. Johnnie remains motionless at the table. Hester reappears a few seconds later.*]

HESTER. You're going to empty those slops in there sometime, I hope?

[*Exit Johnnie left with Hester following.*]

Christ Almighty, no wonder!

[*Johnnie reappears carrying a white enamel bucket.*]

[*Off.*]

And leave it out. Let it get some fresh air!

[*Exit Johnnie up stage. Returns to the table, empty-handed.*]

[*Off.*]

I can't understand why you never got that letter! I posted it. Fifty-seven A Valley Road. Where the hell is my. . . ?

[*Indistinct mumble of words—occasional phrases are heard.*]

. . . good ironing . . . second class . . . all that dust . . . one thing about a good drip-dry. . . .

[*Again loud and distinct.*]

Hell, man, why don't you get the broom in here? It's inches thick. I'm not fussy but this is the bloody limit. Just look at it!

JOHNNIE. Ssssh!

[*Hester appears in her petticoat.*]

He's sleeping.

HESTER. I wasn't making so much noise.

JOHNNIE. He needs all the sleep he can get.

HESTER. So who's stopping him?

JOHNNIE. You were shouting. The doctor said. . . .

HESTER. I know, I know. Good night.

[*Exit Hester. Johnnie waits a few seconds, listening, then follows her to the edge of light.*]

Close your door. Just in case.

[*As soon as he is satisfied that Hester has closed her door, Johnnie moves quickly to the table and looks wildly around the room. Hurried exit into father's room, returning immediately but stopping just inside the light to stare at Hester's room. Another impulsive move this time*]

*to the table to collect two chairs which he stacks up at the entrance
to the father's room, blocking it. But he almost immediately changes
his mind and takes them back to the table.*]

JOHNNIE. Hester, back in the land of the living. It's her all
right. Large as life. Loud as . . . something. Bold! And not
answering questions. The danger signal! Hold your breath
and wait. What else? Think. Go back . . . back . . . all the
days, right back, further than I've ever been . . . memories.
Wind as she said. Dust, and nothing to do . . . and Hester!
I'm crying and she's got her fingers in her ears. Does that
help me? Her fingers in her ears, and shouting or singing at
the top of her voice to drown my crying. How does that
help me? Or those times . . . saying nothing! That way of hers
—can't sit still, ants in her pants and saying nothing. Hester
with a scheme up her sleeve. There's a word—beer does it
in the dark—Brewing! And then trouble. Without fail. She
wants something. The letter!

[*Johnnie exits up stage, returning a few seconds later with a bundle
of mail—mostly commercial circulars. He goes through them hurriedly
and finds a letter, but before he can open it Hester reappears, smoking
a cigarette, a small mirror in her hand. Johnnie quickly tucks the
letter back into the pile of mail on the table.*]

HESTER. What you up to?

JOHNNIE [*picking up one of the commercial circulars*]. Boswell's
Circus. Behind the new Law Courts. Cheap seats five bob.

HESTER. Do you sit up all night?

JOHNNIE. When he's bad.

HESTER. You said he was better.

JOHNNIE. He's getting better.

HESTER. So he was bad.

JOHNNIE. Well on the road to recovery.

HESTER. But he *was*. . . .

JOHNNIE. We mustn't talk loud.

HESTER. I'm not talking loud.

JOHNNIE. I'm just saying.

HESTER. Well say it when I'm talking loud!

JOHNNIE. You're starting.

HESTER. Oh shit!

JOHNNIE. Why don't you get a good night's rest?

HESTER. Are you trying to get rid of me?

JOHNNIE. You look tired.

HESTER. Just now. It's those damn frogs. Were they always so loud?

JOHNNIE. Croak.

HESTER. What?

JOHNNIE. Ducks quack, dogs bark, frogs croak.

HESTER. All right, professor. I still don't remember them being so loud.

JOHNNIE. Some nights they don't croak at all.

[*Back to the mail.*]

Spick! 'Spick for your pots
   Spick for your pans
   Cleans like a shot
   And soft on the hands.'

They're damned clever, you know.

HESTER. There is something I want to ask you.

JOHNNIE. Now in a family pack.

HESTER. Hey! I've got a question.

JOHNNIE. As long as it's not loud.

HESTER. For God's sake! I'm talking at the bottom of my voice.

[*Johnnie goes back to the circular.*]

I haven't asked my question yet! What do *I* look like? When you saw me, and you knew it was me, Hester, did you remember much?

JOHNNIE. Like what?

HESTER. Like I was. I mean, am I changed much?

JOHNNIE [*not looking at her*]. Hard to say. . . .

HESTER. Have you had a good look at me yet?

JOHNNIE. It's the light in here. I feel it when I'm reading. Maybe I need glasses.

HESTER. Rubbish! Look at me. Come close! You're not looking properly! I can see it in your eyes.

JOHNNIE. I'm trying to.

HESTER. What's the matter with you?

JOHNNIE. It's rude to stare.

HESTER. I'm asking you to. Now come on!

JOHNNIE. All right, but don't stare at me. Look the other way.
  [*Pause. He looks at Hester.*]
 Okay.

HESTER. Well?

JOHNNIE. What do you want me to say?

HESTER. What you saw.

JOHNNIE. You—my sister Hester—a few years older. Satisfied?

HESTER. No! Am I also . . . were you shocked? At the changes?
 My face?
  [*Mirror in her hand.*]
 What do I really look like now? I can't see myself. Mirrors
 don't work. I can't watch . . . Me. When I look, *I* look back.

JOHNNIE [*back to the commercial circular*]. One cap-full is enough
 for a sink-full of dishes. That's a hell of a lot of dishes. One
 sink-full! Big families I suppose, and three meals a day.
 Porridge, stews, puddings. You'd need it then. Anything with
 gravy or fat, or soft fried eggs with that yellowy yolk. Once
 it's cold you've had it. As for the pot you've boiled milk
 in . . . ! Bread's the best. Dust off the plate and use it again.
 Also cheese, very hard-boiled eggs, biscuits—anything that
 comes in crumbs. Watch out for jam. It looks easy but once
 it's on the plate. . . .

HESTER. And you, Johnnie?

JOHNNIE. If I could afford it beer and lemon creams three
 times a day.

HESTER. Johnnie!

JOHNNIE. I'm all ears.

HESTER. What happened to you?

JOHNNIE. Who said anything happened to me?

HESTER. All these years! Wasn't it learner-stoker once upon
 a time? At the Kroonstad Railway School? You had the
 forms to fill in and everything. Then I left. What happened?

[*Johnnie is staring straight ahead.*]

Ever since I can remember you always wanted to be an engine driver. What. . . .

JOHNNIE. Ssssssh!

[*Exit into father's room. Returns a few seconds later but doesn't sit.*]

He's sleeping soundly. I gave him a dose of Wilson's Beef and Iron after supper. Instructions on the label. One tablespoon with water after meals. Here's the bottle if you don't believe me. Satisfied?

[*He sits.*]

HESTER. I'm not interested in him. I was asking what happened to you.

JOHNNIE. And I heard you. That was a long time ago. But I remember now. I changed my mind.

HESTER [*not believing him*]. Just like that!

JOHNNIE. Just like that.

HESTER. After all those years?

JOHNNIE. After all those years one morning I changed my mind just like that and didn't go. I tore up the application forms.

[*Back to the mail on the table.*]

We've had Spick, Boswell's Circus . . . what's left? Providential Assurance. Looks like arithmetic. And this?

[*The letter is uncovered.*]

Is this your handwriting?

HESTER. Give here. Hey, yes. This is it.

JOHNNIE [*taking it back*]. Let's see what you said.

[*He opens it.*]

HESTER. But I posted that weeks ago.

JOHNNIE. Isn't there something called surface mail?

HESTER [*watching him open the envelope*]. You going to read it?

JOHNNIE. You wrote it to me.

HESTER. No, wait. That's not fair.

JOHNNIE. Fair?

HESTER. I'm already here.

JOHNNIE. That makes it even fairer. You know . . . in your presence.

HESTER. I said wait! Let me think. NO. Hand over.

JOHNNIE. Strictly speaking it's mine now.

HESTER. Give it!

[*She grabs it out of his hands.*]

I want to read it first.

[*Hester reads the letter. Johnnie waits passively for a few seconds, then starts his next speech while she is reading.*]

JOHNNIE. Yes, it all comes back. Clear as daylight—which it was. Just after breakfast, in fact. I changed my mind! There are bigger things in life than driving an engine, I said. So I tore up the forms in duplicate, and never looked back. It's best, they say, and they're right. I never do. Habit. One of those that help. Good and bad. Onward, always onward. Eyes on the road. Leave the corner and over the bridge, under the cliffs and along the river and no regrets. I never look back. I'll see it all again tomorrow. Always onwards. That's me in a nutshell.

HESTER [*folding up the letter*]. Nothing much. I wouldn't worry about it if I was you.

JOHNNIE [*holding out his hand*]. Who cares?

HESTER [*ignoring the hand*]. Stick to your comics if you want a laugh. It's not worth reading.

JOHNNIE. Let's see what you said.

HESTER. Just that I'm coming by train.

JOHNNIE. Two pages.

HESTER. And how are you and I'm okay. The usual.

JOHNNIE. Two pages on both sides.

HESTER. Mrs. Humphries only had two pages left.

JOHNNIE. So it's really four pages to say you're coming by train and how am I and you're okay.

HESTER. And news.

JOHNNIE. What news?

HESTER. Just news, for God's sake. Don't you know what news is? Anyway you wouldn't be interested.

JOHNNIE. Then why did you write it?

HESTER. You got to write something.

JOHNNIE. I am interested. I've thought about it. I am definitely interested.

HESTER. All right. Don't panic. Remember Pearl Harbor. I said. . . .

JOHNNIE [*holding out his hand*]. Let me read it.

HESTER. I want to have another look.

JOHNNIE. I'll give it back.

HESTER. What you in such a hurry for?

JOHNNIE. I'm not in a hurry.

HESTER. Oh no? Look at your hand.

JOHNNIE [*withdrawing his hand*]. I'll wait.

[*He waits. Hester watches him.*]

HESTER. If you're trying to be funny, Johnnie Smit . . . !

[*Johnnie waits.*]

I'm warning you!

[*Johnnie waits.*]

Right, you asked for it!

[*Tearing up the letter.*]

That . . . and that . . . and that . . . and may God strike me stone dead if I ever write you another one.

[*She lights a cigarette; the letter has brought a tension to her.*]

JOHNNIE. Happy?

HESTER. Why should I be happy?

JOHNNIE. You didn't want me to read it.

HESTER [*vindictive*]. Yes! I didn't want you to read it.

JOHNNIE. That's what I said.

HESTER. And now you *can't* read it.

JOHNNIE. And that's why you're happy.

HESTER. Happy? In here? Don't make me laugh. Nothing in here knows what happy means.

JOHNNIE. 'That way of hers . . . saying nothing!'

HESTER. Who?

JOHNNIE. Hester with a scheme up her sleeve! What was in that letter?

HESTER. My own business.

JOHNNIE. Why didn't you want me to read it?

HESTER. Because it's going to stay my own business.

JOHNNIE. Suppose I found it before you arrived?

HESTER. Suppose, suppose. Suppose I didn't come, what then? Suppose he was dead, what then?

JOHNNIE. You Must Not Say That!

HESTER. I said suppose, for God's sake.

JOHNNIE. He's our father.

HESTER. Here we go again! And I'm his daughter and you're his son and I'm your sister and where's our mother? Well, I'm also ME! Just ME. Hester. And something is going to be mine—just mine—and no sharing with brothers or fathers. . . .

JOHNNIE. Twenty years ago you used to say that.

[*This remark stops her tirade. She moves about restlessly.*]

What are you looking for?

HESTER. I'm not looking for anything.

JOHNNIE. You're looking in all the corners.

HESTER. Twenty years ago. That puts him in his sixties.

JOHNNIE. All the corners—not answering questions.

HESTER. I said that puts him in his sixties.

JOHNNIE. Does it?

HESTER. Work it out.

JOHNNIE. Multiplied by. . . .

HESTER. Add.

JOHNNIE. Multiplication gives you the seconds.

HESTER. Just add. Middle age plus twenty years. Puts him in his old age. He must be getting grey then. Eyesight bad and the shakes. Isn't he grey?

JOHNNIE [*his eyes closed*]. . . . become minutes, become hours, days of the week. . . .

HESTER. Answer me! Is he grey?

JOHNNIE. Ssssssh!

[*Gets up and goes into father's room. Hester waits, lights another cigarette. After a few seconds Johnnie returns.*]

JOHNNIE. I thought I heard a groan. But he's still asleep. That doesn't mean he didn't groan. Sometimes he groans in his sleep. But not from pain in the stump. It's his dreams that make him groan. You know what he's doing in his dreams? He's working again on the railway line to Graaff-Reinet in the olden days. It's the hard work that makes him groan, he says. Other times it's the pain. I can't tell the difference. I've tried to guess. How many nights haven't I listened and said, Is that hard work or is it pain? Then in the morning I go in to him and say: You were dreaming again last night, chum. No, he says, ... the pain in my stump. I never slept a wink. Or when I say: It seemed to hurt last night, Daddy, he looks at me and says, ... Maybe. I didn't feel it. I dreamed we reached Heuningvlei. We're living in tents on the side of the line at Heuningvlei.

[*Pause.*]

You asked if he's grey. I had a good look at him. Yes, he's gone grey, but. . . .

HESTER. That's what I said.

JOHNNIE. BUT ... it suits him. In fact he's looking handsome these days. Don't you believe me?

HESTER. I didn't say that.

JOHNNIE [*watching Hester closely*]. Suppose I were to tell you he's grown a moustache. A smart little Errol Flynn moustache.

HESTER. Good luck to him.

JOHNNIE. And a beard! A voortrekker beard to go with it. And he's getting fat . . . plump!

HESTER. So who cares?

JOHNNIE. You believe me?

HESTER. If you say so.

JOHNNIE. No. He still shaves. Tries to. Cuts himself. Misses little patches where the hairs grow longer and longer until I have to fetch the scissors. He's thin. Skin and bone. He won't eat. I try all sorts of delicacies. Sardines on toast. Warm buttered toast with the silver little fishes. . . .

HESTER. Does he ask about me?

JOHNNIE. No.

HESTER. But he remembers me.

JOHNNIE. I don't know.

HESTER. So then how can you say he still hates me?

JOHNNIE. Because he doesn't speak about you.

HESTER. Maybe he's thinking about me.

JOHNNIE. When you left he said, 'We won't speak about her any more.' You weren't a real Afrikaner by nature, he said. Must be some English blood somewhere, on Mommie's side. He hated you then. He doesn't dream about you. Only the railway line in the old days, the bad old days.

HESTER. Well, just remember that in the eyes of the law it doesn't mean a thing. Just because he doesn't remember or isn't thinking about me doesn't mean a damned thing.

JOHNNIE. Who says it does?

HESTER. Exactly! So when the time comes I want you to be a witness to what you just said.

JOHNNIE. What time?

HESTER. Don't panic. Nothing's happened yet.

JOHNNIE. What's going to happen? I don't like the sound of this. You want something, Hester. You're scheming. You've come back because you want something.

HESTER. I'm saying nothing. I'm passing through and my name is Hester Smit.

JOHNNIE. I know you.

HESTER. No you don't. None of you know me.

JOHNNIE. That's what you used to say.

HESTER. I'll say it again: None of you know me!

JOHNNIE. Just like that, and then there was trouble. None of you know me and you took that job in the café that nearly gave him the stroke, and stayed out late and brought those soldiers home. None of you know me, and you was gone for a week. None of you know me and you went for good. What is it this time? Why have you come back?

HESTER. Must I have a reason to visit my own home?

JOHNNIE. Just leave us alone. We're doing all right.

HESTER. I haven't done anything, for Christ's sake.

JOHNNIE. You're here.

HESTER. Because this is also my home. And him forgetting me doesn't count. She was my mother and he's still my father even if he hates me. So half of everything in here is mine when the time comes.

JOHNNIE. What time is going to come?

HESTER. Something is going to happen some day.

JOHNNIE. Such as what?

HESTER. Such as being dead when your time comes. That happens.

JOHNNIE. The second time.

HESTER. Well, you know what I mean.

JOHNNIE. That's the second time you've said it.

HESTER. You forced me.

JOHNNIE. You're wishing it.

HESTER. I'm not.

JOHNNIE. That's wicked.

HESTER. Dry up, for God's sake.

JOHNNIE. That's sin.

HESTER. It's not Sunday, Dominee.

JOHNNIE [*loudly*]. Wishing for him to die is the wickedest sin in the world!

HESTER. Who's making the noise now?

[*Abrupt silence. Johnnie goes into father's room, returning in a few seconds very nervous and agitated.*]

JOHNNIE. Now you've done it! He's groaning.

HESTER. I've done it?

JOHNNIE. I warned you.

HESTER. Jesus.

JOHNNIE. If there's a stroke you know who's to blame! It looks bad. Wait for the worst, pray for the best.

HESTER. How the hell do you like that!

[*Johnnie now busies himself with the bottle of medicine; a lot of movement in and out of the light to clean the glass, fetch the spoon, measure out the medicine, add water, etc., etc.*]

Fifteen years gone and one hour back but I done it again! Home sweet home where who did it means Hester done it. 'I didn't do it. She did it!' If I laughed too loud that did it. Have a little cry and that will do it. Sit still and mind your own business but sure as the lavatory stinks that will also do it. Well one day I will. And then God help the lot of you.

JOHNNIE. Will what?

HESTER. *Really* do it.

JOHNNIE. Your worst.

HESTER. Worse!

JOHNNIE. There's a word . . . catastrophe. Calamity. Ruin staring us in the face.

HESTER. That's it! In ruins. The lot of you.

JOHNNIE. Smashed to smithereens.

HESTER. And I'll be happy. It's broken and I'm to blame but I'm happy because this time I'll know I did it. So hello be damned and goodbye for good and go back home.

JOHNNIE. You're a rotten egg. There's one in every dozen.

[*Shouting to father's room.*]

Hold on I'm coming!

[*To Hester.*]

For your sake I hope this works.

[*Exit with medicine. Exhausted by her outburst Hester sinks into a chair . . . her elbows on the table, her forehead resting on her palms. She holds this position in silence for a few seconds.*]

HESTER [*without looking up*]. Home.

[*A few more seconds in silence and without movement and then she lifts her head once to look around the room and then drops it back on to her palms. Johnnie returns from his father's room, but stays some distance away from the table in half light.*]

[*Without looking up.*]

You?

JOHNNIE. Yes.

HESTER. I meant a room.

JOHNNIE. What?

HESTER. When I go back. I said I would go back Home. But this is it, isn't it? I'll go back to a room. I'm not hard up for a home.

JOHNNIE [*still in the shadows*]. Leave me your address. I'll write. Let you know how things. . . .

HESTER [*abruptly*]. There's no address.

JOHNNIE. When you settle down and find a new place.

HESTER. There's no address! No names, no numbers. A room somewhere, in a street somewhere. To Let is always the longest list, and they're all the same. Rent in advance and one week's notice—one week to notice it's walls again and a door with nobody knocking, a table, a bed, a window for your face when there's nothing to do. So many times! Then I started waking in the middle of the night wondering which one it was, which room . . . lie there in the dark not knowing. And later still, who it was. Just like that. Who was it lying there wondering where she was? Who was where? Me. And I'm Hester. But what's that mean? What does Hester Smit mean? So you listen. But men dream about other women. The names they call are not yours. That's all. You don't know the room, you're not in his dream. Where do you belong?

JOHNNIE. So what do you do?

HESTER. Wait. Lie there, let it happen, and wait. For a memory. That's the way it works. A memory comes. Suddenly there's going to be a memory of you, somewhere, some other time. And then you can work it all out again. In the meantime, just wait, listen to the questions and have no answers . . . no danger or pain or anything like that, just something missing, the meaning of your name.

[*Pause.*]

It was always the same memory. I was a little girl and I was lying awake one night. I was in here, the kitchen, sleeping in here because you got the mumps in the other room. Mommie and Daddy are in there . . .

[*Pointing to father's room.*]

. . . the door is open and I can hear them talking.

Compensation, he says. They got to. I've only got one leg and a wife and two children. He was talking about the accident, the explosion and everything is just compensation, compensation . . . hundreds of pounds!

JOHNNIE [*stepping forward into the light*]. The earth opened up! Just like in the Bible. And the mountain fell down on top of him! I know it by heart.

[*Clears his throat and tells the story in a strong vigorous voice.*]

Two miles the other side of Perseverance. They were relaying a section of the line to Uitenhage. It was as hot as hell, which isn't swearing because that's what Bible says. He had slipped away when the others weren't looking to eat prickly pears. There was a bush on the hill, covered with them, fat and ripe. So he was standing there in the shade sucking a juicy one when one of the men from headquarters—those in the white coats—saw him and started to shout. At first Daddy pretended he didn't see him. But then this man got more excited, shouting and swearing and running towards him. The others had all stopped working and were watching. Daddy said he knew then he was in trouble . . . maybe the prickly pear bush was on private property or something. So he picked up his spade and started to go back. But then the man in the white coat went completely mad, screaming and swearing in English like nothing Daddy had ever heard. The others also were jumping up and down—old Dolf, Van Rooyen, Elsie, the lot—jumping up and down and shouting and waving at him. This is it, he thought, I'm fired. The spade was heavy, it was uphill—because he was so frightened he had turned around and was running away for good—and then with a tremendous roar the earth opened! Right in front of his own eyes it just opened and half a mountain was coming down towards him!

[*Pause.*]

He woke up in hospital minus one leg. Dynamite! It's a hell of a word.

HESTER. Does he still talk about it?

JOHNNIE. It's my favourite of all the stories.

HESTER. And the compensation? What does he say about the compensation? Don't look stupid. He was paid hundreds of pounds compensation.

JOHNNIE. He never . . . he doesn't talk about that.

HESTER. Well, he was! I heard him myself, in here. And not just once. There was a lot of talk those days about compensation, and him saying they got to pay. Hundreds of pounds! Because it wasn't his fault. They didn't tell him there was dynamite.

JOHNNIE. So?

HESTER. So I'm just saying.

JOHNNIE. He must have spent it.

HESTER. Him? Hundreds of pounds? Don't make me laugh. Does this look like hundreds of pounds was spent in our lives?

JOHNNIE. What about food? Rent?

HESTER. No you don't! I worked it out. He still gets his disability grant, doesn't he?

JOHNNIE. Yes.

HESTER. And his pension. Well, you work it out and you'll see it covers household and upkeep and all we ever got out of life in here.

JOHNNIE. So then it's in the bank or a post-office book or something.

HESTER. Maybe—only I don't think it is, you see. Because I thought about that one too. When Mommie died and he had to pay the expenses—the coffin and all that—he didn't go to no bank or post-office, he went in there!

[*Pointing to father's room.*]

I was sitting here with the man from the funeral firm and Daddy went in *there* and came back and paid cash!

JOHNNIE. So?

HESTER. So I'm just saying for Christ's sake.

[*Johnnie moves closer to the table, watching Hester carefully. She is tensed and restless.*]
[*Uncertain of how to put her next question.*]
Tell me . . . is . . . a . . . ?

JOHNNIE [*quickly*]. What?

HESTER. Hold your horses! Hell you're in a hurry. What's it like in there?

JOHNNIE. It was a bad turn, but I think he's pulling around. Wilson's Beef and Iron did the trick. Double dose. Calms the nerves and eases the pain. With water after every. . . .

HESTER. Yes, yes, I know. What I mean is, all that old junk —those boxes, man, and suitcases, all that old junk that was packed away when Mommie died and he wouldn't let us fiddle in.

JOHNNIE. You mean his private possessions.

HESTER. Is it still in there? On the wardrobe and under the bed, you know the way it was.

JOHNNIE. Yes.

[*Johnnie watching Hester carefully. She knows it but works up enough courage to continue.*]

HESTER. You want to know something?

JOHNNIE. NO!

HESTER. It's in one of them. The compensation. I'll take you any bet you like it's hidden in one of those boxes.

JOHNNIE. So that's it.

HESTER [*embarrassed but determined*]. Is it?

JOHNNIE. That's why you've come back! That was in your letter!

HESTER. Since when are you a mind-reader?

JOHNNIE. Tell me I'm wrong.

HESTER. What's that prove? Can you deny it's there? No. Because it is. And I'm entitled to half. What would have happened to my share if he passed away and I hadn't come? You didn't know where I was?

JOHNNIE [*closing his eyes*]. He Is Not. . . .

HESTER. HE IS! Some day. He's got to. Everybody does. Sooner or later. . . .

JOHNNIE. No.

HESTER. Yes.

JOHNNIE. The Wilson's Beef and Iron. . . .

HESTER. Shut up! And wake up. Open your eyes! You said so yourself. Grey, you said. And thin. Your own words. Old age and grey and bad turns. Well, that's knocking at death's door . . . LISTEN! If you don't want a slap in your face just shut up and listen. I'm still alive, you see. Alive. He's passing away but I'm still alive. And I'm his daughter. So half of that compensation is mine. Ask any lawyer you like. It's legal and I'm entitled. What good is it doing in there? He doesn't need it. The disability and pension keep him going. So it's just lying there rotting away. Maybe the mould has got it. It got everything else in this house. Or the cockroaches. And then one day when we find it it's cockrotted and useless. So what then is the use of anything? I want it now. Not next year, or when I'm ready for the rubbish heap like him, but Now! Is that such a sin?

JOHNNIE. Yes! It's his, and he's your father. . . .

HESTER. And you're my brother and I'm his daughter so we must all love each other and live happily ever after! Well I got news for you, brother. I don't. There's no fathers, no brothers, no sisters, or Sunday, or sin. There's nothing. The fairy stories is finished. They died in a hundred Jo'burg rooms. There's man. And I'm a woman. It's as simple as that. You want a sin, well there's one. I *Hoer*. I've *hoer*ed all the brothers and fathers and sons and sweethearts in this world into one thing . . . Man. That's how I live and that's why I don't care. And now I'm here and waiting. Because when he wakes up I'm going in there to tell him I want it. My share.

JOHNNIE. No.

HESTER. You think I'm scared of him?

JOHNNIE. No, I mean yes. You will. But don't. Wait. One minute. Just stay still. . . . Sssssh! Let me think. I'm coming!

[*Hurried exit into father's room. Hester lights a cigarette and waits. After a few seconds Johnnie returns.*]

If you find it, will you go?

HESTER. Only my share. All I'm asking for. . . .

JOHNNIE. If you find it, will you go?

HESTER. Yes.

JOHNNIE. Straight away?

HESTER. Yes.

JOHNNIE. You won't worry him?

HESTER. No.

[*Pause.*]

Anything else?

JOHNNIE. You won't come back.

HESTER. This is also my home, you know.

JOHNNIE. I'll make a bargain. You take the money, all of it. Leave me the home.

HESTER. Fair exchange.

JOHNNIE. Then you won't come back, ever?

HESTER. No. So what do we do?

JOHNNIE. He's sleeping. I'll bring in the boxes. You say it's in the boxes.

HESTER. Or those old suitcases under the bed. I'm prepared to bet you anything. . . .

JOHNNIE. I'll bring them in.

[*Exit Johnnie. Hester clears the table and waits. Johnnie returns with the first box—cardboard and tied up with a piece of flaxen twine —which he puts on the table. Hester stands to one side watching it.*]

Number one.

[*He starts to untie the string.*]

HESTER [*going to the table*]. I'll do that! You just bring in the boxes.

[*Johnnie sits down and watches her.*]

You think I'm low, don't you?

JOHNNIE. I didn't say that.

HESTER. But you think it.

JOHNNIE. No.

HESTER. So then what you staring at?

JOHNNIE. How much did they pay you?

HESTER. Who?

JOHNNIE. The men. The ones you . . . you know. Your boy-friends. What's the tariff of charges?

[*Hester ignores the question. She has untied the twine and is now opening the box. There is a sheet of brown paper on top.*]

It depends on your age, doesn't it? The older you get, and so on.

HESTER. Mind your own business.

JOHNNIE. Just asking. I'm interested. There's a few in P.E., you know. Jetty Street. I watch them.

[*The first thing to come out of the box is a woman's dress. Hester smells it.*]

HESTER. Hey!

[*Another smell.*]

My God, Johnnie! Smell!

JOHNNIE. What?

HESTER. It's her.

JOHNNIE. Who?

HESTER. Mommie. Smell, man. It's Mommie's smell.

JOHNNIE [*smelling the dress*]. I can't remember.

HESTER. I'm telling you, it's her. I remember. How do you like that, hey? All these years. Hell, man, it hurts. Look, I claim this too. You don't need it. I'll put it on one side and pack it in with my things when I go. Remind me.

[*Back to the box.*]

JOHNNIE [*watching her again*]. Were there many? Hester! On an average, how many times a week?

[*Hester ignores him.*]

I've often wondered, when I see them in Jetty Street. It's illegal of course. You know that.

HESTER [*another dress out of the box—this time a young girl's*]. And this! Jesus, Johnnie. Look.

JOHNNIE. Ribbons.

HESTER. Me, man. Don't you remember? On Sundays? NO!

[*She puts the dress back hurriedly into the box and walks away— sudden fear.*]

JOHNNIE. And now?

HESTER. I've got a funny feeling.

JOHNNIE. What about the money?

[*After a silent struggle Hester goes back to the box and resumes her unpacking. Johnnie watches her.*]

HESTER. Bring in the others.

CURTAIN

ACT TWO

The same, about an hour later.

Three or four suitcases and the same number of boxes—all opened —clutter the stage, their contents spilling out on to the floor, gathered together in piles, etc., etc.

Hester is sitting on a suitcase, a photo album open on her lap. She is studying a loose photo in her hands. Johnnie stands to one side holding another, as yet unopened box from his father's room.

A pair of crutches are leaning against a chair.

JOHNNIE. What about that Jansen girl? What was it? Gertrude! Gertrude Jansen!

[*Hester, still studying the photo, shakes her head.*]

She married a De Villiers.

HESTER. Give me some other names.

JOHNNIE. Bet you anything you like it's Gertrude.

HESTER. I said no. Now come on. Who were the others?

JOHNNIE. Let me see, sayeth the blind man. I'll give it to you in alphabetic order. A. Abel. The Abel boys. Ronnie and Dennis. No good. B. Blank. C . . . C. D. . . .

HESTER. Her brother worked at G.M.

JOHNNIE. I've got it. Carrol. Jessie Carrol.

HESTER. That's the one!

JOHNNIE. Jessica Carrol.

[*Places the box beside Hester and studies the photo over her shoulder.*]
Yes, that's her.

HESTER. She hated me.

JOHNNIE. Doesn't look like it.

HESTER. She hated my guts.

JOHNNIE. Got her arm through yours. Smiling. You too.

HESTER. Because we were having this picture taken! But she hated me all right. That time when I got the job at the Astoria Café—she also tried for it, but they took me. So she hated me more. And Stevie Jackson. He was supposed to be her boyfriend, but when he came home on leave it was me he was always running after and taking to Happy Valley. That's when she started telling everyone I had a price. So I buggered her up.

JOHNNIE. I remember now. Daddy was going to send you to reformatory for fighting in the streets.

HESTER. She started it. Scandalizing my name.

JOHNNIE. Hell of a thought, isn't it? Girls' reformatory! All the tough ones together.

HESTER. Who else was there? Me, her, the Abels, Stevie, Gertrude. There was about ten of us.

JOHNNIE. Magda Swanepoel.

HESTER. Yes.

JOHNNIE. Legransie.

HESTER. The Valley Road gang!

JOHNNIE. That's only eight. Me! Nine. . . .

HESTER. You weren't.

JOHNNIE. Wasn't I?

HESTER. You were too small.

JOHNNIE. I joined in the games.

HESTER. You mean you got in the way. Games! What could you play? Nothing. You were a nuisance. Always hanging around! We cook up an idea for something to do and off we go; and then somebody says: Your little brother is following us, Hester. I look back and there you are, trying to hide behind a lamp-post.

JOHNNIE. You used to throw stones at me.

HESTER. Not really.

JOHNNIE. You did, you know.

HESTER. I mean I never really aimed at you.

JOHNNIE [*persistent in his memory*]. Once or twice. . . .

HESTER. When you wouldn't go back!

JOHNNIE. . . . they came quite close.

HESTER. 'Where you going Hester?' 'Can I come with Hester?'

JOHNNIE. Because you were supposed to look after me.

HESTER. Didn't I?

JOHNNIE. Not always.

HESTER. What you complaining about? You're still alive.

JOHNNIE. That's true.

HESTER. You messed up some good times for me, my boy. When I did take you with me, you was always getting tired and crying and then I had to carry you. And when we got back always telling him . . . what we did.

JOHNNIE. He asked me.

HESTER. No, he didn't. You just told him.

JOHNNIE. Only to make him happy!

HESTER. By getting me in trouble.

JOHNNIE. NO! By telling him the truth. I just wanted to make him happy by telling him the truth. There was nothing else to tell the truth about. After you went there was nothing left. So many times he said: You always used to tell me the truth, Johnnie. I tried to explain. Hester's gone. There's nothing else, Daddy.

HESTER. You and him! There's a picture somewhere here, of him holding you . . . in the backyard.

[*She is paging through the album.*]

JOHNNIE [*moving away*]. I don't want to see!

HESTER. What's the matter with you? Here it is.

[*She studies the photo. Johnnie watches her.*]

JOHNNIE. Describe it.

HESTER. You're crying, and he's not smiling.

JOHNNIE. More.

HESTER. The backyard—just next to the door. . . .

[*Examining it closely.*]

If you look hard you can just see. . . .

JOHNNIE. Him! Daddy!

HESTER. His crutches.

JOHNNIE. Yes.

HESTER. The way he used to lean on them—sort of forward, but his head up, looking up. . . .

JOHNNIE. That's right.

HESTER. Not smiling. It looks like Sunday. What's the bet it was Sunday? He's got his suit on.

JOHNNIE [*turning to the crutches*]. I forgot all about these.

HESTER [*paging through the album*]. Look at them. What a mob!

[*Examining another one closely.*]

Frikkie! Frikkie Who? Relatives, I suppose.

JOHNNIE. Can you believe it? I forgot all about these being in there.

HESTER. Is this what we look like? A lot of mistakes? It's enough to make the dog vomit.

[*Closing the album.*]

Which box did it come from? Doesn't matter.

[*Defeated by the disorder around her, she puts the album aside negligently.*]

So what's going on?

JOHNNIE. There's another one next to you.

HESTER [*pointing*]. We been through that one?

JOHNNIE. Yes. Those old curtains.

HESTER [*pointing to the new box*]. Well, it better be in here.

[*This box is also tied with string.*]

Where's that knife?

JOHNNIE [*pointing to the crutches*]. I put them on top of the wardrobe after he had that fall—he said his walking days were over—and then I forgot all about them.

HESTER. What?

JOHNNIE. These. The crutches.

HESTER [*She can't find the knife and is trying to break the string with her hands*]. Doesn't he use them any more?

[*Pause. Johnnie stares at her.*]

I asked doesn't he use them any more!

JOHNNIE. Sssssssh! I thought I heard a groan. No. I carry him. When I sweep the room I carry him in here. He's not heavy.

HESTER. Where's that knife? This looks good, man. It's tied up tight. Maybe it's in here!

JOHNNIE. It wasn't heavy.

HESTER. That doesn't mean a thing. It would be bank-notes. Come on, use your muscles.

JOHNNIE. You promised you would go, remember.

HESTER. Yes, yes. Hurry up.

[*The box is opened. Johnnie looks in past Hester's greedy hands.*]

JOHNNIE. Shoes!

[*Hester burrows through a collection of old shoes—men's, women's, and children's. From the bottom of the box she brings out a paper bag which she tears open. The contents spill on to the floor. Johnnie retrieves one.*]

Crutch-rubbers. Shoes and crutch-rubbers. Do you get it? Footwear! Amazing!

[*After a final scrabble through the box, Hester sits down wearily on the suitcase.*]

HESTER. What's the time? No, don't tell me. It doesn't matter.

JOHNNIE [*holding up a pair of girl's shoes*]. Yours?

HESTER. Turn them around. Yes.

JOHNNIE. Dainty. How old? Seven, eight, nine . . . ?

HESTER. Older. Ten or eleven.

[*Johnnie drops them carelessly on the floor.*]

Don't do that! Give here.

[*He passes her the shoes.*]

Yes, one of my birthdays. Mommie bought them, I think. I wore them all that day and after that they were my specials —Sundays and so on—until they pinched so much I couldn't wear them any more.

JOHNNIE. They're still in good shape.

HESTER. So what good was it saving them up for best? What's the use of them now? I wanted them then, when they fitted, when the other girls were laughing at my old ones and my father's socks. The second-hand Smits of Valley Road. That was us! You in my vests, me in his socks, Mommie in his old shoes because the best went into boxes, the boxes into cupboards, and then the door was locked. 'One day you'll thank me,' she used to say. *Ai*, Mommie! You were wrong. There should have been more.

JOHNNIE. More what?

HESTER. Anything. Everything. There wasn't enough of anything except hard times.

JOHNNIE. Because we were hard up. Breadwinner out of action.

HESTER. Other people are also poor but they don't live like we did. Look at the Abels—with only an *Ouma*!

[*Shoes in her hands.*]

Even the birthdays were buggered up by a present you didn't want, and didn't get anyway because it had to be saved. For the rainy day! I've hated rain all my life. The terrible to-morrow—when we're broke, when we're hungry, when we're cold, when we're sick. Why the hell did we go on living?

JOHNNIE [*leaving the box*]. This is fascinating. Let's test your powers of observation.

[*He puts three men's shoes on the floor in front of Hester.*]

HESTER. So?

JOHNNIE. Notice anything strange?

HESTER. I didn't come here to play games.

JOHNNIE. I spotted it. They're all left shoes. They're Daddy's. That's the leg he lost in the explosion!

[*Hester pushes the shoes away with her foot.*]

That's not a very nice thing to do.

HESTER. Run and tell him I did it. Go on . . . Run! Waste my time with rubbish.

[*Looking around.*]

That's what this is. Second-hand rubbish. What's it good for?

[*Johnnie is back on the crutches, examining them, tentatively trying one and then the other. He takes two crutch-rubbers out of his pocket and starts to put them on.*]

JOHNNIE. Our inheritance.

HESTER. All I'm inheriting tonight is bad memories. Makes me sick just to look at it. Can't we pack some away?

[*Hester scoops up an armful and goes around looking for an empty box, but can't find one.*]

JOHNNIE. I can't say I'm bored. Some interesting things are coming to light.

[*The crutch-rubbers are on.*]

There! Good as new.

HESTER [*pointing to a box*]. You quite sure we been through all this? Carefully? I can't remember these hats.

JOHNNIE. You should know. You said you would search the boxes.

HESTER. But you're supposed to tell me when you bring in a new one.

[*Drops the armful she is carrying for a greedy scrabble through the box—hats come out.*]

JOHNNIE. I can't get over this. These crutches. . . .

HESTER. Leave them alone. They're getting on my nerves.

JOHNNIE. But they're comfortable. I used to think they hurt, it looked so sore.

HESTER. I saw enough of them in the old days.

JOHNNIE. Remember his fear of banana-skins? How he used to stand at the window and watch the traffic in the street?

HESTER. Spying on us!

JOHNNIE. Hours on end. But no wonder. I could. It's like being propped up.

HESTER. Soon as I did something . . . Hester! I'm watching you! And there he was peeping behind the curtains.

[*Looks into another box.*]

JOHNNIE. You been through that one.

HESTER. I'm just making sure.

[*Sits.*]

Five hundred pounds is a lot of money.

JOHNNIE. Be the biggest wad I ever seen. Fat as a roll of lavatory paper. What you going to do with it?

HESTER. Plenty.

JOHNNIE. Such as?

HESTER. Such as anything I like. Once you got money you can do anything you like. Change my name! Stay at a posh hotel! I could. And then let them try and refuse to serve me just because I'm sitting by myself in the lounge.

JOHNNIE. What do you mean?

[*During Hester's next speech he moves behind her back and there tries out the crutches—a few steps, different positions, opening an imaginary door, etc., etc.*]

HESTER. Some of those big-shot places don't serve you if you're a woman by yourself. I wasn't trying for a pick-up. I just wanted a few beers and a little peace and quiet somewhere nice for a change. They're supposed to be open to the public! But when I walked in they all started staring and then this coolie waiter comes to me and says they don't serve 'ladies' by themselves. Well, this time they will. Because I'll be a boarder. I'll pay in advance. And then let one of those bitches smile as though she's not also selling what she's got between her legs. Give them a chance to say Yes and I DO —because who the hell ever says no—put a ring on their finger and they think they're better! That being married gives them a licence to do it! I'm sick of that lot with their husbands and fashions and happy families. They don't fool me. And I'll tell them. Happy families is fat men crawling on to frightened women. And when you've had enough he doesn't stop, 'lady'. I've washed more of your husbands out of me than ever gave you babies.

JOHNNIE. That's known as exposing your dirty linen in a place of public entertainment.

HESTER. Who the hell do they think they are? Laughing at us like we're a dirty joke or something. Let them live in a back-room where the lavatory is blocked again and the drain is crawling with cockroaches and see if they go on smelling like the soap counter in Woolworth's. Money, brother. Money! You can do anything with money. And my turn is coming. Bring in the boxes. I've wasted enough time.

[*Johnnie leans the crutches against a chair and exits into father's room. Hester moves with a new resolution—clearing a space around her for the next boxes. Johnnie returns with one.*]

JOHNNIE. Light as a feather.

HESTER. Get the others! And put them down here. I don't want them mixed up any more. I mean business now. Soon as I find the money I'm on my way.

[*Johnnie is back with the crutches.*]

And leave those crutches alone for Christ sake.

JOHNNIE. Just—what's the word?—practising.

HESTER. That's mockery.

JOHNNIE. Who?

HESTER. You. You're mocking him.

JOHNNIE. Oh, no.

HESTER. Yes it is. Mockery of a cripple.

JOHNNIE. No, no, no, no.

HESTER. You wait until he catches you.

JOHNNIE. Sssssssh! Keep it down.

[*Exit Johnnie, returning a few seconds later with another load—two bundles of newspapers wrapped up in brown paper and tied with string.*]

HESTER [*still busy with the last box*]. What's all this?

JOHNNIE [*joins her to examine the contents of the box*]. Looks like seeds. Yes. Look here. . . .

[*Pointing to one of the brown paper packets which have come out.*]

. . . Marigolds. Well, I'll be. . . .

[*Taking out other packets.*]

Watermelons, pumpkins, onions . . . beans!

HESTER [*abandoning the box and turning to the bundles*]. And these?

JOHNNIE. Old Mother Earth!

HESTER. Wake up. What's these?

JOHNNIE. Dunno. In the corner next to the wardrobe.

HESTER. Break the strings.

[*Johnnie breaks the string—newspapers spill out. He returns to the seeds.*]

Liewe God!

JOHNNIE. I think they would grow, you know. They've been kept in a cool dry place. All they need now is direct sunlight and Bob's Your Uncle . . . fresh veg.

HESTER. Leave them.

JOHNNIE. But think of it. Ripe watermelons!

HESTER. Get the other boxes.

[*A last scrabble through the pile of newspapers—she picks up one.*]

1937. Six years old. You weren't even born yet.

JOHNNIE. Let's see. 'Roosevelt refuses. . . .'

HESTER [*tearing the paper out of his hands*]. If you don't get those boxes I'll go in there myself!

JOHNNIE. Don't move. I'm on my way.

[*Exit into father's room.*]

[*Hester tries to push back the second flood of rubbish. Johnnie returns with two boxes, puts them down, and exits again. Hester opens these two boxes to find old clothes. She is still busy with them when Johnnie returns with yet another.*]

JOHNNIE. Here's one. Heavy as lead. And listen!

[*He shakes it—Hester abandons the boxes she is busy with and turns feverishly on the new one. It contains packets of old nails, screws, a few tools, a brass door-handle, old keys, etc., etc.*]

Hardware! They thought of everything.

HESTER. More junk. Ten bob on the sale.

JOHNNIE [*holding up a hammer*]. You couldn't buy a ball-pane like this today for love or money.

HESTER. Ten bob on the sale—if you're lucky!

[*She returns to the two half-empty boxes. Johnnie goes through the papers on the floor.*]

[*Holding up a badly torn but clean white shirt.*]

Look at this!

JOHNNIE. 'Chamberlain refuses German offer!' January 1937.

HESTER. A kaffir wouldn't polish the floor with it.

JOHNNIE [*looking at another headline*]. . . . .

HESTER. Other people would have chucked it away.

JOHNNIE. Thirty-six. December 1936.

[*He starts examining the dates on all the papers.*]

HESTER. But we kept it. The Smits of Valley Road washed it, ironed it, folded it up, and packed it away.

JOHNNIE. November 1936. Nearer!

HESTER. Nearer what?

JOHNNIE. 1931, or '30 or '32. Don't you remember? The Bad Years. 1931 onwards. When he worked on the line to Graaff-Reinet. You remember, man. Daddy. He was always telling us. Something terrible had happened somewhere and it was

Bad Times . . . no jobs, no money. That's what he dreams about now.

The kaffirs sit and watch them work. The white men are hungry. Everybody is greedy. Specially about work—more greedy even than with food. Because work is food—not just today but tomorrow is work. So men look at another man's work the way they used to look at his wife. And those that got it work until the blisters burst and their backs break. He queued for a week to get the job—laying sleepers. Last week ten of his friends was fired. So you work like devils. *They got to see you work!*

And all the time the kaffirs sit and watch the white man doing kaffir work—hungry for the work. They are dying by the dozen!

And then one day in the kloof the other side of Heuningvlei he thought the end had come. His back was hurting like never before, his blisters were running blood. So he cried in the wilderness. 'Why hast thou forsaken me, Lord?' Like Moses. 'Why hast thou forsaken thy lamb?' But it wasn't the end.

That night the railway doctor came to the tents with embrocation and bandages—and he carried on. One mile a day. Heuningvlei, Boesmanspoort, Tierberg, Potterstop. . . . He knows them all! And when they reached Graaff-Reinet the Lord's purpose in all suffering was revealed. Because there he met Mommie.

'I was there in the wilderness—like Moses. The sleepers bent my back, the Lord bent my spirit. But I was not broken. It took dynamite to do that!' Hey?

HESTER. Don't make me sick.

JOHNNIE [*attempting another quote*]. 'And God said unto Moses. . . .'

HESTER. Dry up! I've heard it all. Moses said this, and Abraham said that, and Jesus says something else. Sunday School is over. I'm not a kid any more. Get the other boxes.

JOHNNIE [*collecting the newspapers together*]. In a jiffy.

HESTER. What you doing with those?

JOHNNIE. You might not know it but this is history.

HESTER. Chuck them out.

JOHNNIE. I'd like to read them. When you're gone and life settles down again. There's enough here for. . . .

HESTER. You're as bad as them. It's rubbish.

JOHNNIE. That doesn't stop it from being interesting.

HESTER. I'll chuck them out.

JOHNNIE. No, you won't.

HESTER. Who's going to stop me?

JOHNNIE. Hester!

HESTER. You and who? Him?

JOHNNIE. Hester, if you start something and he wakes up and has a stroke . . . God help you.

HESTER. Here we go again. God help you. God help us. No chance of that, my boy. He never gave a damn about what happened in this house.

JOHNNIE. That sort of talk is not for my ears. I'll get the boxes.
[*Exit.*]

HESTER. And I don't blame him! Look at it. Who the hell would have wanted anything to do with us? We weren't just poor. It was something worse. Second-hand! Life in here was second-hand . . . used up and old before we even got it. Nothing ever reached us new. Even the days felt like the whole world had lived them out before they reached us.
[*Johnnie reappears empty-handed.*]

JOHNNIE. Hester.

HESTER. Where's the box?
[*Exit Johnnie.*]
Why the hell did I ever come back?
[*Johnnie reappears, a box in his hand, but he doesn't hand it over immediately.*]

JOHNNIE. Hester.

HESTER. Wasn't there one thing worth saving from all those years?

JOHNNIE. Hester!

HESTER. I'm not talking loud.

JOHNNIE. What will you do if you don't find it?

HESTER. I don't know. I don't even know what it is yet. Just one thing that's got a good memory. I think and think. I try to remember. There must have been something that made me happy. All those years. Just once. Happy.

JOHNNIE. No, I mean the money. The compensation. What will you do if you don't. . . .

[*Pause.*]

Have you . . . ? Yes, you have, haven't you?

[*Hester looks with bewilderment at the chaos around her.*]

You've forgotten what you're looking for!

HESTER. Shut up!

[*She moves among the boxes with growing desperation.*]

You think I've missed it? How long have I been . . . ? Which one did you bring in last? Are you deaf? When did this one come in?

JOHNNIE. I don't know. I've just been fetching. You . . . you said you would. . . .

[*Hester scratches around on the edge of panic.*]

What will you do if you don't . . . ?

HESTER. Something that will make you regret the day you were born.

JOHNNIE [*closing his eyes*]. Dear God, please let Hester find the money!

[*Opening his eyes.*]

Any luck?

HESTER. Get the other!

[*She takes the box from his hand and when he doesn't move immediately gives him a violent shove.*]

Move!

[*Exit Johnnie. As soon as he is out of the room, Hester collapses into a chair, placing the box on the floor at her feet. She stares at it without seeing it—a few seconds of complete vacancy. Then gradually we feel the box intrude itself into her consciousness, challenging her. Without any of the panic of a few seconds previously she opens it and starts to work methodically through its contents. Near the top she finds a bundle of papers.*

Johnnie returns—he is tensed and watches Hester in silence for a few seconds.]

JOHNNIE. All those in favour of sleep hold up their hands!

[*Hester is busy with the papers and ignores him.*]

Hester!

HESTER. What?

JOHNNIE. Bedtime.

HESTER. No.

JOHNNIE. Nothing's going to run away. Tell you what. . . .

HESTER. I said no! Now shut up! Sleep. In here? I'd rather pay a penny and sit all night in a public lavatory. Bring in the other boxes.

[*Goes back to the papers. Johnnie sees the crutches and goes on to them.*]

Documents.

JOHNNIE. I've got something to tell you.

HESTER [*looking at the papers*]. Somebody was born, somebody was baptized, somebody was something else . . . married. . . .

[*Retrieves the paper just discarded.*]

Them. Mommie and Daddy. 1931. Graaff-Reinet. Johannes Cornelius Smit. Anna Van Rooyen.

JOHNNIE. Happily married, faithfully parted by death.

HESTER. Since when?

JOHNNIE. 1931 onwards. Through the years, the setbacks, the hardships. . . .

HESTER. Since when was it happily married?

JOHNNIE. Daddy. He told me. . . .

HESTER. Then tell him from me he's a liar.

JOHNNIE. I've always believed it.

HESTER. Well, you're wrong. What did you know about her? You wasn't even five years when she died.

JOHNNIE. That's true. I've no memories.

HESTER. And I've got plenty. So don't talk to me about happily married.

JOHNNIE. What was she like?

HESTER. See for yourself. There's a picture in the album—it's here somewhere. Smallish. None of her things fitted me when I was big. Always working—working, working, working. . . .

[*Pause.*]

Frightened. She worked harder than anybody I ever seen in my life, because she was frightened. He frightened her. She said I frightened her. Our fights frightened her. She died frightened of being dead.

[*She sees Johnnie staring at her.*]

I saw her face in the coffin.

JOHNNIE. You what?

HESTER. Saw her, in the coffin.

JOHNNIE. You peeped?

HESTER. They gave you a last look.

[*She is talking with the calculated indifference of someone not sure of their self-control.*]

He was there. Some uncles and aunties.

JOHNNIE. Where was I?

HESTER. Somewhere else. You were too young.

They pushed me forward. 'Say goodbye to your Mommie, Hester.' I said it—but I couldn't cry. I was dry and hot inside. Ashamed! Of us. Of her, Mommie, for being dead and causing all the fuss. Of him, Daddy, his face cracked like one of our old plates, saying things he never said when she was alive.

And all the uncles and aunties kissing him and patting him on the back and saying 'Shame!' every time they saw you. It was those cousins of his from Despatch, who never ever came to visit us. The whole mob of them, all in black, the little girls in pretty dresses, looking at everything in the house, and us looking like poor whites because there wasn't enough cups to give everybody coffee at the same time. I hated it! I hated Mommie for being dead. I couldn't cry. I cried later. I don't know, maybe two days. Everything was over, the relatives gone. He was in bed with shock. The house was quiet like never before.

Then there was a knock at the back door. I opened it and it was that coolie who always sold the vegetables. 'Where's your Mommie?' he asked. I couldn't say anything at first. 'Girlie, where's your Mommie?' Then I told him. 'Dead.' I just said, 'Dead,' and started to cry. He took off his hat and stood there watching me until I shouted, '*Voetsek!*' and chased him away—and sat down and cried and cried. Because suddenly I knew she was dead, and what it meant, being dead. It's goodbye for keeps. She was gone for ever. So I cried. There was something I wanted to do, but it was too late.

JOHNNIE. What did you want to do?

HESTER. Nothing.

[*Looking at the certificate in her hand.*]

Johannes Cornelius Smit—Anna Van Rooyen. Biggest mistake she ever made!

JOHNNIE. You don't know what you're saying.

HESTER. Yes, I do! I'm saying this was the biggest mistake she ever made. Marriage! One man's slave all your life, slog away until you're in your grave. For what? Happiness in Heaven? I seen them—Ma and the others like her, with more kids than they can count, and no money; bruises every pay-day because he comes home drunk or another one in the belly because he was so drunk he didn't know it was his old wife and got into bed!

JOHNNIE. Daddy never beat Mommie. He was never drunk.

HESTER. Because he couldn't. He was a crock. But he did it other ways. She fell into her grave the way they all do—tired, *moeg*. Frightened! I saw her.

JOHNNIE. This is terrible, Hester.

HESTER. You're damned right it is. It's hell. They live in hell, but they're too frightened to do anything about it because there's always somebody around shouting God and Judgement.

Mommie should have taken what she wanted and then kicked him out.

JOHNNIE. And the children.

HESTER. So what! If you get them you get them and if you don't want them there's ways.

JOHNNIE. Hester! Hester!

HESTER. Hester, Hester what? Hester who? Hester Smit! That's me. I've done it. And I don't care a damn. Two months old and I got rid of it.

JOHNNIE. When the time comes to face your maker. . . .

HESTER. THIS is my time. Now! And no man is going to bugger it up for me the way he did for Mommie.

JOHNNIE. You can be grateful Mommie didn't think like you.

HESTER. Look, there's a couple of words I hate and grateful is one of them.

JOHNNIE. Suppose she had done what you did, and it was YOU. You wouldn't be here now.

HESTER. So I'm here because she was a fool. We're all somebody else's mistake. You. Him too. This. The whole damned thing is a mistake. The sooner they blow it up with their atom bombs the better.

JOHNNIE. You'd like that!

HESTER. Yes.

JOHNNIE. The end of the world.

HESTER. Couldn't care less.

JOHNNIE. If it really had to happen. . . .

HESTER. I'd die laughing. At the look on your faces.

JOHNNIE. Nothing . . . nothing matters?

HESTER. Such as what? Find it.

[*Pointing to the chaos around her.*]

One thing. Marriage?

[*She crumples up the certificate in her hand and throws it away.*]

Being born? Being dead? They're mistakes. All we unpacked here tonight is mistakes.

JOHNNIE. Hester.

HESTER. And the sooner somebody rubs it out the better.

JOHNNIE. Hester, wait.

HESTER. What?

JOHNNIE. I dare you . . . I dare you to commit suicide. Now!

[*She stares at him.*]

JOHNNIE. You said nothing matters. Prove it. I dare you!

HESTER [*statement of fact*]. You dare me.

JOHNNIE. Yes.

HESTER. *Ja,* that's right.

JOHNNIE. You will?

HESTER [*ignoring his question*]. You were always daring me. You used to find it—the thing you were too scared to do, and dare me, and watch while I did it and got into trouble. That's what you want, hey? You and him. 'Hester's in trouble again, Pa!'

JOHNNIE. You won't?

HESTER. No.

[*She goes back to the papers.*]

JOHNNIE [*to himself*]. Too much to hope for.

HESTER. You won't get rid of me that easily.

JOHNNIE. But I tried. Whatever happens nobody can say I didn't try. Be brave.

HESTER [*reading from one of the papers*]. 'Johannes Albertus Smit.' That's you.

JOHNNIE. Yes, in full. What's it say?

HESTER [*scanning the letter*]. 'Your application. . . .' The Kroonstad Railway School. From the Principal. Saying they accept your application to be a learner-stoker. And a second-class voucher to get there. November, 1958.

JOHNNIE. Too late now.

HESTER. But you said you tore up your application.

JOHNNIE. That's right.

HESTER. Because you didn't want to go.

JOHNNIE. So?

HESTER. So here he says he *got* your application.

JOHNNIE. These things happen.

[*Pause. Hester thinks about this.*]

HESTER. No. No, they don't. He wouldn't tell you to come if you didn't have asked him if you could come.

JOHNNIE. Where does that get us?

HESTER. You *did* post that application.

JOHNNIE. I see.

HESTER. But you told me you didn't.

JOHNNIE. All right I made a mistake. I forgot. I applied. Satisfied?

HESTER. You didn't forget. You lied to me. You know you posted it.

JOHNNIE. I'm telling you I forgot.

HESTER. You knew they said you must come.

JOHNNIE. Can't I forget things too?

HESTER. And you wanted to go!

JOHNNIE. Maybe . . . it's a long time ago . . . ten years . . . my memory. . . .

HESTER. Don't try to get out of it.

JOHNNIE [*desperate*]. What do you want me to say?

HESTER. What are you trying to hide?

JOHNNIE. Nothing. So leave me alone. Understand? Just leave us alone. Take what you want and go!

[*He is squirming—then a clumsy move and the crutches fall—he stands on his feet.*]

Look, what you've made me do!!

[*Pause.*]

Yes, I wanted to go.
They are the most beautiful things in the world! Black, and hot, hissing, and the red glow of their furnaces, their whistles blowing out like ribbons in the wind! And the engine driver, grade one, and his stoker up there, leaning out of the cab, watching the world like kings!
Yes, I wanted to go.
I could have gone. It was up to me. He didn't say anything to stop me posting the forms in duplicate. And when I got the letter saying I must come he even said he was happy because now his son would also work for the railways. I said I'd come home for all my holidays to be with him and give the house a good sweep out. And when I was packing my suitcase he gave me one of his railway shirts—even made a joke, with tears in his eyes—said it would fit when my muscles were big. So there we stood with tears in our eyes, him on his crutches—me with my suitcase. He came to the door and waved to me all the way down Valley Road.

[*Pause.*]

I got as far as the bridge. Nine o'clock in the morning, sun shining, the world a hustle and a bustle, everybody busy, happy—only him, back there. . . .

So, back there. Simple as that. Here. I told him I missed the train. We agreed it was God's will being done. He helped me unpack. Said I could still keep the shirt.

[*Pause.*]

He's not to blame. He was no problem. What he wants, or God wants, I can do. I fetch, I cook, I sweep, I wash, I wait . . . it was ME. What I wanted.

HESTER. What's the matter, Johnnie? Are you scared of hating him?

JOHNNIE. He was my father.

HESTER. He did that to Mommie.

JOHNNIE. She was his wife.

HESTER. Said God and you all felt like sinners. Hate him!

JOHNNIE. How can I hate . . . ?

HESTER. You're frightened of him.

JOHNNIE. Maybe.

HESTER. Yes!

JOHNNIE. All right, yes!

HESTER. You're frightened of hating him!

JOHNNIE. No.

HESTER. You want to hate him.

JOHNNIE. Definitely, no.

HESTER. I hate him! There, I've said it, and I'm still alive. I hate my father.

JOHNNIE. I don't love, I don't hate. I play it safe. I come when called, I go when chased, I laugh when laughed at. . . .

HESTER. Don't make yourself another piece of junk! Hate him! It's clean and new. Let's find something tonight that isn't worn out and second-hand—something bright and sharp and dangerous.

[*Johnnie reacts with terror to this tirade. He picks up the crutches but Hester tries to stop him from going on to them.*]

Don't, Johnnie!

JOHNNIE. Let go.

HESTER. No.

JOHNNIE. I feel faint.

HESTER. They're not yours.

JOHNNIE. They fit.

HESTER. Don't you understand? They're his. They're him.

JOHNNIE. I'll ask him for them—tomorrow—when you're gone—I'll tell him. . . .

HESTER. Are you mad?

JOHNNIE. He doesn't need them. I carry him. . . .

HESTER. YOU don't need them!

JOHNNIE [*anguish*]. I NEED SOMETHING! LOOK AT ME!

[*Hester lets go of them and Johnnie goes on to them with feverish intensity.*]

Aina! Aina!

HESTER. Then take them. Be cripple!

JOHNNIE. God's will be done. . . .

HESTER. You already look like him. . . .

JOHNNIE. . . . in hell as in heaven. . . .

HESTER. . . . and sound like him. . . .

JOHNNIE. I am his son. He is my father. Flesh of his flesh.

HESTER. That's right. Lick his arse, crawl right up it until your feet hang out. Be HIM.

JOHNNIE. God forgive. . . .

HESTER. That's what you want, isn't it?

JOHNNIE. God forgive you for what you are saying.

HESTER. THERE IS NO GOD! THERE NEVER WAS!
We've unpacked our life, Johannes Cornelius Smit, the years in Valley Road, and there is no God. Nothing but rubbish. In this house there was nothing but useless . . .

[*Amok among the contents of the boxes—picking up and throwing about whatever she can get her hands on.*]

. . . second-hand poor-white junk!

[*Realizes too late that she has just hurled her mother's dress to the floor.*]

No, no! Look what I've done. Why didn't you stop me?

[*She retrieves it.*]

Mommie, not you. I forgot, not you.

[*Smelling it.*]

She's gone. The smell. . . . I can't. . . . It's gone.

Too late again. Just a rag. An empty rag.

That's how it happened. She got lost, among the rubbish.
I forgot she was here—in here, alive, to touch, to talk to, to
love. She was a chance in here to love something. I wanted
to. The hating was hard. Hate! Hate! So much to hate I
forgot she was here.

[*Smelling the dress.*]

What was it? Mothballs and blue soap. Mothballs in the
wardrobe, sixpence blue soap from the Chinaman on the
corner. Washing, always washing. She was clean. I stink,
Mommie. I'm dirty and I stink. All the hardships, the hating.
I couldn't stop hating and it hurts, it hurts.

JOHNNIE. Pain?

HESTER. It hurts.

JOHNNIE. Home ground!

HESTER. It hurts.

JOHNNIE. An ache or a throb?

HESTER [*intoning non-stop*]. Aina aina aina. . . .

JOHNNIE [*hobbling around on the crutches*]. Wilson's Beef and
Iron! Double dose! Kill or cure! Hold your nose! Open your
mouth! Down the hatch. . . .

[*He gets a spoonful into Hester's mouth. She spits it out violently and
coughs. Johnnie slaps her on the back.*]

Cough it up! Get it off your chest.

HESTER [*pushing him away*]. What's going on?

JOHNNIE. Double dose down the wrong pipe.

HESTER. Shut up!

[*Pause.*]

Here and now!

JOHNNIE. This? This is . . . was . . . will be for ever and ever.
. . . Let us pray: Oh Lord . . . something . . . our daily bread,

brown bread, the broken loaf and Amen. Grace at supper.
By the grace of God, you me and him in the light of the
lamp with our heads bowed at supper.

This . . . is our home. You've come home. The prodigal
daughter has. . . .

HESTER. The Compensation!

[*Pause.*]

JOHNNIE. That's right. But. . . .

HESTER. Five hundred pounds!

JOHNNIE. According to you.

HESTER. I'll be rich.

JOHNNIE. If you ever find it.

HESTER. So what are we waiting for? Bring in the boxes.

JOHNNIE. There's a catch.

HESTER. Bring in the boxes!!

JOHNNIE. There's none left.

[*Pause.*]

You've had the lot.

HESTER. This . . . ?

JOHNNIE. Is all. The lot. There's nothing left.

HESTER. So where's the money?

JOHNNIE. I tried to warn you.

HESTER. Five hundred pounds. Where is it?

JOHNNIE. I suppose he never got it.

[*Pause.*]

Now you must go. You promised. I'll help you pack.

HESTER. NO!

You've found it.

JOHNNIE. Hester. . . .

HESTER. Let me feel your pockets.

JOHNNIE. You promised you would go.

HESTER. Then he's got it.

JOHNNIE. No.

HESTER. He's awake!

JOHNNIE. NO.

HESTER. He knows I'm looking for it and he's hiding it. Go in there and tell him I want it.

JOHNNIE. 'Strue's there's a living God. . . .

HESTER. If you won't I will!

JOHNNIE. That will kill him. He hates the sight of you.

HESTER [*shouting*]. Johannes Cornelius Smit, I want my share!

JOHNNIE. I'm warning you.

[*Exit Hester into father's room.*]

Something's going to happen now. There's dynamite, some-where in this house. In Hester's heart. The heart that hurts. Was it like this? Did he feel like this? He was running—the others were shouting. I'm standing still, nobody's shouting. . . . 'I was standing still, leaning on my. . . .'

[*Hester returns slowly.*]

Five, four, three, two, one. . . .

HESTER. Where is he?

JOHNNIE. Dead.

HESTER. Dead?

JOHNNIE. Dead as a dud. He died.

[*Hester approaches Johnnie.*]

Gave up the ghost—all the words! . . . called by God, with the singing angels . . . laid to rest. . . .

[*Hester is now in front of Johnnie. She hits him once. He closes his eyes and speaks with bitter violence.*]

The Beef and Iron was a flop! Double dose three times a day! But he died!

[*Hester pulls the crutches out from under his arms. He falls to the ground. She kicks him.*]

More! Explode! Swallow me up. Let the mountain fall! This is the end of the world.

[*Hester goes down on her knees to beat Johnnie with clenched fists—stopping eventually from sheer exhaustion. She gets up and staggers to a chair. Johnnie remains on the floor—he will not move until after Hester's final exit.*]

[*A long pause as the violence ebbs.*]

Don't be fooled. This isn't silence. I can hear you breathing

Silence isn't what you think it is. Silence is waiting—for it to happen, anything—a noise, or a groan or a call.

Sometimes it wasn't any of them—just the sound of his medicine bottles rattling in the dark in the middle of the night. But I was waiting. I'd go in and see if he was all right. 'Have I got enough?' he'd ask me. So I'd look. 'Yes, chum, you've got enough. Six doses if there's a drop.' 'Even so,' he would say, 'get me another bottle tomorrow—the safe side in case of.'

And sometimes when it was like that, the waiting just stopped, the silence went and there were frogs croaking in the river or a cricket in the yard. Little Happy Noises! And we would talk quietly. One night it was all about modern means of transport and he was saying he could still remember the old ox-wagon days and how long it took to go from Despatch to P.E. . . . Suddenly in the middle of it his face went all sort of puffy! His mouth started shivering, he closed his eyes. I thought it was a stroke! Then I saw he was crying.

'Don't let them cut off my other leg,' he said. 'Promise you won't let them.'

'Don't be silly,' I said. 'Of course they won't. Why would they do a stupid thing like that?' 'But promise me you won't let them if they want to all the same.' 'Over my dead body, chum,' I said. 'Over my dead body.'

I went back to bed.

HESTER. Johnnie.

JOHNNIE [*doesn't hear her*]. I missed the end.

HESTER. Johnnie!

JOHNNIE. He died in my sleep.

HESTER. When?

   [*Pause.*]

A long time ago? Yesterday?

JOHNNIE. Something like that.

HESTER. Today?

JOHNNIE. No! The other day.

I woke up on the sofa the other day, just lay there waiting for the first cough or call of the new day. Waited and waited. Started to wonder. Got worried. Went in, 'Rise and Shine!' I said. 'Beef and Iron time, Daddy!'

[Pause.]

Nothing.

[Pause.]

[Hester leaves the room quietly, wearily.]

The room was dark, the curtain still closed. I listened . . . I didn't want to look!

[Loud.]

'Daddy!' I sat on my chair next to his bed.

'Wake up, Lazybones! You'll miss the early worm!' . . . all our little jokes. I waited and waited . . . it might have been days . . . called and called till I knew he was dead.

I tried to work it out. 'This is it,' I thought. 'The end.' Of what? Of him. Of Waiting. Of pain in the other room.

'You're on your own, Johnnie Smit,' I said to myself. 'From now on it's you—just you and wherever you are—you in the middle of a moment. The other room is empty.'

[Hester returns, her coat on, carrying her suitcase. She puts it down and sits on it.]

HESTER. I'm on my way.

JOHNNIE. Where.

HESTER. Back. My room. I'm paid up for the month. There's a week left. She won't even know I'm gone.

JOHNNIE. When's the train leave?

HESTER. Sometime. Ten o'clock.

JOHNNIE. That's right. All stations via Kommodagga.

HESTER. I'll wait at the station. I've had enough of this.

JOHNNIE. There's some bread somewhere . . . butter and jam . . . make yourself sandwiches. It's a long trip.

HESTER. Get up, Johnnie.

JOHNNIE. I'm just resting.

HESTER. I'm sorry about what happened. I didn't mean it. But why did you lie to me? Bluff he was in there?

JOHNNIE. I am. . . . *[Pause.]*

HESTER. What?

JOHNNIE. It's hard to describe. It feels like . . . I'm ashamed. Of me. Of being alone. Just me in my whole life. It was so

different with him. He was in there, something else, somewhere else. Even tonight, just pretending it helped. You
believed he was in there, didn't you?

HESTER. Yes.

JOHNNIE. If only his ghost would come back and haunt me!
Even if I went grey with fright! Do you believe in ghosts,
Hester?

HESTER. Hang on, Johnnie. Listen—pack up and come with
me.

JOHNNIE. Where?

HESTER. Jo'burg. Where else?

JOHNNIE. A holiday?

HESTER. Or for good.

JOHNNIE. And then?

HESTER. Anything! Anything's better than this, *Boetie*. Get a
job, a girl, have some good times. What do you say?

[*Pause. She realizes it is useless.*]

You won't come.

JOHNNIE. Suppose—just suppose there are ghosts, and he did
come back to haunt, and I was gone!
I'll stay. Just in case, I'll wait.

HESTER [*gesture to the chaos on the floor, the house*]. Anyway you
can have it. Okay? It's all yours. The house and everything.
Tell them I said it's yours.

JOHNNIE. Who?

HESTER. The people. There's always people around when
somebody dies. Officials. Tell them I gave you my share.
It was my will. Read the newspapers, plant the seeds, have
a garden. . . .

JOHNNIE. Don't you need dung?

HESTER. That's it! . . . Live happily. Try, Johnnie, try to be
happy.

JOHNNIE. Why? What's this?

HESTER. I don't know. I don't know what it is. But there's
something else—something we never had.

JOHNNIE. And you? Any plans?

HESTER. Back like I said. There's always jobs. And I got my room. That's me—a woman in a room. I'm used to it now.

[*Stands and moves upstage to the edge of the light.*]

It's strange, you know. I can see it—see it happening. All of this. I'll walk out of that door, through the streets to the station, sit in the waiting-room. Then the train at ten and all the way back. It's hard. Things are too clear. This, there, Jo'burg tomorrow when I get there. The rooms—the dark rooms, the many faces—and one of them me, Hester Smit. I'm too far away from my life.

I want to get back to it, in it, be it, be me again the way it was when I walked in. It will come, I suppose. But at this moment—there she is waiting, here she is going, and somebody's watching all of it. But it isn't God. It's me.

Goodbye, Johnnie.

[*Exit Hester.*]

[*Johnnie makes a move as if to get up, then sees the crutches some distance away from him on the floor. He stares at them for a few seconds then very laboriously drags himself along the floor to them. With equal effort he holds them upright and goes on to them.*

He stands still, on one leg for a few seconds, then realizes he is standing on the wrong leg and changes over.]

JOHNNIE. Why not? It solves problems. Let's face it—a man on his own two legs is a shaky proposition. She said it was mine. All of it—my inheritance. These, seeds . . . and memories. More than enough!

They can look now. Shine their lights in my face, stare as hard as they like. I've got a reason. I'm a man with a story. 'I was eating prickly pears, Mister, leaning on my spade having a rest, minding my own business, when suddenly the earth opened and the mountain fell on me. . . .'

They'll say shame, buy me a beer, help me on buses, stop the traffic when I cross the street . . . slowly. . . .

Yes! Everything slower now. Everything changed. The time it takes. Leave at sunset, arrive in the dark, twilight on the bridge. The shadow on the wall different . . . but me . . . a different me!

What's the word? Birth. Death. Both. Jesus did it in the Bible.
 [*Pause.*]
Resurrection.
 [*Pause.*]

CURTAIN

BOESMAN AND LENA

A PLAY
IN TWO ACTS

CHARACTERS

BOESMAN, *a Coloured man*
LENA, *a Coloured woman*
OUTA, *an old African*

BOESMAN AND LENA was first produced at the Rhodes University Little Theatre, Grahamstown, on 10 July 1969 with the following cast:

BOESMAN	Athol Fugard
LENA	Yvonne Bryceland
OUTA	Glynn Day

ACT ONE

An empty stage.

A Coloured man—Boesman—walks on. Heavily burdened. On his back an old mattress and blanket, a blackened paraffin tin, an apple box . . . these contain a few simple cooking utensils, items of clothing etc., etc. With one hand he is dragging a piece of corrugated iron. Barefoot, shapeless grey trousers rolled up to just below the knee, an old shirt, faded and torn sports-club blazer, cap on his head.

He chooses a spot, then drops the corrugated iron, gets down his load, and slumps to the ground beside it. He has obviously walked very far. He waits.

After a few seconds a Coloured woman—Lena—appears. She is similarly burdened—no mattress though—and carries her load on her head. As a result, she walks with characteristic stiff-necked rigidity. There is a bundle of firewood under one arm. Also barefoot. Wearing one of those sad dresses that reduce the body to an angular, gaunt cipher of poverty.

A life of hardship and dissipation obscures their ages, but they are most probably in their fifties.

Boesman looks up slowly as Lena appears. He watches her with a hard, cruel objectivity. He says nothing. She has been reduced to a dumb, animal-like submission by the weight of her burden and the long walk behind them, and in this condition almost misses him sitting to one side, propped up against his bundle. Realizing she has passed him, she stops, but does not turn to face him in case they have to walk still further.

LENA. Here?

[*Boesman clears his throat and spits. She waits a few seconds longer for a word from him, then turns slowly and joins him. The bundle of firewood falls to the ground. Her arms go up and with the last of her strength she gets her bundle down. Her relief as she does so is almost painful. She sits down slowly. For a few seconds she just rests, her head between her knees, breathing deeply. Then she stretches forward and works a finger between the toes of one of her feet. It comes away with a piece of mud. She looks at it, squashing it between her fingers.*]

Mud! Swartkops!

[*She now looks at the world around her for the first time—she knows*

it well—then still higher up, into the sky, searching for something.]
Too late now. [*Pause.*] No. There's one.

[*She is obviously staring up at a bird. Softly . . .*]

Jou moer!

[*She watches it for a few seconds longer, then scrambles to her feet and shakes her fist at it.*]

Jou moer!!

[*Boesman watches her, then the bird, then Lena again. Her eyes follow it as it glides out of sight.*]

So slowly . . . ! Must be a feeling, hey. Even your shadow so heavy you leave it on the ground.

[*She sits down again, even more exhausted now by her outburst. She cleans the mud from between her other toes while she talks.*]

Tomorrow they'll hang up there in the wind and laugh. We'll be in the mud. I hate them.

[*She looks at Boesman.*]

Why did you walk so hard? In a hurry to get here? 'Here', Boesman! What's here? This . . . [*the mud between her fingers*] . . . and tomorrow. And that will be like this! *Vrot!* This piece of world is rotten. Put down your foot and you're in it up to your knee.

That last *skof* was hard. Against the wind. I thought you were never going to stop. Heavier and heavier. Every step. This afternoon heavier than this morning. This time heavier than last time. And there's other times coming. '*Vat jou goed en trek!* Whiteman says *Voetsek!* Eina!*

[*Boesman is watching her with undisguised animosity and disgust.*]

Remember the old times? Quick march! Even run . . . [*a little laugh*] . . . when they chased us. Don't make trouble for us here, Boesman. I can't run any more.

Quiet, hey! Let's have a *dop*.

[*Lena registers Boesman's hard stare. She studies him in return.*]

You're the hell-in. Don't look at me, *ou ding*. Blame the whiteman. Bulldozer!

[*Another laugh.*]

Ja! You were happy this morning. 'Push it over, my *baas!*' '*Dankie, baas!*' '*Weg is ons!*'

It was funny, hey, Boesman! All the *pondoks* flat. The poor people running around trying to save their things. You had a good laugh. And now? Here we sit. Just now it's dark, and Boesman's thinking about another *pondok*. The world feels big when you sit like this. Not even a bush to make it your own size. Now's the time to laugh. This is also funny. Look at us! Boesman and Lena with the sky for a roof again.

[*Pause. ., . . Boesman stares at her.*]

What you waiting for?

BOESMAN [*shaking his head as he finally breaks his silence*]. *Yessus*, Lena! I'm telling you, the next time we walk. . . .

LENA. Don't talk about that now, man.

BOESMAN. The Next Time We Walk! . . .

LENA. Where?

BOESMAN. . . . I'll keep on walking. I'll walk and walk. . . .

LENA. *Eina!*

BOESMAN. . . . until you're so bloody *moeg* that when I stop you can't open your mouth!

LENA. It was almost that way today.

BOESMAN. Not a damn! Wasn't long enough. And I knew it. 'When she puts down her bundle, she'll start her rubbish.' You did.

LENA. Rubbish?

BOESMAN. That long *drol* of nonsense that comes out when you open your mouth!

LENA. What have I said? I'm *moeg*! *Eina!* That's true. And you were happy this morning. That's also true.

BOESMAN. I'm still happy.

LENA. You happy now?

BOESMAN [*aggressively*]. I'm always happy.

LENA [*mirthless laughter, clapping her hands*]. *Ek sê!* His backside in the Swartkops mud, but Boesman's happy. This is a new sort of happy, *ou ding*. The hell-in happy.

BOESMAN. Why shouldn't I be happy?

LENA. *Ja*, that's the way it is. When I want to cry, you want to laugh.

BOESMAN. Cry!

LENA. Something hurt. Wasn't just your fist.

BOESMAN. Snot and tears because the whiteman pushed over a rotten old *pondok*? That will be the day. He did me a favour. I was sick of it. So I laughed.

LENA. And now?

BOESMAN. Yes. You think I can't laugh now?

LENA. Don't be a bastard.

BOESMAN. You want to hear me?

LENA. NO!

BOESMAN. Then shut up, or you will! I'm a happy *Hotnot*. Laughing all the time . . . inside! I haven't stopped since this morning. You were a big joke then, and if you don't watch out you'll be a big joke now.

LENA. Big joke? Because I cried? No, *here*, Boesman! It was too early in the morning to have your life kicked in its *moer* again. Sitting there in the dust with the pieces . . . *Kaalgat!* That's what it felt like! . . . and thinking of somewhere else again. Put your life on your head and walk, sister.
Another day gone. Other people lived it. We tramped it into the ground. I haven't got so many left, Boesman.

BOESMAN. If your legs worked as hard as your tongue then we were here long ago.

LENA. It's not my fault.

BOESMAN. Then whose? Every few steps . . . 'Rest a bit, Boesman.' 'I'm tired, Boesman.'

LENA. *Arme ou Lena se maer ou bene.*

BOESMAN. You weren't resting.

LENA. I was.

BOESMAN. You lie.

LENA. What was I doing?

BOESMAN. You were looking for that *brak* of yours.

LENA. *Brak?*
 [*She remembers.*] *Hond!*
 Haai! Was it this morning?

BOESMAN. You almost twisted your head off you were looking

behind you so much. You should have walked backwards today.

LENA. He might have followed me. Dogs smell footsteps.

BOESMAN. Follow you! You fancy yourself, hey.

LENA. Anyway you weren't in such a hurry yourself. You didn't even know where we were going.

BOESMAN. I did.

LENA. Swartkops?

BOESMAN [*emphatically*]. Here! Right here where I am.

LENA. No, Boesman. This time you *lieg*.

BOESMAN. Don't say to me I *lieg*! I'm not mix-up like you. I know what I'm doing.

LENA. Why didn't we come the short way then?

BOESMAN. Short way? Korsten to Swartkops? What you talking about?

LENA. It didn't use to feel so long. That walk never came to an end. I'm still out there, walking!

BOESMAN [*a gesture of defeat*].

It's useless to talk to you.

[*He goes through Lena's bundle and finds two bottles of water. He uncorks one and has a drink. He then starts unpacking his bundle.*]

LENA. All you knew was to load up our things and take the empties to the bottle store. After that . . . !

[*She shakes her head.*]

'Where we going, Boesman?' 'Don't ask questions. Walk!' *Ja*, don't ask questions. Because you didn't know the answers. Where to go, what to do. I remember now. Down this street, up the next one, look down that one, then turn around and go the other way. Not lost? What way takes you past Berry's Corner twice, then back to where you started from? I'm not a fool, Boesman. The roads are crooked enough without you also being in a *dwaal*.

First it looked like Redhouse, or Veeplaas. Then it was Bethelsdorp, or maybe Missionvale. *Sukkel* along! The dogs want to bite but you can't look down. Look ahead, sister. To what? Boesman's back. That's the scenery in my world. You don't know what it's like behind you. Look back one day,

Boesman. It's *me*, that thing you *sleep* along the roads. My life. It felt old today. Sitting there on the pavement when you went inside with the empties. Not just *moeg*. It's been that for a long time. Something else. Something that's been used too long. The old pot that leaks, the blanket that can't even keep the fleas warm. Time to throw it away. How do you do that when it's yourself?

I was still sore where you hit me. Two white children came and looked while I counted the bruises. There's a big one here, hey. . . .

[*Touching a tender spot under one eye.*]

You know what I asked them? 'Does your mother want a girl? Go ask your mother if she wants a girl.' I would have gone, Boesman.

BOESMAN. And then?

LENA. Work for the madam.

[*Boesman laughs derisively.*]

They also laughed, and looked some more, *ja*, look at Lena! *Ou Hotnot meid*. Boesman's her man. Gave her a hiding for dropping the empties. Three bottles broken. Sixpence. Sixpence worth of bruises.

BOESMAN [*indifferently*]. You should have gone.

LENA [*she has to think about it*].

They didn't want me.

BOESMAN [*another laugh, then stops himself abruptly*].

You think *I* want you?

LENA [*she also thinks about this before answering*].

You took me. You came out with the wine, put it in your bundle, then you said 'Come!' and walked. I wanted to say something. The word was in my mouth! But the way you did it . . . no questions, didn't even look at me . . . just picked up and walked. So I followed you. Didn't even know where until I felt the mud between my toes. Then I knew. Swartkops again! Digging for bait. Mudprawns and worms in an old jam tin. A few live ones on top, the dead one at the bottom. 'Three bob, my *baas*. Just dug them out!' *Lieg* your soul into hell for enough to live.

How we going to dig? We haven't even got a spade.

BOESMAN. I'll get one.

LENA. *Oppas* they don't get *you*. *Blourokkie* next time they catch you stealing.

Haai, Boesman! Why here? This place hasn't been good to us. All we've had next to the Modderspruit is hard times. [*A little laugh.*] And wet ones. Remember that night the water came up so high? When we woke up *pap nat* with all our things floating down to the bridge. You got such a *skrik* you ran the wrong way.

[*She laughs at the memory.*]

BOESMAN. I didn't!

LENA. What were you doing in the deep water? Having a wash?

[*Another laugh.*]

It was almost up with you that night. Hey! When was that? Last time?

[*Pause. . . . Lena thinks.*]

Boesman! When was our last time here? I'm talking to you.

[*Boesman deliberately ignores her, and carries on sorting out the contents of his bundle.*]

Boesman!!!

[*Pause. . . . No reaction from him.*]

Don't be like that tonight, man. This is a lonely place. Just us two. Talk to me.

BOESMAN. I've got nothing left to say to you. Talk to yourself.

LENA. I'll go mad.

BOESMAN. What do you mean, 'go' mad? You've been talking to yourself since . . .

[*Pause. . . . Lena waits, he remembers.*]

Ja! . . . since our first walk.

LENA. First walk?

BOESMAN. That night, in the brickfields.

LENA. Coega to Veeplaas!

BOESMAN. First you cried. When you stopped crying, you started talking. I was tired. I wanted to sleep. But you talked. 'Where we going?' 'Let's go back.' Who? What? How?

Yessus! On and on. Then I thought it. 'Boesman, you've made a mistake!'

LENA. Coega to Veeplaas.

BOESMAN. You talked there too. So I thought it again.

LENA. Mistake.

BOESMAN. Mistake. Every time you opened your mouth . . . until I stopped listening.

LENA. I was somebody to listen.

BOESMAN. To what? That *gebabbel* of yours. When you *poep* it makes more sense. You know why? It stinks. Your words are just noise. Nonsense. *Die geraas van 'n vervloekte lewe.* Look at you! Listen to you! You're asking for a lot, Lena. Must I go mad as well?

LENA. I asked you when we came here last. Is that nonsense?

BOESMAN. Yes! What difference does it make? To anything? You're here now!

LENA [*looking around*]. I'm here now.

[*Surge of anger.*] I know I'm here now. Why? Look at it, for God's sake. Is this the best you could do? What was wrong with Veeplaas?

BOESMAN. What's right with it?

LENA. There's other people there! What's the matter with you? Ashamed of yourself?

[*Boesman turns away from her, dragging their one mattress to the spot where he will build the shelter. He then picks up the piece of corrugated iron and examines it, trying it out in various positions . . . as a roof, a wall, etc.*]

LENA. Or Missionvale! Redhouse! There's a chance of a job there on the saltpans.

Not even a dog to look at us. Everytime we come back here it feels like I've never left. Maybe this is the last time here I'm trying to remember. *Haai!*

[*She shakes her head . . . then pauses.*]

Wasn't it after Redhouse? Out last time here. Remember, that *boer* chased us off his land. Then we came here. Is that right?

[*Boesman ignores her.*]

Then we went to Korsten.

BOESMAN. After here we went to Korsten?

LENA. *Ja.* [*Boesman laughs at her derisively.*] How was it then?
[*Pause.*] You won't tell me.

BOESMAN [*putting down the piece of iron*].
Make the fire.

LENA. Let's have a *dop* first. I'm feeling the cold. Please,
Boesman!

[*Without another look at her he walks off. Lena gets stiffly to her
legs and starts to make the fire. A box is positioned to shield it from
the wind, then the bundle of firewood untied, the wood itself broken
into pieces, a piece of paper to get it started, etc.*]

LENA. Walk our legs off for this! Piece of bread and black tea.
No butter . . . not even for bruises.

[*A thought crosses her mind. She straightens up, thinks hard for a
few seconds, then shakes her head.*]

No. [*She looks around.*] Maybe he's right. What's the difference.
I'm here now.

'Here!' After a long life that's a thin slice. No jam on that
one. Or *kondens melk!* There's *soeterigheid* for you. Maybe if
we get lots of prawns. . . .

[*Another thought. . . . She thinks hard. . . .*]

It was after Redhouse. Collecting prickly pears. Then they
found our place there in the bush. *Loop, Hotnot!* So *Hotnot
loops* . . . to Swartkops. Here. The last time here. I was right!

[*Pause.*]

No, we ran! The *boer* had a gun. When he showed us the
bullets Boesman dropped his tin and went down that road
like a rabbit. . . .

[*Laughing . . . her hands to her backside in an imitation of the scene.*]
. . . *Moenie skiet, baas!*

Me too, but the other way. Where did I find him . . . looking
at the mud, the hell-in because we had lost all our things
again. Just our clothes, and each other. Never lose that. Run
your legs off the other way but at the end of it Boesman
is waiting. How the hell does that happen?

Redhouse—Swartkops! I was right. He must laugh at himself.

[*Back to her chores.*]

And then? Somewhere else! *Ja*, of course. One of them. Veeplaas. Or Missionvale. Maybe Bethelsdorp. Lena knows them all.

[*Pause.*]

But which one . . . that time?

[*She straightens up and looks around.*]

Which way . . . ?

[*Moving around, trying to orientate herself physically.*]

Let me see now. We came. . . . No. Those lights! What's that? Where is . . . it's round all right . . . where the hell is . . . *Yessus!* I'm right in the middle. No wonder I get drunk when I try to work it out. . . .

[*Sudden desperation.*]

Think, man! It happened to you.

[*Closes her eyes in an effort to remember.*]

We were here. Then we left. Off we go. . . . We're walking . . . and walking . . . where we walking? Boesman never tells me. Wait and see. Walking. . . .

Somewhere, his shadow. In front of me. Small man with a long *maer* shadow. It's stretching back to me over the veld because we're walking to the sun and it's going down. . . .

Veeplaas! That's where the sun goes. Behind it there into the bush. So Veeplaas is. . . .

[*Looking now for the sun.*]

Waar die donner is . . . ?

[*Pause.*]

Finished. So what. I got it in here [*pointing to her head*]. Redhouse—Swartkops—Veeplaas!

[*She is very pleased with herself.*]

Get a move on now. I'm nearly here. Redhouse—Swartkops —Veeplaas. . . .

[*She carries on working, laying out mugs, filling a little pot with water, etc. . . . all the time muttering to herself the sequence of places she has established.*]

It's coming! Korsten! Empties, and the dog. *Hond!* How was it now? Redhouse—Swartkops—Veeplaas—Korsten. Then this morning the bulldozers . . . and then. . . .

[*Pause.*] Here! I've got there!

[*She is very happy.*] 'Here', sister. You ran that last bit. Bundle and all.

[*She is humming away happily to herself when Boesman returns with a few odds and ends—an old sack, few pieces of wood, another piece of corrugated iron, an old motor-car door, etc.—out of which he will fashion their shelter for the night. He registers Lena's good humour and watches her suspiciously as he starts to work. Lena realizes this and laughs.*]

Why you looking at me so *skeef*?

[*He says nothing. Lena hums a little song.*]

Remember the times I used to sing for us?
'Da . . . da . . . da. . . .'

BOESMAN. What's the matter with you?

LENA. Feeling fine, darling. I'm warm. You know why? I've been running. You should have seen me! I'm not as old as I thought. All the way from Redhouse. . . .

[*The rest of her sentence is lost in laughter at the expression on his face.*]

. . . and now I'm here. With you.
Da . . . da . . . da. . . .

BOESMAN [*after watching her for a few more seconds*]. Show me the wine!

LENA. Look for yourself.

[*Boesman leaves his work on the shelter. He goes through his bundle and examines two bottles of wine. They are both intact. Lena laughs at him.*]

How's it for a *dop*?

[*He puts away the bottles and goes back to work.*]

Hey, you know what I was thinking just now. *Blikkie kondens melk*. What do you say? If we get lots of prawns. Sugar's not enough, man. I want some real sweetness. Then you can be as *bedonnerd* as you like.

[*She starts singing, shuffling out a few dance steps at the same time.*]

> *Ou blikkie kondens melk*
> *Maak die lewe soet;*
> *Boesman is 'n Boesman*
> *Maar hy dra 'n Hotnot hoed.*

Look at this! Lena's still got a *vastrap* in her old legs. You want to dance, Boesman. Not too late to learn. I'll teach you.

BOESMAN. Just now you get a bloody good *klap*!

LENA. *Ja!* See what I mean. This time I'm laughing, and you . . . ! *Vies!* You don't like it when somebody else laughs. Well, you laughed at me for nothing. Because I was right! Last time here *was* after Redhouse. You won't mix me up this time. I remember, The *boer* pointed his gun and you were gone, non-stop to Swartkops. Then Veeplaas. Then Korsten. And now here. How's that!

[*She laughs triumphantly. Boesman lets her enjoy herself. He waits for his moment.*]

And I'm not finished. Wait and see. I'm going to think some more. I'll work it out, back and back until I reach Coega Kop. Then I'll have it. Coega Kop to here. So what you got to say?

BOESMAN. Nothing.

LENA [*another laugh*]. Now you're really the hell-in. Nothing to laugh at.

BOESMAN. Nothing to laugh at?

[*He disproves this with a small laugh.*]

LENA. You can't laugh at me.

[*Another laugh from Boesman.*]

I'm right, Boesman!

BOESMAN. How was it? Swartkops after Redhouse?

LENA. Yes!

BOESMAN. And from here we went to . . .

LENA. Korsten!

[*Boesman shakes his head with another laugh.*]

It's no good, Boesman. I know what you're trying. You're not going to do it this time. Go laugh at yourself.

[*She goes back to her work, but there is an edge of something now in her voice as she repeats the sequence with exaggerated emphasis.*]

Redhouse—Swartkops—Veeplaas—Korsten . . . Here! Where I am.

[*She looks up at Boesman, but he pretends total indifference. This adds to her growing uncertainty. She looks around. We see her trying hard to remember, to work it out yet again. Boesman waits. He knows. Eventually . . .]*

Is it wrong?

BOESMAN [*strolling up to the fire to fetch something*].
Why do you stop singing?

LENA. Is it wrong, Boesman?

BOESMAN [*he takes his time, finding whatever he is looking for first before answering*].
What about . . . Swartkops—Veeplaas—Redhouse?

LENA [*vacantly*]. Swartkops . . . Veeplaas. . . .

BOESMAN. Or this. Veeplaas.

LENA. Veeplaas.

BOESMAN. Redhouse . . .

LENA. Redhouse . . .

BOESMAN. Korsten!

LENA. Veeplaas—Redhouse—Korsten? [*Pause.*] Where's Swartkops?

[*The sight of her vacant confusion is too much for Boesman. He has a good laugh, now thoroughly enjoying himself.*]

To hell with it! I'm not listening to you. I'm here!

BOESMAN. Where? Veeplaas?

LENA [*closing her eyes*]. I'm here. I know how I got here. Redhouse, then Swartkops. . . .

[*Pause—she has forgotten.*]

Wait . . . ! Redhouse—Swartkops. . . .

BOESMAN. Go on! But don't forget Bethelsdorp this time. You've been there too. And Missionvale. And Kleinskool.

LENA. Don't mix me up, Boesman!

[*Trying desperately to remember her sequence.*]

Redhouse—Swartkops . . . then Veeplaas . . . then. . . .

BOESMAN. It's wrong!

[*Pause . . . she looks at him desperately. He leaves his work on the shelter and goes to her.*]

Yes! It's wrong! Now what you going to do?

LENA [*she moves around helplessly, trying to orientate herself physically*].

It's mixed up again. I had it!

BOESMAN. Look at you! *Babalas!* . . . from yesterday's wine. Yesterday you were drunk. One or the other. Your whole life.

LENA [*staring off in a direction*].
Over there. . . . Where did the sun go?

BOESMAN [*joining her*]. What you looking for?

LENA. Veeplaas.

BOESMAN. That way?

[*Lena studies Boesman's face for a second, then decides she is wrong.*]

LENA. No.

[*Moving in a different direction.*]

That way!

BOESMAN. Wrong!

[*Lena tries yet another direction.*]

Wrong!
Yessus, Lena! You're lost.

LENA. Do you really know, Boesman? Where and how?

BOESMAN. Yes!

LENA. Tell me.

[*He laughs.*]

Help me, Boesman!

BOESMAN. What? Find yourself?

[*Boesman launches into a grotesque pantomime of a search. Lena watches him with hatred.*]

[*Calling.*] Lena! Lena!

[*He rejoins her.*]

Sorry, Auntie. Better go to Veeplaas. Maybe you're there.

LENA [*directly at Boesman, her anger overwhelming her*].
Jou lae donner? Vark. Yes, you. You're a pig. *Voetsek*, you bastard. It's a sin, Boesman.

[*He enjoys her tirade immensely.*]

Wait a bit! One day . . . !

BOESMAN. One day what?

LENA. Something's going to happen.

BOESMAN. That's right.

LENA. What?

BOESMAN. Something's going to happen.

LENA. *Ja!*

[*Pause.*]

What's going to happen?

BOESMAN. I thought you knew. One day you'll ask me who you are.

[*He laughs.*]

LENA. *Ja,* another good laugh for you that day.

BOESMAN. The best one!

'*Ek sê, ou pellie* . . . who am I?' [*More laughter.*]

LENA [*trying her name*]. Lena . . . Lena. . . .

BOESMAN. What about Rosie? Nice name Rose. Maria. Anna. Or Sannie! Sannie who? *Sommer* Sannie Somebody.

LENA. NO!

BOESMAN [*ready to laugh*]. Who are you?

LENA. Mary. I want to be Mary. Who are you?

[*The laugh dies on Boesman's lips.*]

That's what I ask next. *Ja,* you! *Wie's die man?* And then I'm gone. Goodbye, darling. I've had enough. 'Strue's God, that day I'm gone.

BOESMAN. You mean that day you get a bloody *good* hiding.

LENA. *Aikona!* I'll go to the police.

BOESMAN. You tried that before and what happened? 'She's my woman, *baas. Net 'n bietjie warm gemaak.*' 'Take her' . . . finish *en klaar.* They know the way it is with our sort.

LENA. Not this time! My name is Mary, remember. 'Don't know this man, *baas.*' So where's your proof.

BOESMAN [*holding up a clenched fist*]. Here!

LENA. *Oppas!* You'll go too far one day. Death penalty.

BOESMAN. For you? [*Derisive laughter.*] Not guilty and discharge.

LENA. Don't talk big. You're frightened of the rope. When you stop hitting it's not because you're *moeg* or had enough. You're frightened! *Ja.*

[*Pause.*]

Ja. That's when I feel it most. When you do it carefully. The last few . . . when you aim. I count them. One . . . another one . . . wait for the next one! He's only resting.

[*Pause.*]

You're right, Boesman. That's proof. When I feel it I'll know. I'm Lena.

BOESMAN [*emphatically*]. And I'm Boesman.

LENA. Boesman and Lena.

BOESMAN. Yes! That's who. That's what. When . . . where . . . why! All your bloody nonsense questions. That's the answer.

LENA. Boesman and Lena.

BOESMAN. So stop asking them!

[*Pause . . . he goes back to work on the shelter. He tries the 'answer' for himself.*]

Boesman and Lena. *Ja!* It explains. So it's another *vrot ou huisie vir die vrot mens.* Look at it! Useless, hey. If it rains tonight you'll get wet. If it blows hard you'll be counting stars.

LENA. I know what it's like in there!

BOESMAN. It's all you'll ever know.

LENA. I'm sick of it.

BOESMAN. Sick of it! You want to live in a house? What do you think you are? A white madam?

LENA. It wasn't always like this. There were better times.

BOESMAN. In your dreams maybe.

LENA. What about Veeplaas? Chopping wood for the China-man? That room in his backyard. Real room, with a door and all that.

BOESMAN. Forget it. *Now* is the only time in your life.

LENA. No! Now. What's that? I wasn't born today. I want my life. Where's it?

BOESMAN. In the mud, where you are, *Now.* Tomorrow it will be there too, and the next day. And if you're still alive when I've had enough of this, you'll load up and walk, somewhere else.

LENA. Roll up in my blanket and crawl into that! [*Pointing to the shelter.*]
Never enough wine to make us sleep the whole night. Wake up in the dark. The fire cold. What time is that in my life? Another now! Black now and empty as hell. Even when you're also awake. You make it worse. When I call you, and I know you hear me, but you say nothing. Sometimes loneliness is two . . . you and the other person who doesn't want to know you're there. I'm sick of you too, Boesman!

BOESMAN. So go.

LENA. Don't joke. I'll walk tonight. *So waar.*

BOESMAN. Go! Goodbye, darling.

[*Lena takes a few steps away from the fire then stops. Boesman watches her.*]

You still lost? Okay. Boesman will help you tonight. That way is Veeplaas. Through Swartkops, over the railway line, past that big thing with chimneys. Then you come to the veld. There's a path. Walk it until you see little lights. That's Veeplaas. Redhouse is that way. Korsten is over there. What else you want? Bethelsdorp? Coega Kop? There! There! I know my way. I know my world.

[*Lena is standing still.*]

So what you waiting for? Walk!

LENA [*her back to him, staring into the darkness*].
There's somebody out there.

[*Pause. Boesman leaves his work on the* pondok *and joins her. They stare in silence for a few seconds.*]

BOESMAN. Drunk.

LENA. No.

BOESMAN. Look at him!

LENA [*shaking her head*]. Nobody comes to the mudflats to get drunk.

BOESMAN. What do you know?

LENA. He's stopped. Maybe he's going to dig.

BOESMAN. Dark before the water's low.

LENA. Or a whiteman.

BOESMAN. When did you see a whiteman sitting like that!

LENA. Maybe he sees us.

[*She waves.*]

BOESMAN [*stopping her*]. What's the matter with you?

LENA. Go see what he wants.

BOESMAN. And then?

LENA. Do something. Help him.

BOESMAN. We got no help.

LENA. I'm not thinking of him.

[*Boesman stares at her.*]

It's another person, Boesman.

BOESMAN. I'm warning you! Don't start any nonsense.

[*He moves back to the shelter. Lena watches him for a few seconds, then decides.*]

LENA [*calling to the other person*].
Hey, I say.

BOESMAN. Lena!

LENA [*ignoring Boesman*]. We got a fire!

BOESMAN. Lena!

LENA. Come over!

BOESMAN. *Jou verdomde*. . . .

LENA [*sees the violence coming and moves away quickly*].
To hell with you! I want him.
[*Calling.*] Hey, darling! *Kom die kant!*
[*To Boesman.*] Sit in the dark and talk to myself because you don't hear me any more? No, Boesman! I want him! Hey! He's coming.

[*A moment of mutual uncertainty at the approach of the stranger. Lena falls back to Boesman's side. He picks up a stick in readiness for trouble. They stand together, waiting.*
An old African appears slowly.
Hat on his head, the rest of him lost in the folds of a shabby old overcoat. He is an image of age and decrepitude.]

BOESMAN. *Kaffer!*

LENA. *Ou kaffer.*

[*Lena almost turns away with disappointment. Boesman sees this and has a good laugh.*]

BOESMAN. Lena calls out in the dark, and what does she get? Look at it.

LENA [*after a few more seconds of hesitation*]. Better than nothing.

BOESMAN. So? Go on. You wanted somebody. There's a black one.

[*Lena takes a few steps towards the old man. He has remained at a distance. As Lena approaches him he murmurs a greeting in Xhosa.*]

LENA. *Molo, Outa.*

[*Boesman watches this, and Lena's other attempts to communicate with the old man, with cruel amusement. She gets another murmur from the old man.*]

BOESMAN. What you waiting for?

LENA. I am Lena. This is my man, Boesman.

BOESMAN. Shake his hand! Fancy *Hotnot* like you. Give him some smart stuff. 'How do you do, darling.'

[*The old man murmurs something in Xhosa.*]

LENA. What's that? You know his language.

[*Boesman laughs.*]

Does the *Outa* want something?

[*Another murmur.*]

Don't you speak English or Afrikaans? '*Môre, baas!*'

BOESMAN. Give him some help.

LENA. He doesn't look so good.

[*A few steps closer to the old man.*]

Come sit, *Outa.* Sit and rest.

[*Nothing happens. She turns to Boesman.*]

How do you say that in the kaffir *taal*?

BOESMAN. *Hamba.*

LENA. All right, Boesman!

[*Back to the old man . . . she pushes forward a box.*]

It's warm by the fire.

[*Nothing happens . . . a spark of anger in her voice.*]

You deaf? Sit!

[*The old man does so.*]

Ja, rest your legs. They work hard for us poor people.

[*Boesman looks up in time to see her uncorking one of their bottles of water. They stare at each other in silence for a few seconds.*]

Maybe he's thirsty.

BOESMAN. And us?

LENA. Only water.

BOESMAN. It's scarce here.

LENA. I'll fetch from Swartkops tomorrow.

BOESMAN. To hell! He doesn't belong to us.

[*Grabs the bottle away from her and together with the other one puts it inside the* pondok.]

LENA. There was plenty of times his sort gave us water on the road.

BOESMAN. It's different now.

LENA. How?

BOESMAN. Because I say so.

LENA. Because this time you got the water, hey!

[*Back to the old man.*]

Does *Outa* come far?

[*She stands and waits. . . . Nothing.*]

We're from Korsten. They kicked us out there this morning.

[*Nothing.*]

It's a hard life for us brown people, hey.

BOESMAN. He's not brown people, he's black people.

LENA. They got feelings too. Not so, *Outa?*

BOESMAN. You'll get some feelings if you don't watch that fire.

[*Lena is waiting for a word from the old man with growing desperation and irritation.*]

LENA. What's the matter? You sick? Where's it hurt?

[*Nothing.*]

Hey! I'm speaking to you.

[*The old man murmurs in Xhosa.*]

Stop that baboon language! *Waar kry jy seer?*

[*Another unintelligible response.*]

[*Lena turns away in violent disgust.*] *Ag*, go to hell! *Onnooslike kaffer. My bleddy bek af praat vir niks!*

[*Boesman explodes into laughter at this ending to Lena's encounter with the old man.*]

BOESMAN. Finished with him already? *Ag nee, wat!* You must try something there. He's *mos* better than nothing. Or was nothing better?

Too bad you're both so useless. Could have worked a point. Some sports. You and him. They like *Hotnot meide*. Black bastards!

[*Lena is wandering around helplessly.*]

Going to call again? You'll end up with a tribe of old *kaffers* sitting here. That's all you'll get out of that darkness. They go there to die. I'm warning you, Lena! Pull another one in here and you'll do the rest of your talking tonight with a thick mouth. Turn my place into a *kaffer nes*!

LENA [*coming back dejectedly to the fire*].
Give me a *dop*.

BOESMAN. That's better. Now you're talking like a *Hotnot. Weg wêreld, kom brandewyn.*

LENA. A *dop*, please, man!

BOESMAN. You look like one too now. A real one. *Gat op die grond en trane vir 'n bottel.*

LENA [*really desperate*]. Then open one.

BOESMAN. All that fancy talk is thirsty work, hey.

LENA. Open a bottle, Boesman!

BOESMAN. When I'm ready.

LENA [*she stands*]. One of them is mine!

[*She waits for a reaction from Boesman, but gets none.*]

I want it now!

[*Pause.*]

I'm going to take it, Boesman.

[*She moves forward impulsively to where the bottles are hidden. Boesman lets her take a few steps then goes into action.*]

BOESMAN [*grabbing a stick*].
Okay!

LENA [*seeing it coming*].
Eina!

[*Running quickly to the old man.*]

Watch now, *Outa*. You be witness for me. Watch! He's going to kill me.

BOESMAN [*stopping*]. You asking for it tonight, Lena.

LENA. You see how it is, *Outa*?

BOESMAN. He'll see you get it if you don't watch out.

LENA. I got it this morning!

BOESMAN. Just touch those bottles and you'll get it again.

[*He throws down the stick and goes off.*]

LENA [*shouting after him*]. Go on! Why don't you hit me? There's no white *baases* here to laugh. Does this old thing worry you?

[*Turning back to the old man.*]

Look, *Outa*. I want you to look.

[*Showing him the bruises on her arms and face.*]

No, not that one. That's a old one. This one. And here. Just because I dropped the sack with the empties. I would have been dead if they hadn't laughed. When other people laugh he gets ashamed. Now too. I would have got it hard from him if you. . . .

[*Pause.*]

Why didn't you laugh? They laughed this morning. They laugh every time.

[*Growing violence.*]

What's the matter with you? *Kaffers* laugh at it too. It's *mos* funny. Me! *Ou meid* being *donnered*!

[*Pause. . . . She moves away to some small chore at the fire. After this she looks up at the old man, and then goes slowly to him.*]

Wasn't it funny?

[*She moves closer.*]

Hey, look at me?

[*He looks at her.*]

My name is Lena.

[*She pats herself on the chest. Nothing happens. She tries again, but this time she pats him.*]

Outa . . . You . . . [*patting herself*] . . . Lena . . . me.

OLD MAN. Lena.

LENA [*excited*]. *Ewe!* Lena!

OLD MAN. Lena.

LENA [*softly*]. My God!

[*She looks around desperately, then after a quick look in the direction in which Boesman disappeared she goes to the half-finished shelter and fetches one of the bottles of water. She uncorks it and hurries back to the old man.*]

LENA [*offering the bottle*]. Water. *Water! Manzi!*

[*She helps him get it to his lips. He drinks. In between mouthfuls he murmurs away in Xhosa. Lena picks up the odd phrase and echoes it . . . 'Bhomboloza Outa, Bhomboloza' . . . 'Mlomo, ewe mlomo' . . . 'Yes, Outa, dala' . . . as if she understood him.*
The whole of the monologue follows this pattern: the old man murmuring intermittently—the occasional phrase or even sentence quite clear—and Lena surrendering herself more and more to the illusion of conversation.]

LENA. *Safa . . . safa. . . .*

[*Pause.*]

What's all that mean?

[*He hands her back the bottle.*]

If *Outa's* saying. . . .

[*She stops, takes another quick look to make sure Boesman is out of sight, then returns to the old man's side. She speaks secretively and with intensity.*]

It's true! You're right. [*He is still murmuring.*] Wait now. Listen to mine.

I had a dog. In Korsten. Just a *brak*. Once when we were sitting somewhere counting our bottles and eating he came and looked at us. Must have been a *Kaffer hond*. He didn't bark. I left some bread for him there on the ground when we went. He ate it and followed us all the way back to Korsten.

[*Another look over her shoulder to make sure Boesman isn't near. She continues her story in an even lower tone.*]

For two days like that around our place there. When Boesman wasn't looking I threw him things to eat. Boesman knew I was up to something. I'm a bloody fool, *Outa*. Something makes me happy I start singing. So every time Boesman saw the dog, he throws stones. He doesn't like dogs. They don't like him. But when he wasn't looking I threw food.

[*Laughs secretively.*]

I won, *Outa*! One night the dog came in when he was asleep . . . came and sat and looked at me. When Boesman woke up, he moved out. So it was every night after that. We waited for Boesman to sleep, then he came and watched me. All the things I did—making the fire, cooking, counting bottles or bruises, even just sitting, you know, when it's too much . . . he saw it. *Hond!* I called him *Hond*. But any name, he'd wag his tail if you said it nice.

I'll tell you what it is. Eyes, *Outa*. Another pair of eyes. Something to see you.

Then this morning in all the *lawaai* and mix-up—gone!

I wanted to look, but Boesman was in a hurry.

So what! Now I got *Outa*.

[*Nudging him.*] Lena!

OLD MAN. Lena.

LENA [*little laugh*]. You see, I'm not ashamed.

Dè! [*In a fit of generosity she passes the bottle over again.*] Much as you like, darling. Doesn't cost a penny. Drink. Don't worry about him. He's worried about the wine. [*Old man drinks.*]

No heart in that one, *Outa*. Or empty. *Leeggesuip. Tickey* deposit for Boesman's heart. Brandy bottle.

[*She gets the bottle back and takes it to the* pondok, *talking all the time.*]

Outa know the empties. Brandy bottles, beer bottles, wine bottles. Any kind. Medicine. Tomato sauce. Sell them at the Bottle Exchange. We were doing good with the empties there in Korsten. Whiteman's drinking himself to death. Take your sack, knock on some back doors and it's full by no time. It was going easy for us, man. Eating meat. Proper chops! Then this morning: *Loop, Hotnot!* Just had time to grab our things. That's when I dropped the sack. Three bottles broken. I didn't even have on a *broek* or a petticoat when we started walking.

[*Straightens up at the shelter and registers the old man sitting quietly.*]

You're a nice *Ou* . . . [*correcting herself*] . . . you're one of the good *Bantoes*, hey. I can see it. Sit so nice and listen to Lena.

[*Back to the fire where she puts on a few more pieces of wood.*]

That's why we called. I could see it. I said to Boesman: He's one of the good ones. *Arme ou drommel!* Sorry feelings—for you. 'Let's call him over!'

[*The old man starts murmuring again. This time it is accompanied by much head-shaking. Lena interprets this as a rejection of what she has just said.*]

No, *Outa*, I did! *Haai*, it's true! Why should I lie?

[*Her tone and manner becoming progressively more angry.*]

It's true! What do you know? Don't argue! Bloody old. . . .

[*The old man makes a move to stand up. Lena, changing tone and attitude, forces him to stay seated.*]

Okay! Okay! Okay, *Outa*!! I'll tell you the truth. But mustn't say I *lieg*. Sit still.

[*Pause.*]

It's my eyes. They're not so good any more, specially when the thing is far away. But in the old days . . . ! You know those mountains out there, when you walk Kleinskool way. . . . In the old days so clear, *Outa*. When we were resting I used to put my finger on a point, and then up and down, just the way it is.

[*Demonstrates tracing the outline of a mountain range.*]

I haven't seen them for a long time. Boesman's back gets in the way these days.

[*Breaking the mood.*]

It's not so bad, when the thing is near to me. Like Korsten, this morning. That's quite clear. Tomorrow as well.
I can see that too, we'll be digging.
I say! *Ou* Lena's talking her head off tonight. And you sit so nicely and listen to her. Boesman wouldn't. Tell me to shut up.

[*Secretively.*] We must be careful. He'll try and chase you away just now. Mustn't go, you see.

[*The old man starts murmuring again. For a few seconds Lena*

interprets it as small talk as she goes on preparing for their supper.]
That's right. Of course, *Ja*, it's going to be cold tonight. You
never said a truer thing, darling. I know, I know. Don't you
worry. We'll eat just now. Won't take long to boil.

[*Pause. . . . The old man mumbles away, Lena studies him in silence
for a few seconds.*]

LENA [*interrupting him*]. It's about Boesman, isn't it?

[*She laughs.*]

I *mos* know. Why shouldn't you and me talk? Well. . . . Too
small for a real *Hotnot, Outa*. There's something else there.
Bushman blood. And wild! That *tickey* deposit heart of his is
tight, like his *poephol* and his fist.

[*Holds up a clenched fist in an imitation of Boesman.*]

That's how he talks to the world.

[*Much laughter from Lena at her joke, with a lot of nudging and
back-slapping as if the old man was also laughing. He isn't.*]

Ja, so it goes. He walks in front. I walk behind. It used to
be side by side, with jokes. At night he let me sing, and
listened. Never learnt any songs himself.

[*The old man murmurs.*]

I don't know.

[*The old man continues to murmur, Lena gets desperate.*]

Don't start again, *Outa*. I don't know! Behind us. Isn't that
enough? Too heavy to carry. The last time we joked, the last
time I sang. Behind us somewhere. Our rubbish. We'll leave
something here too if there's any last times left.

Yessus! It's so heavy now, *Outa*. Am I crooked? It feels that
way when we stop and the bundles come down. What's so
heavy? I walk and I think . . . a blanket, a few things in a
bucket. . . .

Look! [*Pointing to their possessions.*]

And even when they're down, when you've made your place
and the fire is burning and you rest your legs, something
stays heavy. Hey! Once you've put your life on your head
and walked you never get light again.

We've been walking a long time, *Outa*. Look at my feet.

Those little paths on the veld . . . Boesman and Lena helped
write them.

I meet the memory of myself on the old roads. Sometimes young. Sometimes old. Is she coming or going? From where to where? All mixed up. The right time on the wrong road, the right road leading to the wrong place.

[*A murmur from the old man.*]

He won't tell me. That's a sin, isn't it? He'll be punished. But he says there's no God for us. Do you know? Up there!

[*A vague gesture to the sky. No intelligible response from the old man.*]

Doesn't matter.

[*The old man murmurs loudly, urgently.*]

What's that now? Maybe. . . .

[*Straightening up at the fire.*]

Yessus, Outa! You're asking things tonight. [*Sharply.*] Why do you want to know?

[*Pause.*]

It's a long story.

[*She moves over to him, sits down beside him.*]

One, *Outa*, that lived. For six months. The others were born dead.

[*Pause.*]

That all? *Ja.* Only a few words I know, but a long story if you lived it.

[*Murmuring from the old man.*]

That's all. That's all.

Nee, God, Outa! What more must I say? What you asking me about? Pain? Yes! Don't *kaffers* know what that means? One night it was longer than a small piece of candle and then as big as darkness. Somewhere else a donkey looked at it. I crawled under the cart and they looked. Boesman was too far away to call. Just the sound of his axe as he chopped wood. I didn't even have rags!

You asked me and now I've told you. Pain is a candle *entjie* and a donkey's face. What's that mean to you? You weren't there. Nobody was. Why do you ask *now*. You're too late for that. *This* is what I feel now [*the fire, the shelter, her 'here and now'*]. . . . This!

My life is here tonight. Tomorrow or the next day that one

out there will drag it somewhere else. But tonight I sit *here*. You interested in that?

[*The old man gets slowly to his feet and starts to move away. Lena throws herself at him violently.*]

LENA. Not a damn! I'm not finished! You can't just go, walk away like you didn't hear. You asked me, and I've told you. This is what I'm left with. You've got two eyes. Sit and look!

[*She has forced the old man back on his box. Lena calms down.*]

Lena!

OLD MAN. Lena.

LENA [*trying to mollify him*]. I'll ask Boesman to give you a *dop*. Okay? Won't be too bad. Where could you go now? Dark out there, *Outa*. *Skelms* will grab you.

[*She hears a noise . . . moves away a few steps and peers into the darkness.*]

He's coming. Listen, we must be clever now. Don't look happy. And don't say anything. Just sit still. Pretend we're still *kwaai-vriende*.

[*She goes back to her fire. Another idea sends her back hurriedly to the old man.*]

No. I know what you do. When he comes back you must say you'll buy wine for us all tomorrow. Say you got a job in Swartkops and when you get your pay you'll buy wine. You hear me? [*Violently.*] Hey . . . !

[*Before she can say anything more Boesman appears. He has a few more pieces of firewood, and something else for the shelter. Lena scuttles back to the fire, and makes herself busy. Boesman stops and stares at the two of them.*]

BOESMAN. What you been doing?

LENA [*innocently*]. Nothing. Look at the wine if you don't believe me.

BOESMAN. Then why's he still here?

LENA. I been looking after the fire. Water's nearly boiling.

BOESMAN. *You* called him . . . *you* tell him to go.

LENA [*looking furtively at the old man, waiting for him to speak*]. This wood doesn't mean much. Won't last the night.

BOESMAN. Don't pretend you didn't hear.

LENA. Okay.

[*Tries to lose herself in fussing with the pot.*]
[*Boesman waits.*]

BOESMAN. So when you going to tell him to go?

LENA. Who?

BOESMAN. Don't play stupid with me, Lena!

LENA. Him? Slowly there.

[*Leaves the fire and talks to him with an exaggerated show of secrecy.*]
He's okay.

BOESMAN. What's that mean?

LENA. Good *kaffer*.

BOESMAN. How do you know?

LENA [*to the old man*]. Tell him what you said to me, *Outa*.

BOESMAN. Since when can you speak his language?

LENA. He's got a few words of Afrikaans. *Outa!!*

BOESMAN. What did he say?

LENA. He said he's going to buy wine tomorrow.
[*To the old man.*] Not so?
He's got some jobs there in Swartkops. Some garden jobs.
Ask him.

BOESMAN. Who's going to give *that* a job?

LENA. Somebody with a soft heart.

BOESMAN. You mean a soft head.

LENA [*forcing a laugh*]. Soft head! Bloody good, Boesman.

BOESMAN. Garden job! He hasn't got enough left in him to
dig his own grave.

LENA. Soft heart and a soft head! *Haai!*

[*Lena is laughing too much. Boesman stares at her. She stops.*]

LENA [*weakly*]. Funny *ou grappie*.

[*Boesman's suspicions are aroused. He goes back to work on the shelter,
but watches the other two very carefully. Lena, thinking she has won,
starts to lay out their supper.*]

LENA [*pointing to a loaf of brown bread*]. Can I break it in three
pieces?

BOESMAN. Two pieces!

[*Lena wants to rebuke him, but stops herself in time.*]

LENA [*softly to the old man*]. We'll share mine.

[*Looks up to see Boesman watching her.*]

Pondokkie's looking okay. *Oulike ou nessie.* He's good with his hands, *Outa.*

[*Without realizing what she is doing, Lena starts humming a little song as she works away at the fire. She realizes her mistake too late. Boesman is staring hard at her when she looks up.*]

[*Desperately.*] I'm not happy!

BOESMAN. You're up to something.

LENA. 'Strue's God I'm not happy.

BOESMAN. He must go.

LENA. Please, Boesman!

BOESMAN. He's had his rest. Hey!

LENA. It's dark now.

BOESMAN. That's his troubles. Hey! *Hamba wena!*

LENA. He's not doing any harm.

BOESMAN. He'll bring the others. It's not far to their location from here.

LENA. Boesman! Just for once a favour. Let him stay.

BOESMAN. What's he to me?

LENA. For me, man. [*Pause.*] I want him.

BOESMAN. What for? What you up to, Lena?

[*Pause. . . . Lena can't answer his questions.*]

LENA [*impulsively*]. You can have the wine. All of it. Next time as well.

[*She dives to the shelter, produces the two bottles of wine.*]

There!

BOESMAN [*unbelievingly*]. For that!

LENA. I want him.

BOESMAN. This is wine, Lena. That's a *kaffer.* He won't help you forget. You want to sit sober in this world? You know what it looks like then?

LENA. I want him.

BOESMAN [*shaking his head*]. You off your mind tonight.

[*To the old man.*] You're an expensive *ou drol.* Two bottles of wine! *Ek sê.* Boesman has party tonight.

[*He tantalizes Lena by opening a bottle and passing it under her nose.*]
Smell! *Hotnot's* forget-me-not.

[*First mouthful.*]

Weg wêreld, kom brandewyn.

LENA [*restraining the old man*].
No, *Outa*. I've paid. You can stay the night with us. If we all
lie together it will be warm in there.

BOESMAN [*overhearing*]. What do you mean?

LENA [*after a pause*]. You can have the mattress.

BOESMAN. To hell! He's not coming inside. Bring your *kaffer*
and his fleas into my *pondok*. Not a damn.

LENA. He won't sit there by himself.

BOESMAN. Then sit with him!

[*He sees Lena's dilemma . . . enjoys it.*]

Ja! You can choose. Inside here or take your fleas and keep
him company.

[*Pause. . . . Boesman works away, tries to whistle.*]

I said you can sleep inside with me or. . . .

LENA. I heard you, Boesman.

BOESMAN. So?

[*Lena doesn't answer. Boesman rubs it in.*]

It's going to be cold tonight. When it starts pushing and the
water comes back. Boesman's all right. Two bottles and a
pondokkie. Bakgat!

[*He watches Lena. She moves slowly to their things. For the first
time he is unsure of himself.*]

What you going to do?

[*Lena doesn't answer. She finds one of their blankets and takes it
to the old man.*]

LENA. Here, *Outa*. We'll need it.

BOESMAN [*suddenly on his feet*]. I've changed my mind. He
must go.

LENA [*turning on him with unexpected ferocity*].
Be careful, Boesman!

BOESMAN. Of what?

LENA [*eyes closed, fists clenched*]. Be careful.

[*Her tone stops him. He sits down again, now even more unsure of himself.*]

BOESMAN. You think I care what you do? You want to sit outside and die of cold with a *kaffer*, go ahead!

LENA. I'd sit out there with a dog tonight!

[*Turns back to the old man.*]

We'll need more wood. And something in case it rains. I'm not so handy at making shelter, *Outa*.

[*To Boesman.*] Where did you find that stuff? Anything left out there?

[*This time Boesman doesn't answer. He stares at her with hard disbelief.*]

I'll see what I can find, *Outa*.

[*She wanders off. Boesman, in front of his shelter with the two bottles of wine, watches her go. When she has disappeared he studies the old man. Takes a few more swallows, then gets up and moves a few steps in the direction that Lena left. Certain that she is not about he turns and goes back to the old man.*]

BOESMAN [*standing over him.*] Hond!

[*The old man looks up at him. Boesman pulls the blanket away from him.*]

I want two blankets tonight.

[*Still not satisfied, he sends the old man sprawling with a shove. The old man crawls back laboriously to his seat. Boesman watches him, then hears Lena returning. He throws back the blanket.*]

If you tell her, I'll kill you.
Bulala wena!

[*He returns to his shelter, sits down, and continues drinking. He will remain in this position, watching Lena and the old man, until the end of the Act.*]

LENA [*a few small pieces of wood are all she has found*].
It's too dark now.

[*She goes to the fire. Their tea is now ready. She pours it into two mugs, taking one of them and half the bread to Boesman. Then she joins the old man with her share. She sits beside him.*]

As long as it doesn't rain it won't be so bad. The blanket

will help. Nights are long, but they don't last for ever. This wind will also get tired.

[*Her mug of tea and bread are placed before them.*]

It's a long time since we had somebody else with us. Sit close to the fire. That's it!

[*She throws on another piece of wood.*]

It won't last long, but it's big enough. Not much to see. This is all. This is mine.

Look at this mug, *Outa* . . . old mug, hey. Bitter tea, a piece of bread. Bitter and brown. The bread should have bruises. It's my life.

[*Passing him the mug.*]

There, don't waste time. It's still warm.

[*They drink and eat. Boesman is watching them from the shelter, his bread and tea untouched before him.*]

CURTAIN

ACT TWO

An hour later.

Lena and the old man are still sitting together on the box, huddled together under the blanket. Boesman is on his legs in front of them, the second bottle of wine in his hands. Under the influence of the wine his characteristic violence is now heightened by a wild excitability.

His bread and tea are still untouched on the ground.

BOESMAN. Again.

LENA. No.

BOESMAN. Yes!

LENA. You said that was the last time.

BOESMAN. You didn't do it right.

LENA. Have a heart, Boesman. Leave us alone now, man!

BOESMAN. Come on! 'Please, *my baasie!*'
[*Pause.*] Lena!

LENA [*giving in*]. ' Please, *my baasie.*'

BOESMAN. Properly. The way you did it this morning.

LENA. 'Please, *my baasie.*'

BOESMAN [*pointing to the old man*]. Him too. Hey!

LENA. Say it, *Outa.*

[*The old man mumbles something.*]

BOESMAN. '*Ag siestog, my baas.*'

LENA. '*Ag siestog, my baas.*'

BOESMAN. No bloody good.

LENA [*reaching breaking-point, she jumps up*].
Enough, Boesman!

BOESMAN. Not enough. Whiteman won't feel sorry for you.

LENA. Then you try!

BOESMAN. You must make the words crawl to him, with your tongue between their back legs. Then when the *baas* looks at you, wag it just a little . . . '*Siestoggies, my baas! Siestoggies, my groot* little *baasie!*'

LENA. Whiteman! Whiteman! Whiteman's dog. *Voetsek!*

[*Boesman laughs.*]
I'll pick up a stone, Boesman.

[*Boesman growls at her.*]

[*Sitting down beside the old man again.*] That's what he is, *Outa*. Make life hell for anything that smells poor. He's worse. They stop barking when you've walked past. This one's following me to my grave.

BOESMAN [*launching into a vulgar parody of Lena, with the appropriate servile postures and gestures*].
'*Sommer a ou Hotnot, baas. Lena, baas. Van ou Coega, baas. Ja, my baas.*'

[*He turns on her.*]
You!

[*He extends the pantomime to a crude imitation of the scene that morning when the Korsten shacks were demolished.*]

[*Peering at something.*] '*En dit? Nee, moer!* Boesman. Hey, Boesman! *Daar kom'n ding die kant.* Save our things! [*In and out of the shelter.*] Give us time, *my baas. Al weer sukke tyd.* Poor old Lena. Just one more load, *baas. Arme ou Lena!*'

[*Abandoning the act and turning on Lena again.*]
This morning! That's how you said it. That's what you looked like.

LENA. And did somebody feel sorry for us?

BOESMAN. The lot of you! Crawling out of your holes. Like worms. *Babalas* as the day you were born. That piece of ground was rotten with *dronkies*. Trying to save their rubbish, falling over each other . . . !

'Run you bastards! Whiteman's bulldozer is chasing you!'
[*Big laugh.*]

LENA. And then he hit me for dropping the empties.

BOESMAN [*the bulldozer*]. Slowly it comes . . . slowly . . . big yellow *donner* with its jawbone on the ground. One bite and there's a hole in the earth! Whiteman on top. I watched him. He had to work, *ou boeta.* Wasn't easy to tell that thing where to go. He had to work with those knobs!
In reverse . . . take aim! . . . *maak sy bek oop!* . . . then horsepower in top gear and smashed to hell. One push and it was flat. All of them. Slum clearance! And what did we do? Stand and look.

[*Another imitation*].

'*Haai! Kyk net. Witman is'n snaakse ding.*'

[*Boesman laughs.*]

But the dogs knew. They had their tails between their legs. They were ready to run.

LENA. He laughed then too, *Outa*. Like a madman. Running around shouting and laughing at our own people.

BOESMAN. So would you if you'd seen them.

LENA. I did.

BOESMAN. You didn't. You were sitting there with our things crying.

LENA. I saw myself.

BOESMAN. And what did that look like?

LENA. Me.

BOESMAN. Only one.

LENA. One's enough.

BOESMAN. Enough! Leave that word alone. You don't know what it means.

LENA. It was the same story for all of us. Once is enough if it's a sad one.

BOESMAN. Sad story? Those two that had the fight because somebody grabbed the wrong *broek*? The *ou* trying to catch his donkey? Or that other one running around with his porridge looking for a fire to finish cooking it? It was bioscope, man! And I watched it. Beginning to end, the way it happened. *I* saw it. *Me*.

The women and children sitting there with their snot and tears. The *pondoks* falling. The men standing, looking, as the yellow *donner* pushed them over and then staring at the pieces when they were the only things left standing. I saw all that! The whiteman stopped the bulldozer and smoked a cigarette. I saw that too.

[*Another act.*]

'*Ek sê, my baas . . . !*' He threw me the *stompie*. '*Dankie, baas.*'

LENA. They made a big pile and burnt everything.

BOESMAN. Bonfire!

LENA. He helped drag what was left of the *pondoks*. . . .

BOESMAN. Of course. Full of disease. That one in the uniform told me. '*Dankie, baas!*'

LENA. Just like that.

BOESMAN [*violently*]. Yes! *Dankie, baas.*
You should have said it too, sitting there with your sad story. Whiteman was doing us a favour. You should have helped him. He wasn't just burning *pondoks*. They alone can't stink like that. Or burn like that.
There was something else in that fire, something rotten. Us! Our sad stories, our smells, our world! And it burnt, *boeta*. It burnt. I watched that too.
The end was a pile of ashes. And quiet.
Then . . . 'Here!' . . . then I went back to the place where our *pondok* had been. It was gone! You understand that? Gone! I wanted to call you and show you. There where we crawled in and out like baboons, where we used to sit like them and eat, our head between our knees, our fingers in the pot, hiding away so that the others wouldn't see our food. . . . I could stand there! There was room for me to stand straight. You know what that is? Listen now. I'm going to use a word. Freedom! *Ja*, I've heard them talk it. Freedom! That's what the whiteman gave us. I've got my feelings too, sister. It was a big one I had when I stood there. That's why I laughed, why I was happy. When we picked up our things and started to walk I wanted to sing. It was Freedom!

LENA. You still got it, *ou ding*?

[*Boesman stares at her dumbly. He wanders around aimlessly, looking at the fire, the other two, the shelter, as if he were itemizing every detail in his present situation. Lena watches him.*]
You lost it?

[*Boesman doesn't answer.*]
Your big word? That made you so happy?

BOESMAN. When I turned off the road, when I said Swartkops. I didn't want to! Say it, or think it. Any of the old places. I didn't want to. I tried!
The world was open this morning. It was big! All the roads . . . new ways, new places. *Yessus!* It made me drunk.

Which one? When the robot said 'Go' there at Berry's Corner I was nearly *bang in my broek*.

LENA. So that's what we were looking for, that *dwaal* there in the back streets. Should have seen us, *Outa*! Down one, up the other, back to where we started from . . . looking for Boesman's Freedom.

BOESMAN. I had it!

It was you with your big mouth and stupid questions. 'Where we going?' Every corner! 'Hey, Boesman, where we going?' 'Let's try Veeplaas.' 'How about Coega?' All you could think of was those old rubbish dumps. 'Bethelsdorp . . . Missionvale. . . .'

Don't listen to her, Boesman! Walk!

'Redhouse . . . Kleinskool. . . .'

They were like fleas on my life. I scratched until I was raw.

LENA. We had to go somewhere. Couldn't walk around Korsten carrying your Freedom for ever.

BOESMAN. Every time you opened your mouth it got worse.

LENA. Bad day for Lena. Three empties and Boesman's Freedom in pieces.

BOESMAN. By the time you shut up we just a *vlenterbroek* and his *meid* in the backyard of the world.

I saw that piece of *sinkplaat* on the side of the road, I should have passed it. Gone on! Freedom's a long walk.

But the sun was low. Our days are too short.

[*Pause.*]

Too late, Boesman. Too late for it today.

So I picked it up. Finish and *klaar*. Another *pondok*.

[*Shouting violently.*]

It's no use, *baas*. Boesman's done it again. Bring your bull-dozer tomorrow and push it over!

[*To the old man.*] Then you must run. It will chase you too. *Sa! Sa vir die kaffer!*

LENA. Don't listen to him, *Outa*. There's no hurry. When it's over they let you walk away. Nobody had to run. One by one we went, a few things on the head, different ways, one by one.

BOESMAN. Whiteman's wasting his time trying to help us.

Pushed it over this morning and here it is again. Push this one over and I'll do it somewhere else. Make another hole in the ground, crawl into it, and live my life crooked.

One push. That's all we need. Into gaol, out of your job . . . one push and it's pieces.

Must I tell you why? Listen! I'm thinking deep tonight. We're whiteman's rubbish. That's why he's so *beneukt* with us. He can't get rid of his rubbish. He throws it away, we pick it up. Wear it. Sleep in it. Eat it. We're made of it now. His rubbish is people.

LENA. Throw yourself away and leave us alone.

BOESMAN. It's been done. Why do you think we sit here like this? We've been thrown away. Rubbishes. Him too. [*Pointing to the old man.*] They don't want him any more. Useless. But there! You see what happens. Lena picks him up. Wraps him in a blanket. Gives him food.

LENA. You picked up yours. I picked up mine.

BOESMAN. I got mine for nothing. It made a *pondok*. What you going to do with him.

[*Pause.*]

Hey! I'm speaking to you. You paid a lot for that *ou drol*. Bottle of wine. You happy now?

LENA. I didn't buy *Outa* for happiness.

BOESMAN. So then what's the use of him. Is he hot stuff? Keeping you warm there?

LENA. No.

BOESMAN. You two up to something under that blanket?

[*Lena doesn't answer.*]

Lena and *ou* better-than-nothing. Waiting for me to go to sleep, hey. *Vuilgoed!*

LENA. No, Boesman.

BOESMAN. You're cold, you're hungry, you're not making Happiness but still you want him.

LENA. Yes.

BOESMAN [*turning away with a forced laugh*].

Nee, God! She's gone mad. Lena's gone mad on the mudflats. Sit there with a *kaffer*. . . .

[*His laughter spirals up into violent bewilderment. He faces her savagely.*]

Why! Why!!!

[*Pause.*]

LENA [*she takes her time*].

What we doing to you, Boesman? Why can't you leave us alone? You've had the wine, you've got the shelter. What else is there? Me?! *Haai*, Boesman, is that why he worries you? You jealous . . . because Lena's turned you down, your *pondok*, and your bottle?

Must I tell you why?

That's not a *pondok*, Boesman. [*Pointing to the shelter.*] It's a coffin. All of them. You bury my life in your *pondoks*. Not tonight. Crawl into darkness and silence before I'm dead.

No! I'm on this earth, not in it.

Look now. [*She nudges the old man.*] Lena!

OLD MAN. Lena.

LENA. *Ewe*, Lena.

[*To Boesman.*] That's me.

You're right, Boesman. It's here and now. This is the time and place. To hell with the others. They're finished, and mixed up anyway. I don't know why I'm here, how I got here. And you won't tell me. Doesn't matter. They've ended *now*. The walks led *here*. Tonight. And he sees it.

BOESMAN. What's there to see? Boesman and Lena on the mudflats at Swartkops. Like any other night.

LENA. That's right.

BOESMAN. And tomorrow night will be the same. What you going to do then? Maybe I'll kick you out again.

LENA. You didn't kick me out.

BOESMAN. Tomorrow night I will. And you'll sit alone. Because he won't be here. That I tell you. Or anybody else.

LENA. He's here now.

[*Boesman leaves her and sits down in front of his shelter, drinking in a withdrawn and violent silence.*]

[*To the old man.*] Not yet, *Outa*. [*Shaking him.*] It's not finished. Open your eyes.

[*To Boesman.*]

If you don't want your bread and tea pass it this way, man.

[*Boesman studies Lena in silence for a few seconds then stretches out a leg and pushes over the mug of tea. He watches Lena for a reaction. There is none. In a sudden fury he picks up the bread and hurls it into the darkness.*]

BOESMAN. I've told you, we've got no help.

[*Disappears into the shelter with his bottle of wine, reappears, on his knees, almost immediately.*]

I'm kicking you out *now*. Even if you change your mind you can't come in.

LENA. I won't, Boesman.

[*Boesman disappears into the shelter.*]

Maybe he'll sleep now.

[*The old man leans forward.*]

No, *Outa*, not us. [*Shaking him.*]
Listen to me. You'll never sleep long enough.
Sit close. *Ja! Hotnot* and a *Kaffer* got no time for apartheid on a night like this. We must keep that bit of wood for later. After that there's nothing left. Don't think about what you're feeling. Something else. Warm times. Let's talk about warm times. Good walk on a nice day! Not too long, not too hot. Otherwise you're back in hell again . . . as hot as this one's cold. In and out, hey, *Outa*, we poor people. But when it's just right! It's a feeling. And a taste, when you lick your lips. Dust and sweat.
Hard work too. Watch tomorrow. You start to dig for prawns, your hands are stiff, the mud and water is cold, but after a little while you start to sweat and it's okay.
Outa must help us dig tomorrow. Get nice and warm. And a good dance! *Yessus, Outa.* There's a warm feeling. If we had a *dop* inside now we could have tried. Hard to make party without a *dop*.
[*Humming.*] Da . . . da . . . da.
Outa know that one? *Ou Hotnot* dance. Clap your hands. So.

[*She starts clapping and singing softly.*]

'*Die trane die rol vir jou bokkie!*'
Coegakop days! Lena danced the moon down and the sun up. The parties, *Outa!* Happy Christmas, Happy New Year,

Happy Birthday . . . all the Happies. We danced them. The sad ones too. Somebody born, somebody buried. We danced them in, we danced them out. It helps us forget. Few *dops* and a guitar and it's *voetsek* yesterday and to hell with tomorrow. [*Singing.*] Da . . . da . . . da . . . da. . . .
Outa's not clapping. So.
[*Clapping and singing.*] Da . . . da . . . da . . . da. . . .

> *Ou blikkie kondens melk*
> *Maak die lewe soet ;*
> *Boesman is'n Boesman*
> *Maar hy dra 'n Hotnot hoed.*

Not like your dances. No war-dances for us. They say we were slaves in the old days. Just your feet on the earth and then stamp. Hit it hard!
[*Still seated, she demonstrates.*]
Da . . . da . . . da . . . da. . . .
Nothing fancy. We don't tickle it like the white people. Maybe it laughs for them. It's a hard mother to us. So we dance hard. Let it feel us. Clap with me.
[*Lena is now on her legs. Still clapping she starts to dance. In the course of it Boesman's head appears in the opening to the shelter. He watches her.*]
[*Speaking as she makes the first heavy steps.*]
So for Korsten. *So* for the walk. *So* for Swartkops. *This* time. *Next* time. *Last* time.
[*Singing.*]

> Korsten had its empties
> Swartkops got its bait
> Lena's got her bruises
> Cause Lena's a *Hotnot meid.*
>
> Kleinskool got prickly pears
> Missionvale's got salt
> Lena's got a Boesman
> So it's always Lena's fault.
>
> Coegakop is far away
> Redhouse up the river
> Lena's in the mud again
> *Outa's* sitting with her.

[*She stops, breathing heavily, then wipes her forehead with her hand and licks one of the fingers.*]

Sweat! You see, *Outa*, Sweat. Sit close now, I'm warm. You feel me? And we've still got that wood!

[*They huddle together again under the blanket. Boesman is watching from the shelter. He lets them settle down before speaking.*]

BOESMAN. I dropped the empties.

[*Lena looks at him, she doesn't understand.*]

This morning. When we had to clear out of the *pondok*. I carried the sack.

[*It takes Lena a long time.*]

I dropped it.

LENA. [*She understands now. She speaks quietly.*]
You said I did.

BOESMAN. Yes.

LENA. You blamed me. You hit me.

BOESMAN. Yes.

LENA [*to the old man*]. He wanted to count the bottles before we left. Three were broken. He stopped hitting when the white-man laughed. Took off his hat and smiled at them. '*Jus a ou meid, baas.*' They laughed louder. [*Pointing to her bruises.*] Too dark to see them now. He's hit me everywhere.

[*Her arms open . . . looking down at her body. She has a sense of her frail anatomy. She feels herself.*]

Haai, Yessus! Look at it. *Pap ou borste, ribbetjies.*

[*She looks up at Boesman. He is still watching her from the shelter.*]

For nothing then. Why do you tell me now?

[*Pause. . . . He stares at her.*]

You want to hurt me again. Why, Boesman? I've come through a day that God can take back. Even if it was my last one. Isn't that enough for you?

[*Pause.*]

No.

Why must you hurt me so much? What have I really done? Why didn't you hit yourself this morning? You broke the bottles. Or the whiteman that kicked us out? Why did you hit me?

BOESMAN [*now out of the shelter*].
Why do I hit you?

[*He tries to work it out. He looks at his hands, clenches one, and smashes it into the palm of the other.*]

Why?

LENA. To keep your life warm? Learn to dance, Boesman. Leave your bruises on the earth.

BOESMAN [*another blow*]. Why?

LENA [*still quietly*]. Maybe you just want to touch me, to know I'm here. Try it the other way. Open your fist, put your hand on me. I'm here. I'm Lena.

BOESMAN. Lena!

[*Another blow, the hardest. He looks at her and nods.*]

Lena . . . and I'm Boesman.

LENA. Hit yourself!

BOESMAN [*holding up his palm*]. It doesn't hurt.

LENA [*the first note of outrage*].
And when it's me? Does that hurt you?
What have I done, Boesman? It's my life. Hit your own.

BOESMAN [*equally desperate, looking around dumbly*].
Show it to me! Where is it? This thing that happens to me. Where? Is it the *pondok*? Whiteman pushed it over this morning. Wind will do it to this one. The road I walked today? Behind us! Swartkops? Next week it's somewhere else. The wine? Bottles are empty. Where is it?!!

[*Pause.*]

I look, and I see you. I listen, I hear you.

LENA. And when you hit . . . ?

BOESMAN. You. You cry.

LENA. You hear that too?

BOESMAN. Yes.

LENA [*now almost inarticulate with outrage*].
Moer! Moer!

Outa hear all that? Hey! [*She shakes him violently.*] You can't sleep now! [*Changing her tone, pleading.*] Please, *Outa*. Just a little bit longer. I'll put the wood on the fire.

[*She does so.*]

Wake up. This is the truth now. Listen.

BOESMAN [*watching her*]. You have gone mad tonight.

LENA. He's got to listen!

BOESMAN. He doesn't know what you're saying. *You* must wake up!
You've wasted your time with him. You've been talking to yourself tonight the way you've been talking to yourself your whole life. You're dumb. When you make a hole in your face the noise that comes out is as good as nothing, because nobody hears it.

LENA. Say it in the *kaffertaal*. 'You hit me for nothing.' Say it!

BOESMAN. No.

LENA. Then let him see it.

[*She crawls to Boesman in an attitude of abject beggary.*]

Hit me. Please, Boesman. For a favour. My last one, 'strue's God. Hit me now.

[*To the old man.*] I've shown you the bruises. Now watch.

[*Pause. . . . Boesman is staring at her with disgust.*]

What you waiting for? You don't need reasons. Let him see it. Hit me!

BOESMAN [*withering disgust*]. Sies.

LENA. Who?

BOESMAN. *SIES!*

LENA. Me?

[*This is too much for Lena. She wanders around vacantly, almost as if she were drunk.*]

Nee, God! Nee nee nee nee, God!

I've got the bruises . . . he did it, he broke the bottles, but I've got the bruises and it's '*Sies*' to me?

What have I done?

BOESMAN. He doesn't know what you're saying!

LENA. Look at me, *Outa* . . . Lena! Me.

BOESMAN. There's only me. All you've got is me and I'm saying '*Sies!*'

LENA [*beside the old man on the box . . . softly . . .*]. *Outa?*

BOESMAN. You think I haven't got secrets in my heart too?

That's mine. *Sies!* Small little word, hey. *Sies.*
But it fits.

[*Parodying himself.*] '*Ja, baas! Dankie, baas!*'
Sies, Boesman!
And you? Don't ask me what you've done. Just look. You
say you can see yourself. Take a good look tonight! Crying
for a bottle, begging for bruises.
Sies, Lena! Boesman and Lena, *sies!*
We're not people any more. Freedom's not for us.
We stood there under the sky . . . two crooked *Hotnots.*
So they laughed.
Sies wêreld!
All there is to say. That's our word. After that our life is
dumb. Like your *moer.* All that came out of it was silence.
There should have been noise. You pushed out silence. And
Boesman buried it. Took the spade the next morning and
pushed our hope back into the dirt. Deep holes! When I
filled them up I said it again: *Sies.*
One day your turn. One day mine. Two more holes some-
where. The earth will get *naar* when they push us in. And
then it's finished. The end of Boesman and Lena.
That's all it is, tonight or any other night. Two dead *Hotnots*
living together.
And you want him to look? To see? He must close his eyes.
That's what I'll say for you in the *kaffertaal.*
Musa khangela! Don't look! That's what you must tell him.
Musa khangela!

LENA. He can't hear you, Boesman.

BOESMAN. *Musa khangela!*

LENA. Don't shout. I'm alone.

BOESMAN. What do you mean?

LENA. He can't hear you.

BOESMAN. Then wake him up.

LENA. Does it look like sleep? *Outa's* closed his eyes. The old
thing must have been tired. I tried to keep them open, make
him look. When he closed them his darkness was mine.

[*Pause. . . . Boesman now realizes. Lena looks up at him.*]
Ja! He's dead.

BOESMAN. How do you know?

LENA. He let go. He was holding my hand. He grabbed it, held it tight, then he let go.

BOESMAN. Feel his heart.

LENA. He's dead, Boesman. His hand is empty.

BOESMAN [*unbelievingly*]. He didn't cry, or something. . . .

LENA. Maybe it wasn't worth it.

BOESMAN. *He* wasn't worth it. Bottle of wine! And now . . . ? Didn't last you long.
[*The bottle in his hand.*] Mine too. Finished.
[*Throws the bottle aside.*] There goes mine.
[*Pause. . . . He looks at Lena and the old man again.*]
Morsdood?

LENA. *Ja.*

BOESMAN [*walking away*]. All yours.

LENA. Help me put him down.

BOESMAN [*quickly*]. He's got nothing to do with me.
[*Sits down in front of his shelter, nervous and uncertain.*]
You wanted him. You called him to the fire.

LENA [*gently easing the body down*].
Hey, heavy! No wonder we get *moeg*. It's not just the things on your head. There's also yourself.
[*She moves away.*]

BOESMAN [*after a pause*]. And now? What's going to happen now?

LENA. Is something going to happen now?

BOESMAN. Dead man.

LENA. Only a *kaffer*. *Outa.* Didn't even learn his real name. He said mine so nicely. Sorry, *ou ding*. Sorry.

BOESMAN [*false indifference*]. *Ja*, well . . . *môre is nog'n dag*. I'm tired. Low water early. We'll have to *woel* if we want prawns. I'm going to sleep.
[*Pause.*]
I said I'm going to sleep.

LENA. I heard you.

BOESMAN [*before disappearing into the shelter*]. He's got nothing to do with me.

LENA. '*Môre is nog'n dag.*' Maybe, hey, *Outa.* Maybe. So that's all. Hold on for as long as you can, and then let go.

BOESMAN [*shouting from inside the shelter*].
What are you doing?

LENA. Put your hands on the things in your life. Yours were full. Mug of tea, piece of bread. . . . Me.
Somebody else. Touch them, hold them. . . .

BOESMAN [*his head appearing in the opening of the shelter*].
What you doing?

LENA [*looking at him*].
. . . or make a fist and hit them.

BOESMAN. You can't just sit·there. You better do something.
[*Pause.*]
Listen to me, Lena!

LENA. Why must I listen to you?

BOESMAN [*coming out*].
This is no time for more bloody nonsense! It's serious.

LENA. When *you* want somebody to listen, it's serious.

BOESMAN. That! [*Pointing to the body.*]

LENA. *Outa* still worry you? *Haai,* Boesman. He's dead.

BOESMAN. Dead men are dangerous. You better get rid of it.

LENA. Real piece of rubbish now, hey. What must I do?

BOESMAN. I don't give a damn. Just do it.

LENA. How do you throw away a dead *kaffer*?

BOESMAN. Your problems. He's got nothing . . .

LENA. . . . to do with you. Go back to sleep, Boesman.

BOESMAN. I am! Why must I worry? I did nothing. Clear conscience! Come and do his nonsense here! This is my place. I was here first. He should have stayed with his own sort. Then when I wanted to get rid of him, *you* stopped me.
[*There is no response from Lena to Boesman's growing agitation. This provokes him even more.*]
Are you a bloody fool?

LENA. You say so.

BOESMAN. That's big trouble lying there.

LENA. His troubles are over.

BOESMAN. And ours? What do you think is going to happen tomorrow?

LENA. I don't care.

BOESMAN. Well, I'm just warning you, you better have answers ready. Dead man! There's going to be questions.

LENA. About him? About rubbish? Hey, hey, hey! *Outa* hear that. '*Môre is sommer* a special *dag.*' They're going to ask questions!
About you! Hot stuff, hey. 'What's his name?' 'Where's he come from?'

BOESMAN. Never saw him before in my life!

LENA. 'Who did it?'

BOESMAN [*sharply*]. Did what? He died by himself.

LENA. Too bad you can't tell them, *Outa*.

BOESMAN. I did nothing.

LENA. Why don't they ask some questions when we're alive?

BOESMAN [*interrupting her*]. Hey! You saw.

LENA. What did I see?

BOESMAN. I did nothing to him. You saw that.

LENA. Now you want a witness too.

BOESMAN. I didn't touch him. You tell them.

LENA. What?

BOESMAN. The truth.

LENA. You got some words tonight, Boesman. Freedom. Truth. What's that? *Sies?*

BOESMAN. Stop your jokes, Lena! When they come tomorrow you just tell them. I was minding my own business. I only come here to dig for prawns.

LENA. Teach me again, Boesman. You *mos* know how the whiteman likes to hear it.
'He's just a *Hotnot, baas.* Wasn't doing any harm.' How's that? Will that make him feel sorry for you?

BOESMAN. Then the *kaffer* came. And *you* called him to the fire.

LENA. '*Siestoggies, my baas.*'

BOESMAN. I didn't want him. I didn't touch him.

LENA. 'Boesman didn't want him, *baas*.'

BOESMAN. I hate *kaffers*.

LENA. 'He hates *kaffers, baas*.'

BOESMAN. NO!!

LENA. 'He loves *kaffers, baas*.'

BOESMAN. God, Lena!

[*He grabs a bottle and moves violently towards her. He stops himself in time. Lena has made no move to escape or protect herself.*]

LENA. *Ja*, got to be careful now. There's one already.

[*Boesman is now very frightened. Lena watches him.*]

Whiteman's dog, his tail between his legs because the *baas* is going to be cross. *Yessus!* We crawl, hey. You're right, Boesman. And beg. 'Give us a chance.' *Siestog*. I'm sorry for you. Hey. Maybe he's not dead.

[*Boesman looks at her.*]

That's a thought, hey! Maybe he's not dead, and everything is still okay.

BOESMAN. You said he was.

LENA. You believe me? You mean you're listening to Lena tonight. Are we talking to each other?

BOESMAN. Is he dead?

[*Lena laughs softly. Boesman moves uncertainly towards the body unable to ignore the possibility with which she is tormenting him. He looks down at the dead man.*]

LENA. Go on.

BOESMAN. Wake up!

LENA. Doesn't speak our language, remember.

BOESMAN. Hey!

LENA. That's better.

BOESMAN [*nudging the body with his foot*]. *Vuka!*

LENA. Didn't he move there? Imagine he stands up now? Happy days! Dig prawns tomorrow, buy another bottle, give me a hiding.

[*Boesman is hesitating, uncertain of what to do next.*]

Feel his heart.

[*The nudge becomes a kick.*]

Much better. Let him feel your foot.

BOESMAN. Get up!

LENA. Don't let him play stupid with you. Make him get up.
Tell him to go.

BOESMAN. *Voetsek!*

LENA. Louder! These *kaffers* are *onnooslik*.

BOESMAN [*his violence building up—another kick*].
Go die in your own world!

LENA. *Nog'n een!*

[*Pause. . . . Boesman, rigid with anger and hatred, stares down at the
inert body.*]

No bloody good. He's dead. And you, *ou boeta*, you're in
trouble'!

BOESMAN [*his control breaking*].
Bloody fool!

[*He falls to his knees and beats the body violently with his fists. Lena
watches in silence. When Boesman is finished he goes back to his place
in front of the shelter.*]

LENA. So that's how you do it. I know what it feels like. Now
I know what it looks like. What do you think about, in between
when you rest? Where to hit next?

[*Boesman is breathing heavily.*]

Hard work to beat the daylights out like that. Too bad there
wasn't any left in him. *Outa's* in darkness. He won't be sore
tomorrow, sit and count his bruises in the light. But he'll
have them. When you hit me I go blue.

[*Pause.*]

You shouldn't have hit him, Boesman. Those bruises! Finger-
prints. Yours. On him. You've made it worse for yourself.
Dead *kaffer* and a *Hotnot meid* with bruises . . . and Boesman
sitting near by with no skin on his knuckles. What's that look
like? The answer to all their questions. They won't even ask
them now. They'll just grab you . . . [*carefully*] . . . for something you didn't do!

That's the worst. When you didn't do it. Like the hiding
you gave me for dropping the empties. Now you'll know
what it feels like. You were clever to tell me. It hurt more

than your fists. You know where you feel that one? Inside.
Where your fists can't reach. A bruise there!
Now it's your turn!

[*Boesman, barely controlling his growing panic, gets stiffly to his legs.
He looks around . . . the dead man, Lena, the darkness . . . then
makes up his mind and starts to collect their things together.*]

BOESMAN. Come!

[*Lena doesn't respond.*]

On your legs! We're going.

LENA. *Haai*, Boesman! This hour! Where?

[*Boesman doesn't answer.*]

You don't know again, do you? Just crawl around looking
for a way out of your life.
Why must I go with you? Because you're Boesman and I'm
Lena?

BOESMAN [*urgently packing up their belongings . . . rolling blanket,
etc.*]

Are you coming? It's the last time I ask you.

LENA. No. The first time I tell you. No.
I've walked with you a long way, *ou ding*! It's finished now.
Here, in the Swartkops mud. I wanted to finish it this morning,
sitting there on the pavement. That was the word in my
mouth. NO! Enough! I wasn't ready for it yet. I am now.

[*Boesman is staring at her.*]

Don't you understand? It's over.
Look at you! Look at your hands! Fists again. When Boesman
doesn't understand something, he hits it.
You didn't understand him [*pointing to the dead man*], did you?
I chose him! A *kaffer*! Then he goes and buggers up every-
thing by dying. So you hit him. And now me.
'No, Boesman! I'm not going with you!'
You want to hit me, don't you?

[*Barely controlling his panic now, Boesman goes on packing.*]

Run! It's trouble. Life's showing you bullets again. So run.
But this time you run alone. When you think you're safe
don't rest and wait for me to find you. I'm not running the
other way that leads me back to you. I'm not running at all.
I'm *moeg*. When you're gone I'll crawl in there and sleep.

[*Boesman stops his packing and looks up at Lena. He realizes her intention.*]

BOESMAN. That's what you think!

[*Boesman starts to smash the shelter with methodical and controlled violence.*]

LENA. *Hotnot* bulldozer! Hey, hey!

[*Jumps to her legs and prances around.*]

Dankie, baas Boesman! Smash it to hell! This is my laugh. Run, you old bastard. Whiteman's chasing you!

BOESMAN [*the shelter is totally demolished. He collects their things together with renewed energy.*]

Don't think I'm leaving you anything.

LENA [*pursuing him ruthlessly*].

Take the lot!

[*Helping him collect it all together.*] This . . . this. . . .

Don't forget my blanket.

[*It is still wrapped around the dead man. Boesman hesitates.*]

You frightened? There!

[*She pulls it off and throws it at Boesman.*]

Everything! I want *boggerall*. It's my life but I don't want to feel it any more. I've held on tight too long. I want to let go. I want nothing!

What's your big word? Freedom! Tonight it's Freedom for Lena. Whiteman gave you yours this morning, but you lost it. Must I tell you how? When you put all that on your back. There wasn't room for it as well.

[*All their belongings are now collected together in a pile.*]

You should have thrown it on the bonfire. And me with it. You should have walked away *kaal*!

That's what I'm going to be now. *Kaal.* The noise I make now is going to be new. *Maybe I'll cry.* . . . Or laugh? I want to laugh as well. I feel light. Get ready, Boesman. When you walk I'm going to laugh! At you!

[*Boesman is loading himself up with their belongings . . . blankets, mattress, boxes. It is a difficult operation, the bundles are awkward, things keep falling out. But he finally manages to get it all on his back and under his arms. He stands before Lena, a grotesquely overburdened figure.*]

Eina! Look at you. 'Here' Boesman, the roads, going to be long tomorrow. And hard. You'll sweat.

What way you walking? Veeplaas? Follow the sun, that's where it goes. Sand between your toes tomorrow night.

[*Violently.*] So what you waiting for? Can't we say goodbye? We'll have to do it one day. It's not for ever. Come on. Let's say it now. Goodbye! Okay, now go. Go!! Walk!!

[*Lena turns her back on him violently and walks away. Boesman stands motionless. She ends up beside the old man.*]

Outa, why the hell you do it so soon? There's things I didn't tell you, man. And now this as well. It's still happening! [*Softly.*] . . . *Moer moer moer.* Can't throw yourself away before your time. Hey, *Outa.* Even you had to wait for it.

[*She gets up slowly and goes to Boesman.*]

Give!

[*He passes over the bucket.*]

Hasn't got a hole in it yet. Might be whiteman's rubbish, but I can still use it.

[*It goes on to her head.*]

Where we going? Better be far. Coegakop. That's our farthest. That's where we started.

BOESMAN. Coega to Veeplaas.

LENA [*slowly loading up the rest of her share*].
First walk. I always remember that one. It's the others.

BOESMAN [*as Lena loads*]. Veeplaas to Redhouse. On *baas* Robbie's place.

LENA. My God! *Ou baas* Robbie.

BOESMAN. Redhouse to Missionvale . . . I worked on the salt-pans. Missionvale to Bethelsdorp.

Back again to Redhouse . . . that's where the child died. Then to Kleinskool. Kleinskool to Veeplaas. Veeplaas to here. First time. After that, Redhouse, *baas* Robbie was dead, Bethelsdorp, Korsten, Veeplaas, back here the second time. Then Missionvale again, Veeplaas, Korsten, and then here, now.

LENA [*pause. . . . she is loaded*].
Is that the way it was? How I got here?

BOESMAN. Yes.

LENA. Truly?

BOESMAN. Yes.

[*Pause.*]

LENA. It doesn't explain anything.

BOESMAN. I know.

LENA. Anyway, somebody saw a little bit. Dog and a dead man.

[*They are ready to go.*]

I'm alive, Boesman. There's daylights left in me. You still got a chance. Don't lose it. Next time you want to kill me, do it. Really do it. When you hit, hit those lights out. Don't be too late. Do it yourself. Don't let the old bruises put the rope around your neck. Okay. But not so fast. It's dark.

[*They look around for the last time, then turn and walk off into the darkness.*]

CURTAIN

GLOSSARY

Ag: exclamation, roughly equivalent to the English Oh.

Ag nee, wat!:   literally, Oh no, what! Exclamatory phrase.

Ag siestog, my baas!:   literally, Oh pity, my master!

Ai: exclamation, roughly equivalent to the English Ah

Aikona: corruption of an African phrase meaning No; oh no! not likely, etc.

Aina: exclamation of pain, like *Eina*; Ow!

Aitsa!:   Whoops!

Al weer sukke tyd!:   roughly equivalent to Here we go again!

Arme ou drommel: poor old thing.

Arme ou Lena se maer ou bene: poor old Lena's skinny old legs.

Baas: master.

Baasie: familiar equivalent of *baas*; literally, little master.

Babalas: drunken stupor.

Bakgat!:   Great!

Bang in my broek: shit scared; literally, frightened in my trousers.

Bantoes: Bantu, black Africans in South African official terminology.

Bedonnerd: abusive adjective; being difficult, bloody-minded.

Beneukt: mad; fed up.

Bioscope: cinema.

Blikkie kondens melk: tin of condensed milk.

Bliksem!:   dammit!

Blourokkie: prison slang for long-term prisoner; literally, blue dress.

Boer: farmer.

Boeta: literally, brother; mate.

Boetie: familiar equivalent of *boeta*; literally, little brother.

Boggerall: bugger all.

Brak: mongrel.

Broek(s):   trousers, pants.

Bulala wena!:   African phrase, I'll hit you!

Capie: a Cape Coloured; South African of mixed race.

Chik-a-doem: onomatopoeic for a fast tune.

Coolie: abusive term for an Indian.

Daar kom 'n ding die kant: literally, There's something coming there; something's coming!

Dankie, baas: thank you, master.

Dè!:   There!

Die geraas van 'n vervloekte lewe: the noise of a cursed life.

Die trane die rol vir jou bokkie: I'm crying for you, baby; literally, Tears are rolling for you, baby.

Doek: head-scarf, worn particularly by Coloureds and Africans.

Dominee: preacher, minister.

Donner: (verb) beat up; (noun) fury; literally, beater up.

Dop: tot, drink (of hard liquor).

Drol: turd.

Dronkies: drunkards.

Dwaal: directionless confused state.

Eina: exclamation of pain, like *Aina*.

Ek sê!:   Hey!; literally, I say!

Ek sê, ou pellie!:   elaboration of *Ek sê!* Hey, mate!

En dit?:   And that? What's that?

En klaar: and done with.

Entjie: end; stub-end; cigarette-butt.

Ewe: African word, Yes.

Gat op die grond en trane vir 'n bottel: backside on the ground and crying for a bottle (a drink).

Gebabbel: babble.

Ghoen: a large marble; the master marble in the game.

Goggas: insects.

Goosie: cutie.

Grappie: joke.

Groot: big.

Haai!:   exclamation of surprise, Well I never!

Hamba!:   African word, Go!

Hamba wena!:   You must go! Get out! Bugger off!

Hoe's dit vir 'n ding: How about that!; literally, How's that for a thing?

Hoer: whore.

Hond: dog.

Hotnot: corruption of Hottentot, one of the indigenous African peoples of Southern Africa; now a term of abuse.

Ja: yes.

Jou lae donner: abuse, You dirty bastard.

Jou moer!:   ultimate obscenity; contraction of *Jou ma se moer*, Your mother's womb.

Jou verdomde....   you damned ...

Jus a ou meid, baas: just an old (Coloured) servant, master.

Kaal: naked, bare.

Kaalgat: naked; literally, bare-arsed.

Kaffer: abusive name for an African; nigger, kaffir.

Kaffertaal: African language.

Kaffertjie, Kaffertjie, waar is jou pas? . . .
  Maar, jou ma was 'n Bantoe,
  So dis nou jou ras:
      jingle referring to identity papers (pass) every African in South Africa must carry:
      Little Kaffir, little Kaffir, where's your pass? . . .
      But your mother was a Bantu,
      So that's now your race.

Klaar: finished, ready.
Klap: clout, blow.
Kom die kant!:   Come over here!
Kondens melk: condensed milk.
Koppies: little hills.
Kwaai-vriende: 'bad' friends; not on speaking terms.
Kyk net: just look.
Lawaai: noise, row.
Leeggesuip: empty; literally, drunk dry.
Lieg: lie.
Liewe God!:   dear God!
Links draai, regs swaai: turn left, swing right.
Loop!:   move! bugger off!
Luisgat: louse (*-gat* adds to the abusive meaning).
Maak sy bek oop: opens its mouth.
Maer: thin.
Manzi: African word, water.
Meid: Coloured servant; woman.
Moeg: tired, exhausted.
Moenie skiet, baas!:   Don't shoot, master!
Moer!   literally, womb; obscene exclamation, roughly equivalent to Fuck!
Molo, Outa: Hello, old man.
Môre: tomorrow.
Môre is nog 'n dag: tomorrow is another day.
Morsdood: stone dead.
Mos: just.
Musa khangela!:   Don't look!
My bleddy bek af praat vir niks!:   Talk my bloody jaw off for nothing!
Naar: sick, nauseated.
Nee: No.
Nes: nest, haunt.
Net 'n bietjie warm gemaak: just warmed up a little.

Nog 'n een: another one.

Onnooslik: stupid, witless.

Onnooslike kaffer: stupid black man.

Oom: uncle.

Oppas!: Be careful! Look out! Watch it!

Opskut en uitkap: fast dance; literally, Get up and get moving; shake a leg.

Ou: guy, fellow.

Ou blikkie kondens melk	Old tin of condensed milk
Maak die lewe soet;	Makes life sweet;
Boesman is 'n Boesman	Boesman is a Bushman
Maar hy dra 'n Hotnot hoed:	But he wears a Hottentot's hat.

Ou ding: old thing.

Ou pellie: pal, fellow, mate.

Oulike ou nessie: cute little nest.

Ouma: granny.

Outa: old man; used as a familiar or affectionate term to Africans.

Outjie: diminutive of *ou*; chappie.

Pap nat: sodden, sopping wet.

Pap ou borste, ribbetjies: loose and shrunken breasts, thin ribs.

Poep: fart.

Poephol: arse-hole.

Pondok, pondokkie: little shack or lean-to.

Poopy: terrified (cf. *poep*-scared).

Robot: traffic lights.

Sa vir die kaffer!: After the kaffir! Get the kaffir!

Safa: suffer; pain.

Shame!: How nice!

Sies! Sis!: exclamation of disgust, Ugh!

Siestoggies: exclamation of pity.

Sinkplaat: corrugated iron.

Skeef: crooked, skew.

Skelm: rascal, rogue, scoundrel; devil.

Skof: stretch, lap, stage.

Skrik: fright.

Sleep: drag.

So waar!: Truly!

Soeterigheid: sweetness.

Sommer: just, merely.

Stompie: cigarette-butt.

Sukkel: struggle, toil.

Swartgat: abusive name for a black African; literally, black arse.

Taal: language.

Tackies: rubber-soled canvas shoes.
Tickey: small coin; the old (silver) threepenny piece.
Tickey-draai: a lively country dance.
Totsiens: goodbye.
Van ou Coega, baas: from old Coega, master.
Vark: pig.
Vastrap: a fast country dance; literally, quick-step.
Vat jou goed en trek!:   Take your things and go!
Vies: furious.
Vlenterbroek: torn trousers.
Voetsek!:   Bugger off!
Vrot: rotten.
Vrot ou huisie vir die vrot mens: literally, rotten old house for the rotten people.
Vuilgoed: rubbish, garbage.
Vuka!:   Wake up!
Waar die donner is...?:   Where the hell is...?
Waar kry jy seer?:   Where does it hurt?
Weg is ons!:   We're off!
Weg wêreld, kom brandewyn: literally, Go away world, come brandy.
Wie's die man?:   Who's that man?
Witman is 'n snaakse ding: White man is a funny thing.
Woel: hurry.
Yessus!:   Jesus!